Erica Buist is a writer, journalist and lecturer living in London. She writes mostly for the *Guardian* but has also contributed to publications such as the BBC, the *Mirror*, Medium and *Newsweek*, as well as various literary anthologies. She has been a writer-in-residence at the Wellstone Center in the Redwoods, Vermont Studio Center, Faber, Virginia Center for the Creative Arts and Arte Studio Ginestrelle. She has lived in Mexico and Paris, and speaks five languages – mainly to her dog. She tweets @ericabuist

Photos and video footage of the death festivals can be found on Instagram @thispartysdead

This Party's
Dead

Grief, Joy and Spilled Rum at the World's Death Festivals

ERICA BUIST

unbound

First published in 2021
This paperback edition first published in 2022

Unbound
Level 1, Devonshire House
One Mayfair Place
London W 1J 8AJ

www.unbound.com

This book is a work of non-fiction based on the
experiences and recollections of the author. In some cases,
names of people have been changed to protect the privacy of
others. Except in such minor respects not affecting the substantial
accuracy of the work, the contents of this book are true.

Skull illustrations by José Guadalupe Posada

Designed and typeset in Baskerville by Patty Rennie

A CIP record for this book is available
from the British Library

ISBN 978-1-80018-139-7 (paperback)
ISBN 978-1-78352-954-4 (hardback)
ISBN 978-1-78352-955-1 (ebook)

Printed in Great Britain by Clays Ltd, Elcograf S.p.A

1   3   5   7   9   8   6   4   2

SPOILER
ALERT

We're all going to die.

Love is not a reward, and death is not a punishment.
If you were taught they were, this book is for you.

Contents

Prologue

The revolving door spits me into my all-different-now office. I'm still deciding whether to go right back out and run for it when I realise I'm already on the escalator. I do a quick mental run-down of who knows about what happened last Tuesday. There's my boss, Malik... actually, that's probably it. I doubt he told anyone else. He's busy, and anyway it's customary to treat a death as private, like the first trimester of pregnancy, or prostate troubles. As if it isn't announced in the paper. As if a no-longer-existent human isn't something we'll all have to acknowledge at some point. As if bereaved people *want* to be asked by disgruntled colleagues, 'Where have you been, bloody part-timer? Off on holiday again?' Oh, please, let me have that conversation.

I glide my fob across the pad. The gates open, obliging, even welcoming, but I jog through at a pace that suggests I don't trust them not to get impatient and crush me. I then resolve to act normally. I'm not allowed to be devastated by this. Bereaved parents, children and siblings are expected to be destroyed. Distraught grandchildren, nieces and nephews are permissible too, for a limited time only. 'Daughter-in-law-to-be' doesn't even feature in the grief hierarchy, which can only exist in a culture where kindness is at a premium. Bereaved people get treated inordinately well. No one barks at the bereaved. No one crowds them or lets them make their own tea. No one accuses them of incompetence, idiocy or thoughtlessness, or starts a sentence with a brusque, 'Look . . .' If I tell anyone, they'll think I'm stealing Dion's thunder, milking it for sympathy or slack. I can't be imagining this: if I'm as sure as I am that I have no right to be this upset, someone here probably agrees with me.

As the bottleneck of the corridor widens out into the open-plan of the office, my heart quickens and my vision swims. I can see the back of my chair in the distance, my blue cardigan flung carelessly over it, way back on Monday when everything was fine. I focus on it as I make my way through the bobbing sea of desks. Dion is fifteen minutes down the road, organising the funeral. I walk past a subeditor eating a sandwich. The smell of cold bacon registers as putrescine and cadaverine; I shudder, shake off the olfactory flashback, focus on my chair. Nearly there.

The thudding quietens as I reach my desk, next to Homa and across from Archie. I pull out my chair and sit, completing the action in a way I'm almost positive looks ordinary. I switch on my computer as if it's not pointless. Then I type in my password as if it's the most natural thing in the world. *God, that looked amazing,*

I think, and internally high-five myself. Oh yeah. Nailed it. Gettin' my normal on.

'Morning, Erica,' says Homa, pleasantly.

'Morning!' I shout. Right, that was a fail. I was going for cheerful. I smile, and say in a quieter, more Monday-morning voice, 'How's it going?' *There we go*, I think, *that sounded good*. I am in control. Things aren't tinged green and terrifying. The air is not thicker than usual. The lid is firmly on my jam jar of horror. I could turn myself upside down and not a drop of trauma would leak out.

'Good, thanks. How was your weekend? You've been on holiday, haven't you?'

Oh no.

Mayday.

Leakage. LEAKAGE.

'HE WAS DEAD. DION GOT A CALL FROM HIS CLEANER AND SHE COULDN'T GET IN BECAUSE HE WAS DEAD. HE WAS DEAD FOR OVER A WEEK AND WE FOUND HIM THERE AND THERE WERE PAPERS AND MILK AND THE DOG WAS TRAPPED BECAUSE HE WAS DEAD.'

She looks at me, stunned. Across the desk bank, Archie's head snaps up. They present the whites of their eyes and the backs of their throats for a moment, without comment.

Well, fuck.

CHAPTER ONE

The Worst Tuesday

I'm snooping in a dead man's fridge. It's not an official post-mortem, but he's still upstairs in his bed and I need an answer now.

It confirms the assumption I've already made. Everything I know he's been eating for years is stacked on the shelves, a to-do list for how to stop a heart. Hard cheese. Soft cheese. Cream cheese. Wheels of brie. Chocolate. Bacon. Chorizo. Sausages. And a few cursory baby tomatoes, wrinkled with age.

I don't know why I bothered opening it. What was I expecting to find? Dion and I lived with his father for two years before we got engaged, while we studied and muddled through the worst of the job crisis, and Chris's routine never wavered for a second – except for the time I made him a cup of tea and he said, 'Oh! It's...in a different mug!' I gathered he'd always been prone to

4

Groundhog Day living, even in his early years on a farm in outback Australia. But after his wife died of oesophageal cancer on Christmas Day 2008, he didn't so much stick to his daily routine as become fossilised in it. When his memory showed the slightest signs of wavering, he started setting alarms. The house the three of us shared in north London was pierced by an infernal beeping seven or eight times a day, yet he always remembered what each was for.

He even had an 8 p.m. alarm to remind him to go to bed and read, and a 9.15 p.m. alarm to remind him to sleep. The 12.30 p.m. alarm meant lunch: a stack of crackers, a bunch of grapes and a pile of cheese.

Every day.

Sylvia had been dead for two years when Chris told Dion he was thinking of getting a lodger. Rattling around in a town house that was bought to be filled with family and dogs, even Chris had to admit it was simply too large for him. Such a predicament has two possible answers: move house, or fill it. Of course for Chris, who we nicknamed Don Inertia, there was only one option.

'So...' said Dion, 'I offered to be his lodger.'

'You did?' I said, surprised. 'Do you want to be?'

'Well...sure. Highgate is nice. He only wants to charge me £250 a month, but I got him up to £350.'

I was living in a west London studio with a shared bathroom. The place was so small I basically wore it like a jacket, and I was paying £650 a month.

'Wow, good deal. But, living with your dad? I mean, he's lovely, but...'

'Oh, it's going to be a nightmare,' Dion said. 'He's rigid and inflexible, and ridiculously loud in the mornings. But Highgate is lovely...'

'You said that already.'

'Yeah, and, well...a lodger. No. It's too sad. I'm not having a stranger move in with my widowed dad.'

'Did you tell him that?'

'God, no. I told him he'd be doing me a favour. I said that Sam and Hayley want to get their own place and are sick of having me as a housemate anyway.'

'Well, that's bollocks – they love you more than each other.'

He laughed and ran a hand through his hair.

'I'll tell them tonight. Also, Dad's cooking a roast on Sunday – do you want to come? He says he's going to do something exciting with the parsnips, something about turning them purple.'

I shook my head. 'He has no respect for plants, that man.'

'I know. But you'll come?'

'Oh, please, beef and neon root vegetables? I'm there.'

I knew he was dead an hour before Dion found him. It was all there, in his text: 'Bobbi's at Dad's and he's not answering the door or phone. Milk and paper haven't been collected and the dog is barking. He's probably just asleep or out, right?' Suspicion that something's wrong, confirmation that something's wrong, denial that anything's wrong. It was practically a death certificate.

He sent the text at 8.30 a.m. on a Tuesday. Of course Chris wasn't asleep. He once whispered to me, conspiratorially, that he'd had a lie-in until 6 a.m. Any time I got up after 8 a.m., he would exclaim, 'Half the day's gone!' Papers left uncollected? He'd have read them and assumed the opinions as his own by now. Milk left on the doorstep, with half the day gone? Unthinkable.

One of us had to go and find him dead. And it had to be Dion.

'I don't have the key,' I texted. 'You should check on him. Shall I meet you there?'

'Don't worry – I'll go at lunch. He's clearly just gone out and forgotten to tell anyone.'

My heart thudded. I texted back: 'He could have had a fall – you really should check on him now.' The poisoned apple from *Snow White* flashed into my mind.

'Getting on the bus now,' he replied, followed by, 'Thanks for making me go.'

We were sitting in the garden, the late-afternoon sun on our faces, the smells of fallen apples cooking in the sun and fresh fruit in our drinks. Chris sat back in a plastic garden chair cradling a glass of red wine, his big round stomach full of his latest culinary triumph. Somehow the conversation had turned to Dion's old girlfriend, who he dated after me at university. Dion and I met a week into our first term and lasted three weeks before we broke it off, assuming we couldn't possibly have found The Person so early. I found Alex in my philosophy class, who never left university and later married a local girl; and Dion found Ines from Guernsey, who he brought back to London after graduation in a short-lived attempt at living together. I was living in Mexico, came home for a visit and we bumped into each other in Piccadilly Circus. Dion, newly single, spent two years respectfully trying to convince me to leave my Mexican boyfriend for him. Eventually I moved home and only took another four months' convincing. I'm a slow learner.

'I thought you and Mum didn't like Ines,' said Dion.

'It certainly wasn't that . . .'

Chris started speaking slowly and deliberately, as if trying not to be misunderstood. He also seemed to be making a point of not looking in my direction. 'I think the concern was that you would want to bring her to live with you in our house.'

'What? We were renting our own place, Dad, why would we—'

'It was just when things were a bit slow going with jobs and such, after you graduated. The thing is, we didn't want that to be an option,' he said, and fixed him with a look, 'but that has changed.'

There was a pause as what he had just said hung in the air. He was avoiding my gaze still. I smiled, not quite sure if I was supposed to be part of the conversation.

'Now, trooperoos,' he said, putting his glass on the floor, clapping his hands together and heaving himself up, 'I've got port and some very nice dark chocolate in the pantry, will you have some?'

He didn't wait for an answer. Dion looked at me. I sipped my wine, enjoying the warmth as the sun slipped away.

Feeling like I'd had seven cups of coffee, I marched around the flat getting ready for work, singing loudly to drown out the cartoon anvil whistling down towards my head. I deliberated about whether to go straight to Highgate, or make a show of going to work, as if everything might be somehow, miraculously, fine.

I was halfway to the Tube station when my phone rang.

'You have to come,' Dion said, his voice strangled.

'OK,' I said. 'What happened?'

'He's dead.'

My vision blurred. People crossed the road around me.

'I'm coming.'

Before taking another step, I sent Malik a garbled email, saying I couldn't come to work because of a dead body. It might have been more eloquent than that, but not much.

On the train from Bow Road to Archway, realisations went off in my head like explosions. *We're not seeing him next weekend. He won't be at our wedding. We're*

9

not going to South Africa next month. Dion has no parents left.

It was rush hour, standing room only, nowhere to hide my face as tears ran off the bottom of my cheeks. A woman, squashed up against me, reached into her bag and silently handed me a tissue, which I accepted with a watery 'thank you'. I don't know why, but I said it. Maybe just to hear if it was true.

'My fiancé's dad died.'

She reached back into her bag and handed me the pack. A man halfway down the carriage waved and offered me his seat, which I declined with a grateful smile. I might have imagined it, but at busy stops, I was sure I felt the passengers around me quietly and strategically moving themselves to shield me from clanging commuters as they barrelled onto the Tube.

It took for ever. Then the 43 bus from Archway took for ever. Dion had just found his father's corpse and I was taking two for evers to reach him. The bus sat in traffic and I couldn't take the wait; I pressed the emergency exit button and ran to the house.

Bobbi, Chris's cleaner, was standing in the driveway with a woman I didn't know.

'Bobbi...' I said, breathlessly through tears, 'thank you f-for calling.'

She took my hand and rubbed it in hers, warming it up, saying something soothing in Polish. I stumbled through the open front door and never saw her again.

*

Chris proposed a toast. I'd been accepted onto a journalism programme. No sooner had our glasses clinked than was Dion moaning about the flat-share I'd just seen in Oval.

'You can't move in there, hon – it's a poky little place. You should have seen it, Dad – there wasn't even a living room. The housemates are a couple of greasy computer nerds.'

'They were not – they were nice, normal guys, and they'd probably just run out of shampoo.'

'They talked to your chest.'

'They didn't talk to my chest; they just weren't big on eye contact. You've just got that north-Londoner phobia of anywhere south of the river.'

Chris held up a hand, as he often did to interject in our back-and-forth. 'Why are you looking for a new flat?'

'Well, it's a full-time programme, so I won't be able to do as many teaching hours, so I have to find a cheaper place.'

'Move in here!' Chris said, practically bouncing in his chair.

'Now there's an idea,' said Dion, smirking. That little sneak. That's why he was so down on the greasy south Londoners. They made a long and supposedly impromptu pitch as to why I should move in, conveniently leaving out the phrases 'annoying each other' and 'civilising influence'. Two months later I had a key and was plugging in my coffee machine in the little attic room.

11

Living with Chris was sometimes frustrating but often hilarious. He went on twenty-mile bike rides and came back looking comical in his reflective gear, red-faced and happy. Then he hung his sweaty clothes on the shower rail in the bathroom just off the kitchen. That's also where he kept a shoe rack full of disused and still-muddy shoes, a filing cabinet, a stack of cycling magazines and medical journals, coats and jackets he never wore, and a supply of damp toilet paper. The shelf above the sink was crowded with discarded toothbrush heads that were browning at the roots of the bristles, and a few scattered floss picks, old and new. He liked the downstairs bathroom best, and if he was trying to bogart it by making it too disgusting and confusing for anyone else to use, it worked.

We went about our lives, weaving around each other in the common areas of the house. If he was reading, he wouldn't look up. If he was eating while reading, he would nod. I usually breezed down at around 8 a.m. to grab a jug of milk from the fridge to take upstairs to make coffee in my room. I would say hi to Troy, Chris's dog, tickle him behind his ears and call him '*cachorrito*', Spanish for 'little puppy', which I realise is a ridiculous thing to call a great lumbering Dobermann. A few months later, as I was making my way upstairs to bed, I heard Chris coaxing Troy outside for his last pee with a jolly, 'Come on, cho-ree-toe!', his Australian vowels stretching around the half-remembered word.

The garbage truck in Highgate came early and announced itself with beeping, grinding, clanging, everything short of a marching brass band in its wake. One morning they woke me at 6 a.m. When my optimism that I might fall back to sleep waned at around 6.50 a.m., I decided to give up and start my morning. I made my way downstairs and opened the kitchen door. There, hanging his clothes on the dining-table chair, stood Chris, butt-ass, newborn-baby naked.

'Oh!' I said, turning around and shutting the door.

'Oops!' he said, chuckling with embarrassment, skipping towards the open bathroom door. 'Sorry!'

I had my coffee black that morning.

'I can't believe this is a conversation we have to have,' said Dion that afternoon while I was in class, 'but, Dad: you can't walk around the house naked now we have a girl living with us.'

'I was getting ready for a shower and there's not much space in the downstairs bathroom,' he protested. 'I wasn't *walking around the house*; I was in the kitchen.'

'All right, let me rephrase it: Dad, you can't walk around the *kitchen* naked now we have a girl living with us.'

'But it was before seven; she doesn't usually come down that early.'

'But she *might*, Dad, that's the central bullet point here; she *might* walk into *any* room that isn't yours or locked, so if you're in a room that isn't yours or locked, you're going to need to not be naked.'

'Hmm,' he said, nodding, the way he did when someone had made a new and interesting point, 'I suppose that does make sense.'

After that, whenever Dion had to leave the house early, he would sneak in and leave me a jug of milk by the coffee machine.

We had our own rooms because we could. He had his mum's old office, with a chilly en-suite bathroom that we shared. I didn't like Dion's room much – the floorboards bled noise from the kitchen below; you could hear the ting of a butter knife on a plate. I loved the romance of my attic room: its slanted ceilings, the cast-iron fireplace, the built-in bookshelves. It had been Dion's room growing up, and now he was too tall to move about without hitting his head. We slept apart at first, but my bed was where we lived. On weekends he would wake me up with toast, a kiss and a jug of milk, and I made frothy cappuccinos. We planned our days and heckled morning television. Then, when it was cold – and an attic room with no insulation usually is – we snuggled under three blankets, giggling at nothing, rubbing our feet together like crickets.

The house was freezing. The heating must have been off for days. Dion was in the kitchen mopping up dog mess. Troy had been trapped in there – unfed, unwatered, unwalked.

'Di!' I gasped, letting my bag fall to the floor.

Dion put the mop down, collapsed on me and sobbed. He pulled back and put his forehead on mine and I held his face, ran my thumbs across it, wiping his tears away as they appeared.

'I haven't got any parents left,' he whispered. Something cracked inside me. Troy whined and leaned his head on my leg, and I let one hand go to stroke him.

After a few minutes Dion took a deep breath and pulled back to face me.

'Do you realise what you texted me right before I got the call?'

I thought for a second, and clamped my hands over my mouth, 'Oh God...'

'Right before I found out Dad had died, you sent me a text that said, "We're out of coffee, I want to die."'

Which is how the police arrived to find us in the kitchen, wet-faced and leaning on each other, surrounded by dog shit, gasping for air through peals of laughter.

I'm snooping in a dead man's computer. It's not an official time-of-death investigation, but the paramedics are still upstairs, and I need an answer now.

As I search his desktop for the Outlook icon, I can hear Dion rummaging around in the cellar, looking for a key to the back door. I knew Chris had a daily alarm for checking and sending emails; I should have responded to the twist of worry in my gut when Dion told me the second and third times, 'No reply yet.'

I think about the last time we saw Chris. It was that Sunday, two weeks ago. He cooked a roast. As always, and despite my protests, he bought the wine according to what he thought I'd like – this time, it was Vouvray. He

15

didn't even like white wine. A year earlier, we'd all taken a road trip to Tours in France. This was the wine we had on the first day, he said, and I'd really liked it. I didn't remember, probably because of Chris's strict policy that I must always have a full glass.

Over dessert, he started quizzing us about house prices: 'Do you think you two could afford to buy a place big enough to have kids?'

'God, no,' we replied.

'House prices have probably gone up thirty per cent since you peeled the potatoes,' I said. 'If we had a baby, we'd have to put it in a drawer.'

'Filing-cabinet drawers are huge,' said Dion. 'We could get it a filing cabinet.'

'Then it would have, like, four rooms.'

'The thing is,' Chris said, interrupting our millennial brainstorm, 'this place is too big for just me. But I don't much fancy moving. So I thought I'd renovate it so I could have the bottom floor and you could have the top two. Then you could start a family at some point. Does that interest you at all?'

That's how he offered to set us up for life. Like it was popping in to feed our cats while we were away. We sat, stunned for a moment.

'I think … yeah, Dad, it would. Hon?'

He looked at me. I was still dumbfounded. When he finally convinced us he meant it, he waved away every whisper of thanks and instead talked about getting an architect to turn his one house into two.

Chris kept all his passwords in a Word document on his desktop. Shaking my head, I open his inbox. Looking at the last email he opened, and the last email he sent, I can see when he died. It was eight days ago, hours after he went to his lawyer and changed his will to leave us this house.

Dion comes upstairs from the cellar. 'Look what I found.'

I look up.

He's holding an entire case of Vouvray.

It was a favourite game of ours to try to convince Chris to spend some – any – of his money. When Sylvia got sick, he retired from his job as director of public health for Lewisham to care for her. At sixty-eight he found himself a retired, widowed workaholic, so he amused himself by investing his savings and pension in stocks and bonds. They made money; he called it a win. But that was the end of it: he never spent his winnings.

The road trip to France was to celebrate him buying a car (second-hand, of course). We'd barely left London when he remembered he loathed driving. He seemed to think the way to stop the car was to SLAM on the brakes – the traffic jam in Rouen was particularly nauseating. We arrived frazzled and ready to strangle each other. But once we settled into the bright Airbnb flat, we eased into the holiday spirit – cheeseboard out, glass of wine in hand, abstemious defences down – and spent a full hour trying to convince Chris to buy a new suit.

Wouldn't it be nice to arrive at the opera in a jacket without rips under the arms? Wouldn't it be lovely to sit on a park bench without someone giving you their change? Would spending the money affect your life even one little bit? And on it went. By the time we reached the bottom of the bottle, he was cautiously convinced.

We found a Hugo Boss and set the French sales assistants on him. He started mortifying us less than thirty seconds in by speaking 'loud enough for them to understand'. Then he mentioned that Hugo Boss made uniforms for the Nazis – except the sales assistants didn't understand the word 'Nazis' in his Australian accent. So he demonstrated – by goose-stepping.

We hid behind a shoe rack until it was over.

'This is our own fault,' I told Dion as we tried to pretend we didn't know this loon. 'This is the cost of your dad parting with his cash.'

'I know,' he whispered back. 'It's way, way overpriced.'

He died fourteen months later. He got to wear the fabulous suit he bought maybe three or four times. I wouldn't care if he had never got to wear it: I'll always be glad he bought that suit.

I'm snooping in a dead man's toolbox. I'm not an accomplished handyman, but the handle on his bedroom door has come off and we need to fix it now.

Chris's face could usually be found buried in a textbook about ancient Greece, and he was always slow to take care of his physical surroundings in the boring present. When I told him I'd heard mice in the walls, he did nothing about it until they were joined by rats the size of canoes. The kitchen cupboard doors are falling off and the wallpaper is peeling; the handle on his bedroom door has been merely decorative for years, and now, on this horrible Tuesday morning, the undertakers are paying the price.

It has been less than three hours since Dion found him. He arrived this morning at 9.30 a.m., opened the door and called, 'Dad!' He went to the kitchen and saw the mess, and Troy's ribs. He fed him twice, already knowing what he'd find upstairs.

He opened the bedroom door and saw his dad in bed, with a book on his chest and his glasses on his head. He must have nodded off while reading. But it had been eight days. The sight and smell of what was in that room will linger in our minds for months, wake us up at night and randomly pierce our thoughts like knitting needles through the temple. Dion slammed the door shut, and the handle came off in his hand. He slotted it back in and dialled 999.

'Nine-nine-nine: police or ambulance?'

'I . . . I think both.'

He gave the address, and the paramedics, who happened to be two streets away, arrived within minutes. Dion opened the door and one of them charged in, asking where the patient was.

'Upstairs.'

She took one look, came out, leaned over the banister and called to her partner, 'Don't hurry.'

There's a knock at the living-room door. We've closed it to keep Troy from running upstairs. Everyone should be spared the sight of what happens to a corpse after a week, even a dog. He's distraught and has attempted to curl up on my lap as if he were a puppy rather than a fully-grown Dobermann with paws the size of burger buns. Dion opens the door and the police officer comes in.

'Hi,' he says, gentle and professional, but his lips are pursed, as if he's trying not to laugh. 'Sorry to disturb you. We have, um…a situation. The undertakers are here to remove the body, but the handle on the bedroom door has come off. The window was open, and unfortunately the wind slammed the door shut. So they can't get out. We, um, we need your permission to break down the door.'

There is a silence. It takes a moment for us to comprehend that the undertakers are trapped in the room with an eight-day-old corpse, and we're now being asked, ever so politely, if we might authorise their release.

'Right,' Dion says. He cocks his head to one side and says, 'That's pretty funny.'

The three of us laugh so loud and hard that the dog scurries away. It dawns on us that the trapped undertakers can probably hear us, which makes us feel terrible for laughing, which of course makes it all the funnier. Dion leans against the wall, authorising the breaking of the door with a thumbs-up and a nod, and I'm quickly yanked away from my toolbox search, because, 'They deserve to get out of there quicker than you can fix a doorknob.'

They break down the door. The smell fills the air. We cower in the kitchen as they bring the body downstairs, put it in a van, and drive it away.

I'm wiping up spilt honey in a dead man's pantry. It's an easy meal for the ants that are crawling through the cracks in the walls, but I scrub until paint comes off the wood. This house has been more than generous to the local insect population lately. Dion clears out the fridge, gingerly passing dripping packs of green-tinged chicken to the bin. At least meat doesn't bloat, I think, and wonder if, given equal conditions, food and humans decay at similar rates. Even the cherry tomatoes have grown furry colonies advanced enough to go to war.

We only moved out a year ago. While Dion studied and I struggled through the lowest ranks in journalism, Chris charged us rent high enough that we didn't feel like charity cases but low enough for us to not have to sell toenail clippings to weirdos on the internet. After two years, we found full-time jobs and moved into our own bolthole flat in a converted match factory in east London, with a rickety mezzanine bedroom and windows that rattled when it rained. I love our tiny flat, usually. Today it feels like an indulgence, a place we've been horsing around in like kids playing house while Chris lay in bed, waiting for us to come home, waiting to be found. If we'd held off a year, I think, we'd have been here. We wouldn't have been alerted by a cleaning lady. The dog wouldn't have been trapped for a week, barking and howling to no one. I catch my breath and stop scrubbing. The honey is definitely gone, now. The sponge has splinters.

It's not the first time this house has smelled of death. Last time it was the colony of rats Chris did nothing to discourage. Chris's house is Victorian. No one has ever described a Victorian house without using the word 'draughty'; they seem to always be full of holes, as if punched in by a well-meaning giant who thinks we're defenceless animals, unable to breathe inside our boxes. The holes usher in a safari of creepy-crawlies: the cold, damp downstairs bathroom has a permanent ant regiment marching up and down the walls, passing by the toilet paper and disappearing behind the incongruous shoe rack.

A holey house is also an invitation for rodents. I liked to think I was a conscientious tenant, so I told Chris I'd heard mice in the walls. The rats had not ventured as high as the attic room – my wildlife problem was more usually a pigeon tumbling down the chimney. Rain and snow also got in that way. But the mice were making themselves comfortable on the lower floors.

Chris's style was less 'landlord' than 'eccentric housemate', and he couldn't motivate himself to take action on anything non-urgent – and reaching his bar for 'urgent' could cause altitude sickness. It probably involved uncontrollable blood loss. As such, the mice gave way to an under-floor rat kingdom. These were fat rats. I could hear the heft of their bodies in their gait. Dion and Chris let slip that they'd seen one in the garden but refused to describe how big it was, so naturally I assumed it was wearing a saddle, or sitting at the garden table reading *War and Peace*.

Before long, the house smelled like a poorly maintained pet shop. Eventually Chris called an exterminator.

'RATS!' he hissed, making claws with his hands. 'Not mice. RATS!' He made the claws again. Of course it was rats; mice don't fill every corner of a house with the stink of their nest, and they don't sound like a swarm of chihuahuas scuttling about in the walls. But it was impossible not to laugh at his hissing rat face.

The exterminator came and wiped out the kingdom. A heatwave arrived, speeding up the mass decomposition happening out of sight. The stench was almost visible. Our home was abuzz with flies, which no doubt travelled from all over to gather for the bountiful feast.

I didn't catch the trauma-clean man's name. I should have. He was there to confront chemical compounds like putrescine and cadaverine, to act as a rubber-gloved buffer between us and our mortal terror, to do a job we couldn't do, while we stayed downstairs throwing out chicken, like children. He and Dion seemed far away and distorted as they discussed the job, as if I was watching them through the wrong end of a telescope. I sat at the kitchen table, watching the trauma-clean man's papery hands gesticulate as he went over the particulars of how he would clean up the fluids left by the body of my

father-in-law-never-to-be. The trauma-clean man was
dusty, what you'd call rugged. About fifty years old, but
with grooves in his face so deep you could file tax forms
in them. He had worn-out, sandpapered vocal cords,
and a voice like shovelling gravel. Tobacco-stained teeth
flashing under pale, dry lips, which cracked as he chat-
ted about clearing blood, dirty needles and rotting bodily
excretions from otherwise lovely homes. I watched him,
thinking, *You were a baby once*.

It was when he said 'fluids' for the sixth or eighth or
thousandth time that everything went dark. The kitchen
table pressed against my forehead, comforting and sticky.
Nothing in Chris's house was ever quite clean.

The night Chris died, Dion and I were arguing about
flossing. He said he tried it once and it made his gums
bleed. I told him that means he needs to floss, damn it.
Then I asked if Chris had replied to his email.

'Is she all right?' asked the trauma-clean man.

The day after Chris died, Rhik invited me to that PR
event for the launch of Hotel Chocolat's Christmas line
of chocolate. Chris was probably stiff with rigor mortis
by the time we left with our freebies and went to see that
weird grunge band in Soho. The lead singer was dressed
as a giant rag doll, and scream-sang, 'WHY DON'T
YOU MISS ME?' over and over again.

'I'm fine!' I chirruped, infusing my voice with sunshine and exclamation points but not lifting my head
from the table. 'Just resting my eyes!' Tears dripped onto
my shoes.

On the third day I'd posted a picture of my coffee, on the fourth day a picture of Dion smiling with a tankard of beer.

And I asked if Chris had replied to his email.

'Let me know if you'd like a tea or anything!' Had I really just offered tea while pretending to be cheerful? I'd never been more English.

On the fifth day I took my cat to the vet, then asked Dion if Chris had replied to his email.

'No thanks, love, you're all right,' said the trauma-clean man. 'I'll go and get started.'

At the weekend I'd met an old friend in Camden and she'd cried with worry over a rash on her back. It turned out to be nothing. Chris was already bloated and green when I sent her a text saying, 'You worry too much.'

I heard the trauma-clean man turn and walk to the stairs, coughing like he had a badger in his chest.

'Are you OK?' said Dion.

The day before Dion found Chris, I was at the vet for a follow-up appointment for my cat. He was fine. The loss of his testes hadn't bothered him at all. I asked Dion if his dad usually took so long to respond to emails. Eight days. Eight days. How could it have been eight days?

Dion laid a hand gently on the back of my neck.

'That guy,' I said, still faux-chipper as I clasped Dion's fingers in mine, 'was a baby once.'

He cleaned away the trauma beautifully. Going into the bedroom, now missing both Chris and the bed, you'd never know death ever touched it. But the grief is visible enough. That this was his room at all is the first sign; the master bedroom is on the other side of the wall, with the four-poster bed and wardrobes he shared with Sylvia left practically untouched. He had retired from medicine to look after her when she was diagnosed. She died on Christmas morning, and he shoved a bed into what used to be his office, and became the cliché of the doctor who never went to the doctor. His accolades in the world of public health still hang on the wall, right above the spot where he died of undiagnosed heart disease.

'Hon,' I say, cocking my head to the side and squinting, 'is that a Christmas present?'

'Where?'

'Under the desk.'

Dion moves the bulky wooden chair and slides out a box wrapped in red paper with golden reindeers, layered thick with dust. A tag on it reads, in faded black ink, 'love, Sylvia'.

'He never opened it? For six years?' Don Inertia, this is some commitment to not feeling pain. Where did he get the willpower? And a blind spot the size and shape of a big box? I'm impressed, and sad. But mostly I want to shake him.

'We've got to open it,' says Dion. So we do. It's a turntable.

'Of course,' he says as he pulls back the paper, letting the thick dust fall onto the freshly cleansed floor, 'the one in the living room broke eight years ago. It's still sitting there.'

We donate the turntable, and hope it gets to play something soon.

It's amazing how quickly people can get from 'Sorry for your loss' to 'God, you're so lucky'.

The UK government requires a medical certificate of cause of death. A doctor can provide that, if they know what killed you and you've seen them in the last four-teen days. But Chris hadn't been to his GP in over a year (because why go for screening when he knows the Latin name for anything they might find? If having been to medical school isn't sufficient immunisation against dis-ease, then what is?), so off to the coroner's office he went. They came back with the same conclusion I reached after looking in the fridge: Chris died of undiagnosed heart disease. Shortly after, Dion receives a letter that says (and I'm paraphrasing):

> Condolences to you and your family, and congratula-tions to us: you owe us 40 per cent of your dad's estate! It amounts to more money than you could possibly make between you in a decade, and you owe it terrify-ingly soon. Get selling that house you grew up in and find somewhere else to raise a family.
> Sincerely,
> The Government

That's awful, friends say, but they have to know: how much is left for you? And that's when the 'no parents left' and 'decomposing cadaver' parts of the story dissolve into petty detail. Because what's left for us will be enough for a flat.

'So, you'll have ... no mortgage?'

'No mortgage,' Dion says, simply.

He understands the significance of what he's saying, but it's obvious he doesn't feel guilty. He watched cancer erase his mother – gradually at first, then all at once – then he found his father's week-old corpse. He figures a flat is the least the universe owes him.

But I feel weird. I know how people see me now. From the outside, this couldn't have worked out better for me if I'd dug for it. I spend five years with someone, he proposes, and a few months later he's getting a life-changing inheritance? It's like sticking money in a slot machine moments before it pays out. Inheritance isn't supposed to come when you're twenty-nine, when jobs are insecure and debt is just part of the furniture; inheritance is supposed to come when you're fifty, when your savings are plump and your vote already counts. I've won the lottery. A strange, sad lottery. And as I swallow yet another lump in my throat I think, *I'm supposed to feel lucky right now.*

We lived with Chris for two years, during which Dion quit his job and got a master's in the hope it would give him better job prospects. Desperate for a place of our own, we found somewhere we could just about afford.

The entire flat was barely bigger than the attic room in Chris's house. When people came over, their first comment was often, 'Wow, you two must really love each other.'

Chris seemed pleased we'd found somewhere but, truth be told, was kind of a dick about our stuff. We wanted to leave a few things until we could afford a bigger place, but he made it clear that we couldn't leave so much as a flip-flop in any of the rooms he never used.

'He's forgotten why I moved in,' Dion said to me one evening. We were sitting on my bed, surrounded by piles of stuff yet to be packed.

'Do you think?'

'Yep. When I started my master's, he began thinking of himself as doing *me* a favour, I can tell. So now, in his mind, I'm the kid he's "letting" live here and he's dying for his freedom back.'

'Are you going to remind him?'

'I don't know. I don't want to hurt his pride. It's really important to him to . . . I guess . . . to be seen to be coping. But on the other hand, it's a bit rich, casting me as the needy millennial. I was living with my best friends, I had control of when the heating went on, I didn't move here because I had to, and I haven't asked him for *anything*. He even tried to lower the rent when I started studying and I wouldn't let him.'

'He did? That was nice of him.'

'Yeah, it was. But I didn't need it. So, I don't know. I'm a bit hurt, to be honest.'

It made the last week a little tense, but we removed every last stick ourselves from the house, as requested.

On moving day, Dion went back for one last trip.

'That's the last of it. Cheers, Dad. See you next week-end for lunch?'

'Right-oh, kiddo. Hang on to your key, won't you?'

'Yeah, of course, I've had it since I was fifteen.'

'Good, good. See you next Sunday. We're having Julia Child's beef bourguignon.'

'Amazing.'

Dion made his way through the living room, navigating around Troy, who was asleep across the doorway.

'Dionini?'

Dion stopped and turned, assuming he'd dropped something.

'Yeah?'

Chris had his hands in his pockets, and was rocking back and forth on his feet, gently nodding.

'Thanks for moving in.'

If I have a 'guilty pleasure', it's property porn: trawling through online pictures of well-appointed nests I'll never afford, constructing imaginary identities for myself that would suit them. A Parisian *chambre de bonne*: if I lived there, my wit would be drier and I'd be so much better at walking in heels. A beach house in the Hamptons: if I lived there, I'd have smooth, tanned skin and 60 per cent more friends. A stone cottage in the Cotswolds: if I lived there, I'd read more poetry and bake trays of perfect madeleines. If I'm really committed to the daydream about being a different, sexier, smarter version of myself, one that wouldn't be out of place in these pictures, I check out a floor plan, look at dimensions, work out where my furniture would go, all the while knowing the dimensions of a house are as irrelevant as the song that was on the radio while it was being painted. Houses are compacted dirt that expand with memories and things. Clothes, trinkets, books bought and never read. Rugs you love the stitching on, but that irritate by slipping around underfoot. Dogs and their awful smells and the plastic toys they chew with destructive delight. An under-floor rat cemetery. A system of announcing you're about to shower so no one scalds or freezes you by running the kitchen tap. Conversations, fights, burnt coffee, roast beef on alternate Sundays, tables dotted with dried-on candle wax, toasts to successes, with glasses stained by the supermarket's second-cheapest wine. Celebrations, hurtful words, naked kitchen dashes, countless loads of laundry and hugs goodbye. Houses expand to the size of the world.

It takes Dion and I two days to strip away the imprints and adornments of the dead: his fluids, his furniture, the settled dust, the optimism of a stocked fridge. With every wipe, every donation, every item we throw out or squirrel away in memorial, we shrivel our old home into something saleable – if buyers can look past the rat-nibbled skirting boards, hideous pink wallpaper and oblivious ant army. Yet another London assemblage of overpriced walls, ready to be expanded with the daily mundanities of another family's love.

And we close the front door as we've done a thousand times. We hold hands, go back to our matchbox, and climb into bed. We tuck the blanket under our legs and hold on to each other like we're falling. I find myself thinking of the ants, marching with purpose to whatever lies behind the shoe rack, so oblivious to the tragedy around them, and I wish I'd left a splash of honey.

I'm snooping in a dead man's phone. I need to access his contacts to make a funeral invite list, and trying to guess his passcode is a good distraction from the fact that I'm afraid to go outside. It's 9.45 a.m., and I have to go to work. I've been dressed and ready for twenty minutes. I'm sending and replying to emails so no one notices I'm not in the office. It's nearly 11 a.m. when I realise I'm now knotted in the corner of the sofa, hugging myself and trembling. I have no idea how I'm going to get all the way to the front of the flat, find my shoes and put them on.

Soon someone's going to ask where I am. What can I say? 'I'm scared to go outside because my fiancé's dad is dead'? Is that better or worse than, 'I need to work from home because my fiancé's dad is dead'? Maybe, 'I'm on my way, but I'm not wearing shoes, because my fiancé's dad is dead'?

I don't feel entitled to this level of grief, and that's reinforced with every 'How is Dion?' No one asks how

I am. I don't begrudge their thinking this has little to do with me. No one assumes you're cut up about the death of an in-law-to-be. Even as the 'traditional family' falls by the wayside, we all revert back to traditional ideas when it comes to grief. People assume I haven't lost anyone. Not really. Chris wasn't my dad. I didn't have to see the body. I didn't even have to clean up the dog mess.

So when family and friends ask, 'How is Dion?' I tell them he's coping heroically. I tell them his mother was a psychoanalyst and that she taught him how to talk about and deal with trauma. I tell them we took the Vouvray home and toasted Chris, started calling the cats 'trooperoos', and stayed up late laughing about funny things he used to say.

But there are things I don't tell them. I don't tell them that Dion is coping, but I, for some reason, am not. I don't tell them what a loss this is for me, too, because my grief feels as unearned as the inheritance. I don't tell them just being here talking to them took forty-five minutes of courage-mustering at my front door this morning. I don't tell them that when I saw someone on the train with grey hair and a gut, I wanted to grab him and shake him, yelling, 'You're going to die!' Or that I had the urge to knock a bacon sandwich out of a man's hand and say, 'This will kill you – and I don't mean "turkey's healthier", I mean that one day, because you ate that sandwich and hundreds like it, your heart will stop beating and you will lie in your bed with a book on your chest and glasses on your head until your family realises what a week with no contact means.' I don't tell them Chris did more for me in the five years I knew him than many people do for their real children. I don't tell them how it feels to be set up for life.

But if anyone ever asks, I'll tell them that it's way, way overpriced.

CHAPTER TWO

The Sandwich

There are things we say when someone dies that no one ever questions, they just kind of go unexamined... 'Listen, if there's anything I can do, anything at all, please don't hesitate to ask.' ... You know what you should tell a guy who wants to help? 'Oh fine, why don't you come over this weekend? You can paint the garage. Bring your plunger; the upstairs toilet overflowed and there's shit all over the floor up there... Bring your chainsaw and your pickaxe, we're going to put your ass to work.' He wants to help? Fuck him, call his bluff.

– George Carlin

I doubt my father remembers breaking the news to me, with all the tact of a rhinoceros crapping on a drum, that everybody dies. I'm pretty sure I brought it up. As the first shards of awareness slice into young children's brains, it's not uncommon for them to randomly announce, 'I'm never going to die!' so that may have been what prompted my dad to correct me: 'You will. Everybody does.'

I frowned and peered up at him as he opened a tin of something for dinner, seemingly unaware of the problem he'd just given me to solve. There must be a concession somewhere. *Ah, I've got it*, I thought: '*You* won't die though, Daddy.'

'Of course I will.'

My younger sister Lydia and I started wailing, as children do in the face of things with which they have no resources to cope. And at ages three and five, that's basically everything. We weren't exactly sure what dying meant, of course; our awareness of it wasn't much more profound than 'that terrible thing that, in Disney films, happens as a punishment for bad people'. When it came to good people, like us, Disney would never, ever allow it (except to Bambi's mum. For some reason, Disney really had it in for Bambi's mum. Presumably they had to put Bambi in the sort of peril that would allow him to grow as a deer).

Children between the ages of five and nine tend to view death as something that can be dodged if you're clever enough,* and you don't have to look very far to

---

* This is according to Sheldon Solomon, Jeff Greenberg and Tom Pyszczynski's *The Worm at the Core: On the Role of Death in Life* (Allen Lane, 2015): 'In many children's stories, death is personified by bad characters...If death were a person, he or she could be reasoned with, bargained with, tricked, or overwhelmed by one's own superior wit or strength or that of a magical intercessor. Between the ages of five and nine, children think of death as avoidable if you are swift or smart enough to avoid getting caught.'

see where they got that idea. From the moment we were handed a chocolate egg and some well-meaning adult added the disclaimer, 'It's not all about stuffing your face – we're celebrating Jesus rising from the dead,' the idea was planted with a sugar hit to boot: be special and you can avoid death. Switch on the TV or open a book, and there it is again: one fatal situation after another, and the good guys are almost always magically excused. Aladdin is saved by the genie. Tinkerbell is saved by clapping. Ariel is saved when Ursula the Sea Witch gets impaled by a ship's mast. Dorothy escapes the Wicked Witch. ET is saved by the telepathic magic of fellow extraterrestrials, who arrive – as saviours do – just in time. J. K. Rowling even called her villain *'vol de mort'*, French for 'flee from death' – and, much as in life, 'you-know-who' has to be talked about in euphemisms.

And let's not forget the medicinal power of love, a veritable CPR in the world of children's stories: the Beast is saved because Belle says she loves him; Snow White and Sleeping Beauty both get revived by a kiss from a foppish landowner; and I'm jealous of kids with early exposure to *Frozen*, in which, in an unprecedented statement for feminism, death is thwarted by an act of *sisterly* love. In fact, love is better than CPR: contrary to what movies would have us believe, less than 8 per cent of people who suffer cardiac arrest outside a hospital survive, but I'm yet to see a film where love, when deployed, doesn't do the trick.

The message was clear, even to little children. Death

is for baddies. Not us. And certainly not our parents: our protectors, our providers of cuddles and plasters and Monster Munch. When Dad realised we were weeping for the loss of him, our mum, our brother, ourselves, the entire human race and everything we had ever known, he pointed and laughed.

'It's not going to happen for AGES!' he said. 'You'll be eighty or ninety, you'll be an old woman. How old are you now?'

'Five and three quarters,' I said, which I would have hoped he'd know, and anyway I didn't see what my age had to do with it. This was still very bad news. Quite shoddy, actually. I wanted to speak to the manager. Lydia looked at me for confirmation that this was her cue to recommence wailing.

'So it's not going to happen for years and years, you silly girls! And one day the sun will die too, and there won't be anyone left at all.'

I stared at him. What? How can the sun die? It's . . . it's *there*. It's the *sun*.

'But that won't happen until you've been dead for *thousands* of years.'

For some reason, that worked. I gave Lydia the signal that all was fine – for now. I don't know if it was the perspective, the word 'thousands' when I couldn't count to a hundred, and 'years' when I'd lived the lifespan of a hamster. Maybe he trivialised my worries by laughing at them. Either way, we stopped crying and continued about our lives as small children.

I only thought about death every few hours after that.

I'm in the office bathroom, pulling myself together. I just took my supervisor, Tara, into a little room to calmly explain why I might not be on top form today. The moment the words 'he was dead' left my face, I burst into fitful sobs and apologised over and over. She hugged me and told me, in not so many words, that it's OK to be this completely mental at work. It isn't, though, of course.

I splash water on my face in an attempt to de-puff my eyes. I learned this from movies. Just like 'people who love you chase you to the airport' and 'wedding ceremonies get interrupted', it turns out to be bollocks. My face is still puffy and red, and now it's wet and so is my shirt. So it's obvious I've been crying, but at least I also look like I have a toddler's comprehension of how to handle a glass of water.

I stick my chest under the hand dryer, then walk back to my desk with slow, deliberate steps, hands shaking, head still thick with the fug of the outpour. As I sit, I see Suzie making her way over to me. Oh God. Suzie doesn't know. Suzie's going to expect gargantuan things of me, like eye contact, appropriate facial expressions, and linguistic comprehension.

'Rororororororo?' she says. I stare at her. What?

'Rorororo…roro?' she repeats, slower, looking at me quizzically. I squint, which doesn't help. The self-important clatter of the printer sounds like fireworks, and someone's using a keyboard to deliver a CLACK-CLACK-CLACK directly to the gooey, melting centre of my brain.

She's saying something else. Concentrate.

'Rorororo Malik?' Something about Malik. I have to speak soon or my 'pretend to be normal' plan will be shot to hell. What's a good blanket response to literally anything she might be saying?

'I . . . don't know.'

She looks puzzled and starts to speak again. Tara scurries over and pulls her away. They put me in a taxi home, where my unspoken brief is to spend two weeks becoming fit to be around humans.

I start the process with a nice sit-down on the sofa.

Ugh. It's happened again. I unknot myself from the corner, get my trembling under control, and look at my calendar. Ah. I had a *meeting* with Malik; that's what Suzie was saying. Thank God I didn't take that meeting and go and sit in front of my busy editor with my dumb puffy eyes, deaf and mute, like a fucking effigy of myself.

Oh, great, now my right fist has curled itself into a ball.

I work on prising my uncooperative digits out of my palm. *Be a hand again, you fucker.*

My palm stings where my fingernails have left grooves, four shallow letter 'U's etched into the skin.

We spend two weeks on the death chores movies don't mention – clearing the house, moving Troy to his new home with a family member in Kent, meeting with lawyers, telling everyone we can think of about Chris's death, organising the funeral, drinking just a little more than usual.

Back at the office, I spend the last month of my contract wandering around like a zombie. I don't mean I try to consume the flesh of my colleagues – I'm like a replete zombie. Listless, shuffling, staring into space. Being this useless is a unique privilege of those who have recently happened upon a loved one's corpse: presumably for fear of setting me off, no one gives me anything to do. Though it may also be because I hardly seem like a font of journalistic brilliance. From their perspective, I'm getting into the office around 11 a.m., disappearing for over an hour at lunchtime, and leaving at 4 p.m. – and sending sporadic crap ideas for articles from 8 a.m. to 8 p.m. isn't fooling anyone into thinking I'm capable of producing *Guardian*-level content. And of course, I don't explain to any of my editors that my mornings are spent psyching myself up to leave the house, that I'm walking to a different postcode at lunch to minimise the chances of having to talk to anyone, or that I'm leaving at 4 p.m. so the panic attack hits on the Tube, rather than under their noses.

Luckily, my pre-zombie work has already scored me a writing contract, a pre-agreed number of words to be completed over the coming year – and, neatly fitting my increasing reluctance to leave the house, it's a work-from-home job.

I don't *decide* to stop going out. But in the first few weeks of my freelance life, I only go out when invited, and have to spend hours mustering energy and courage. *It's London's fault*, I think. *All those people. All that noise. The way the air sometimes looks wobbly and feels thick to breathe. Why do we all just accept the maxim that it's healthy to get outside? What's the benefit of fresh air if getting it leaves you frazzled? Isn't it healthier to be inside and calm than outside and stressed?*

'Why is everyone so big on going outside *every day*?' I ask Lydia on the phone one day. I make a coffee as I rant in the voice I used to use when I did stand-up comedy, clanging around cups and spoons, so the sounds of my life don't match my outfit — pyjamas at 2 p.m. 'Seriously,' I continue, 'who is Outside's PR team? I have a window. You can get vitamin D from leeks, and I have *four*.'

I google that as the coffee brews — you can't get vitamin D from leeks, it turns out, and the reason there are so many in the fridge is because Dion has been keeping it stocked, knowing if there's no food in the house, I'd rather stay inside than eat. Lydia laughs, but I think she's worried. Which is annoying. I don't just want to stay inside; I want it to be normalised.

One weekday evening I meet my friend Rhik at a pub in Brixton, and announce, 'I haven't been outside in two days. And it's been *lovely*. Everyone just accepts the wisdom that it's good to get outside, but lately I've been thinking, "But is it?"'

He leans forward, hunches his back and waves a pointed finger around, saying, 'AH, but IS IT?' like a mad scientist. I also hunch and do the rest of my Remain Indoors pitch in the voice of a mad scientist. It's funny, and we laugh, but I'm left with the impression that I am mad, and in no way a scientist.

Did you know that English adjectives absolutely must be in the following order: opinion, size, age, shape, colour, origin, material, purpose, noun? Yes, you did. You'd never have been able to list it like that because you were busy getting on with your life, but you know that you can have a lovely big old round green Spanish porcelain dinner plate, and that if you changed that order you would sound like a thesaurus in a tumble dryer. You know she's a little old Chinese lady, not a Chinese old little lady. You didn't know you knew it, never thought about it, but now that you think about it, it's utterly irrefutable.

That's how I feel about the realisation that anyone outside my field of vision might be dead.

Dion bends down over the sofa and kisses me on the forehead. He's freshly showered, suited, professional. Upright working man. I'm groggy, in pyjamas, unshowered, lost in the internet. Human puddle-woman. But bollocks to you, society, I think: I don't *have* to get dressed. I'm *allowed* to be in pyjamas and staring at a screen. Anyone looking at me would surely assume I was investigating a story, rather than flexing a skill no one else seems to care to cultivate, that of ascertaining the continued existence of anyone I'm not looking at.

Dion calls it stalking. It's not stalking. It's just seeing if the Potentially Deceased Person has posted on social media in the last few hours, and, if not, sending a text to see if the 'seen message' icon appears. If it does, they're probably alive and I'll move on. Until tomorrow, obviously. Because what if they were dead when I messaged but the messages app happened to be open on their phone and there I am, assuming they're alive, *like an idiot*? The logic is simple, and frankly I don't know how it escaped my notice before: if they're dead, they won't charge their phone and by the next day, the battery will have run flat. So, when I text again tomorrow, if the 'seen' icon doesn't light up, it's entirely possible they're dead. At that point it makes sense to go to their house, knock, or get the police to break down the door. Finding dead bodies must have been a nightmare when tech wasn't around to do all the legwork; maybe you could investigate one or two people to check they haven't died, but how on earth could you find time to do it for *everyone you know*?

Look, I know. I have moments of lucidity. Yes, death hangs over us like a watch-tapping chaperone, but in response I'm behaving like a ghost, haunting my friends and family, sending veiled signals that I'm watching them from a place in which I'm trapped. Holed up in my flat, staring at my laptop screen – my portal to the world – I force myself to see what the dead are probably spared: the horror of how easily the world carries on without you.

But I always snap out of this self-pitying train of thought. There's work to do; because the dead *do* send signals to let you know they've gone. It takes time and effort to spot them, because we're calibrated to the messages of the living. We notice calls and emails more readily than a week of silence, and we're quicker to register a neighbour walking his dog than a front door that hasn't been opened, milk and papers left uncollected on the doorstep, cobwebs billowing from a car's wing mirrors. I'm not going to wait until the signals turn into the deafening howl of a bloated corpse ever again. I will not miss another signal.

So, as the weeks drop away from the calendar, my habit of digital stalking becomes a full-time job. No news is good news, but no amount of no news seems to satisfy me: someone has passed out on the panic button. I spend a morning checking that family and friends are fine, and instead of feeling relief, I remember another person I should check on, and then another. I move on to people I haven't seen in a while. Then people I haven't seen in years. My concern spreads to people I barely know, metastasises to people I've never met.

I hear the faintest alarm bells during a text exchange with Dion. He texts, 'Claude Littner's going to replace Nick Hewer on *The Apprentice*!' Dion insists we watch *The bloody Apprentice* every time it's on, not because it's good (it's not), but because he's endlessly entertained by my 'hate-watching'. Every week I swear I will not heckle, nor point out the various ways in which it's designed to raise the blood pressure of anyone with an espresso serving of sense. And every week, Dion ends up hollering with laughter, thoroughly entertained by my rage.

Suffice to say, I do not give one solitary donkey turd about Claude Littner replacing Nick Hewer on *The Apprentice*.

And yet, before I can think, my fingers have sprung to action and typed, 'That's great! He will have had to do a medical, so even though he's overweight, he's probably not about to drop dead.' Hmm. Is that true? I google 'Does heart disease show up during a medical?' The results are vague. I make a mental note to ask a doctor friend.

Dion starts to type back. The little oval with the three dots comes up, then disappears. My heart quickens. Why did he stop typing? I see flashes – a mugger, a bomb, a train crash – and his text comes through: 'Hon, that's a really weird response.'

It is, isn't it? I think, then snap myself out of it. *Pff. Whatever.* I plug in my charger and pull myself up to the screen. *I'm just thinking ahead. Unlike all of you idiots, content to be blindsided, the next time someone I know dies alone in their house, I'll be ready.*

I open Spotify and blast out some playlist that professes to be uplifting. I walk over to the window and look down to the street. Before I can even recall the last time my feet touched it, I shudder with disgust and horror, and scurry back to my computer. The screen is dark and in its reflection I see myself. My unwashed, pyjama-clad, housebound body hunched over a screen. A body that spends its days indoors, feverishly typing breezy hi's, breezy lies. I only talk to the people I love to see if they're still here. I'm not a friend; I'm a head counter. A satellite botherer.

I take a few deep breaths, google 'How to get over agoraphobia', then quickly switch tabs.

It's there, on that last tab, waiting for me. All the information I need. And then I can google more: people's experiences and stories and tips, maybe a listicle on what the hell I'm supposed to do.

I'll read it.

I'll check on a few more people, then I'll read it.

It's days before I check the agoraphobia tab, and the internet enrages me with its verdict. I was hoping the cure would be a glass of orange juice and an hour of Netflix, but it turns out the cure for agoraphobia is just to go outside. Which, frankly, seems fucking insurmountable and not a little bit rude.

But I have to try it. There's no orange juice in the house.

With quivering hands, I get dressed, which I remember how to do without googling – small victories. I pull on a sky-blue hoodie with big white letters spelling out the ironic sentiment 'Life's a Beach'. I am going to buy a sandwich.

I am going.

I AM going.

To buy a sandwich.

I punch the air, Rocky-style. This is happening.

I'm not sure how long I spend in front of the door doing the agoraphobic salsa (an arrhythmic and very unsexy dance involving stepping towards the door and then stepping away multiple times). When my feet force me outside, I immediately retreat inside my hood, moaning. The sun pummels down like it hates me. The sense of danger quivers across my skin. As I start to walk down the high street with my head down, the air thickens in my lungs and touches my face like a creepy uncle. I cringe in terror as people pass – when a yummy mummy, probably on her way to Zumba, approaches at a narrow section of the pavement, I panic. Desperate to avoid her and her pram-bound spawn, I step into the path of an oncoming bus.

If the air outside is oppressive, the air in the supermarket is screaming in my face. With my hood up and my neck almost at a right angle towards the floor, I find the sandwiches and stand in front of them. The air is so thick it's like breathing melted chocolate. The triangular packaging of the sandwiches is utterly alarming – *That's a NIGHTMARE*, I think, *look at all those corners... What if I drop it? I'll NEVER reach it all the way on the floor*. I choose a baguette just for the ease of grip and start wading over

48

to the tills – and then someone approaches me. She is, in real life, just a nice lady trying to offer me a discount on Jaffa Cakes, but I treat her as if she's a toothless demon with open sores, growling, 'Give me a kiss!'

Which is to say, I panic. My exact words are, 'N . . . no!'

I throw the sandwich down and run home.

I tumble through the front door, panting, sweating. My cat Ollie is sitting at the top of the stairs, judging the sorry mess I've become. I tear off my coat and climb the stairs with all four limbs, like a shit Spider-Man.

When I'm back at my kitchen table, where the air is gentle and thin enough to breathe without effort, I wonder what my street's CCTV footage would say about where I am in the grieving process. It's possible I've made a sideways step. I'm pretty sure it's not denial, anger, fear, sandwich throwing, acceptance. I put on the song '(Don't Fear) The Reaper' by Blue Öyster Cult to take the piss out of myself – my ludicrous, friend-stalking, sandwich-throwing self – and google the words 'death anxiety'.

'Death anxiety is anxiety caused by thoughts of death,' says Wikipedia. No shit. '. . . a feeling of dread . . . when one thinks of the process of dying, or ceasing to "be". Also referred to as thanatophobia (fear of death), death anxiety is distinguished from necrophobia, which is a specific fear of dead or dying people.' I fall into an internet hole and find a quote from psychiatrist Irvin D. Yalom's *Staring at the Sun*: 'Adults who are racked with death anxiety are not odd birds who have contracted some exotic disease, but men and women whose family and culture have failed to knit the proper protective clothing for them to withstand the icy chill of mortality.'

He's blaming my mum. And Britain. Is he right? Was it my upbringing in a country where we avoid direct mention of death that made me throw a sandwich in a supermarket? It's hard to dismiss out of hand – when people started meeting up to talk about death in the form of 'death cafés', that made the news. People openly discussing death makes *headlines* in this country.

Or is it me? Why don't I have the protective clothing to ward off the icy chill of mortality? And where can I get it? Do they make it in my size?

Día de Muertos.

Day of the Dead.

It just pops into my head like a marble someone's pushed through my ear.

I lived in Mexico for two years after university. I'd only been there six weeks before the place exploded into colour. Orange, pink, yellow, green and purple streamers hung from tables and across courtyards; marigolds covered entire surfaces of altars lit with candles and littered with skulls constructed from compacted sugar with intricate patterns rendered in icing around the hollow eye sockets.

My first year there, I went to dinner with my Mexican boyfriend's family in Tepoztlán. There was an altar in the corner, decorated with pictures of the deceased and dotted with refreshments – water, tequila, bread, cookies.

'Do you eat the food after the festival's finished?' I asked one of the attendees.

He wrinkled his nose. 'Well, you could, but there's no nutritional value in it any more once the spirits have eaten it.'

'So, there'll be no calories in those cookies tomorrow?' I asked, smiling.

'Yes, exactly.' He wasn't kidding.

And people told me – everyone I asked, in fact – '*No tenemos miedo*.' We are not afraid. We are not afraid of death.

My hands have stopped shaking.

I google 'death festivals around the world'.

There are many, many results.

They celebrate the dead in Japan. They welcome their ancestors' visit with a dance, leave them refreshments, update them on what they've missed, and send them off by setting bonfires and floating lanterns on water.

They celebrate the dead in Nepal. With a cow festival, no less. A decorated cow leads a procession of everyone who has lost someone that year, to send the message that you are not alone in your grief. The festival is joyful and funny, infused with comedy performances. Newspapers publish comedy issues. I giggle with joy at the detail 'if a cow is unavailable, a boy dressed as a cow will do'. I love the notion of a cow being unavailable, like it has a dentist appointment or something.

They celebrate the dead in the highlands of Madagascar. Pictures show a corpse wrapped in a shroud, held aloft by grinning young men, shafts of sunlight cutting across their faces. The tradition is to dig up their dead every seven years, wrap them in fresh sheets, dance around with the body, get drunk, and have a party. They then rebury them, throwing money, rum and old photographs into the tomb with the body, and write the name of the deceased on the sheets, so they'll be recognisable in seven years.

They celebrate the dead in a remote area of Indonesia called Tana Toraja. This area's economy runs largely on death. When someone dies, they are placed in a wooden house with a roof that sweeps up to the sky like the bow of a ship, and there they stay until the family has saved enough money for a funeral – which, given that Tana Toraja's funerals are extravagant, days-long affairs, can take months or years. The deceased is regarded as 'ill', not dead, and family members bring them meals and talk to them. The actual festival is called Ma'nene; people retrieve their relatives from burial caves and dress them in smart new clothes. They then 'walk' them around the village. I find a pearl-clutching piece about it in a British tabloid, with phrases like 'EVEN CHILDREN!' – and they use the word 'zombies' more than once, as if these exhumed grannies somehow endanger the lives of the living.

They celebrate the dead in Sicily. On All Saints' Day or Ognissanti, children wake up to a treasure hunt, the gifts supposedly hidden by the ghosts of family members. Some put their shoes outside their doors in the hopes of waking up in the morning to find them filled with sweets. Up until a few decades ago, it was the only day of the year that children would receive presents of any kind. I try to imagine growing up associating the dead with sugar, instead of an obligatory sad silence.

They celebrate the dead in China. It's called the Pure Bright Festival, and people spend the morning sweeping and cleaning their relatives' tombs, replacing weeds with flowers. They take some time to feel sadness for the loss, light joss sticks and offer prayers for their ancestors' protection. They burn paper representations of money as a way of sending it to them, and in recent years people have even burned paper versions of iPads. Then they go out and live; a spring outing to appreciate life at a time when the seasons are changing.

Two hours and countless renditions of '(Don't Fear) The Reaper' later, I look down to see I've made a list of death festivals. Seven of them. I clutch the list, peer at it. These are places, I think, where people respond to death by throwing a party, not a sandwich.

I'd better go and see how they managed that.

'Hey!' Dion says, pleasantly surprised that for once I'm not on the sofa like an upturned beetle in distress – and I babble for twenty minutes. I tell him about the sandwich mission and the throwing and yes, I know I've made myself agoraphobic, and I've got a few ideas about how to fix it, and by the way I think we should get a dog because then I'd definitely go outside every day, but we'll talk about that later because I've found out there are death festivals basically everywhere but here, and I think I might go, and that's probably the opposite of agoraphobia, so I think I'm starting a writing project, maybe a book.

He looks at me.

'Sorry…what are you saying, exactly, hon? Break it down for me.'

'I'm going to go to seven festivals for the dead,' I say.

His eyes widen. I've barely left the house in weeks, I failed to buy a sandwich in a supermarket 900 feet from my front door, and I've just announced I'm travelling to seven countries.

'OK. Why seven?'

I pause. I look at my hands.

'One for every day we didn't find him.'

CHAPTER THREE

Let's Go Out and Vivir Un Poco

A mí la muerte me pela los dientes.
— Mexican expression, meaning,
'Death can't do anything to me.'

Al diablo la muerte, mientras la vida nos dure.
— Mexican expression, meaning, 'To hell
with death while we're still alive.'

'*Despierten!*' The command for everyone to wake up is yelled into my ear by a mattress-sized man on whose shoulder I've fallen asleep. Jolted back into consciousness, I register the chilly wind whipping at my face, the creeping smell of petrol from the engine underfoot. The boat is barrelling through the dark waters of Lake Pátzcuaro at a speed that's indecently fast for 4 a.m. Spray and splashes jump in through the open sides like licking tentacles. The mattress-sized man continues his urgent message: 'We're going to crash!'

I snap my head to the right to see where we're headed, but in the blackness, I can't focus on anything but the tiny screen on another passenger's video camera. He's pointing the lens towards the front of the boat, following the blaze of the headlights. Even to the bleary-eyed, the pixels form the obvious conclusion that we're careering into a patch of reeds on the edge of an island. Our driver stands at the helm, showing no hint of trying to slow down.

'*Agárrense a lo que sea!*' yells the mattress-sized man. Grab hold of what? There's nothing to hold on to besides the *lancha* itself, the boat that's about to smash and splinter into pieces, so I grab the back of his shoulders and crouch behind him, tensing my whole body in preparation.

I can't believe this. I'm going to die. On Day of the Dead. That's so embarrassing.

I tighten my grip on the human shield and squeeze my eyes shut.

I'm cutting the heads off flowers. It's OK, I've been asked to. Victoria, the American owner of the B & B I'm staying in, seemed slightly surprised that I was volunteering to help build their Day of the Dead altar. She climbed down from her ladder, where she was hanging skull-printed bunting, and slotted me into a casually organised assembly line: my job is to behead the marigolds, leaving an inch or two of stem. Then a young Mexican boxer called Luis weaves them onto the altar. Forty-five minutes later, we're really cooking: Luis is weaving the marigolds almost as fast as I can decapitate them, and when I'm running low, a Canadian called Tanya hauls in fresh ones from the pile at the entrance that was delivered early this morning.

The clippers have etched a sore red groove onto the inside base of my thumb. I give it a quick rub, plus another for my jetlagged eyes, which are convinced it's already bedtime. I glance around the rectangular, red-tiled courtyard. Lush bushes and flowers and trees frame a small stone fountain, paved with tiny glass shards, glinting in the sun. The courtyard is bordered by hotel-room porches. A few of the guests sit on wicker furniture in the tranquillity of the leafy courtyard, watching as it's steadily strung with festive images of death. The guests are almost exclusively retired Americans. Some are here to see Day of the Dead; in the indigenous population of the colonial town of Pátzcuaro, Michoacán, Día de Muertos is celebrated in a collision of tradition and artistic flair. Others are here because they retired to Jalisco, which has just been hit by a hurricane – this is high-end displacement.

In the centre of La Casa Encantada's courtyard stands a statue of La Catrina – an elegantly dressed skeleton in a big hat. Like cobblestones and the smell of cooking corn, La Catrina is omnipresent here, and particularly in the run-up to November. She's in countless paintings.

She's on t-shirts, notebooks, keychains, phone cases; she's formed into figurines and elaborate sculptures; she's carved onto wooden chairs. Often depicted surrounded by other skeletons drinking and dancing, La Catrina is a symbol of death that is jarringly irreverent to those of us who were taught from a young age that death isn't to be smirked at.

And sure enough, La Catrina emerged from satire. In the late nineteenth century the Mexican president wanted to modernise his country. To him, the modern world was epitomised by France, so he imported French fashion. Sometime between 1910 and 1913, cartoonist José Guadalupe Posada sketched a skeleton in a large feathered hat and called her 'La Calavera Garbancera' – literally 'the garbanzo-bean skull'. His message was directed at the Mexican poor, the people with nothing to their name but a few garbanzo beans: don't bother with fruitless efforts to be acceptable to the elite. With or without those great posh hats, we all end up the same way. The word *'garbancera'* later became a nickname for indigenous people who tried to deny their heritage by imitating this imported European style. The artist Diego Rivera started using La Calavera in his murals, and she became known by the slang word for elegant or well-dressed, *Catrina*.

Today, La Catrina is omnipresent in Mexico as Day of the Dead approaches – I took a quick stroll around the town market before we started on the altar, and saw her grinning out of vibrant paintings and standing tall in clay form, looking out over endless street stalls stocked with *pan de muerto* (an intensely sweet bread left for the spirits to 'eat' when they arrive at midnight), choco-late coffins, and sugar skulls with pink-icing eyebrows and glittery blue eye sockets. Everywhere you look in the run-up to 1 November is another grinning, impec-cably dressed reminder that we're all dead, dead, dead. Casa Encantada's Catrina statue stands year-round, and grins across the courtyard at us with her bony fingers upturned. I smile back and carry on snipping in con-tented silence.

Then it happens. Polite conversation. It always ruins everything.

'So, Erica,' says Tanya, dumping a pile of fresh mari-golds at my feet, 'what brings you to Mexico?'

I hesitate. The truth is a bit heavy for small talk, but the question is firmly in the small-talk category. I can't say, 'Well, since my father-in-law dropped dead last year, half my mobile phone bill goes on texts that say, "Are you OK?", I answer calls with the word "Good" and google "terrorist attack London" whenever my hus-band's phone goes to voicemail. Unfortunately, since I live in a country where everyone more or less agrees that death is the worst thing that can happen to you, I'm stuck in a fear spiral with nothing to pull me out. So I decided to visit death festivals in the hope of finding out how others deal with death anxiety. I'm over my agora-phobia though – high five! You?'

But what I do say is basically a garbled version of

that, and predictably, she doesn't know what to say. She flits between Sad Face and Shocked Face, the expressions people seem legally required to do when you tell them someone died. So I try to make her laugh with the anecdote about the undertakers getting trapped in the room with Chris's half-decomposed body. She does not laugh. She does Get-Me-Out-Of-Here Face, pretends to have something to do literally anywhere else, and I don't clap eyes on her again.

The finished altar goes up in the hotel breakfast room. It's cosy, heated with a gas fire, and filled with art: colourful rugs, sculptures, large clay flowerpots and decorative masks. Throughout the day, people wander in and out adorning the altar with candles, pictures of dead friends and relatives, and *ofrendas* – offerings of food and drink. We're in the heart of the indigenous Purépecha territory of Mexico. In the Purépecha tradition, home altars have to include fire (candles), earth (fruit), air (something that hangs off the altar so it can be blown in the wind) and water (though most choose shots of tequila). The *ofrendas* are the nucleus of Day of the Dead, an ancient tradition in a celebration that was forcibly blended with Catholic customs when the Spanish took over Mexico. They even moved Day of the Dead from a month-long celebration around June to two days in early November in an attempt to pass it off as the Catholic All Saints' and All Souls' days.

When my phone finds wifi, it buzzes with messages

on the family WhatsApp group about my grandfather's birthday party. I get a pang of homesickness, and it suddenly feels absurd to be missing a living grandparent's birthday to spend time with dead strangers.

As night falls, hotel guests gather in the breakfast room for a talk from Jaime, a tour guide, on the history of Day of the Dead. The breakfast chairs have been rearranged to form a little audience in front of a screen and projector. The other guests have splintered into groups and chatter excitedly, clutching glasses of wine and crunching *tacos dorados*, probably my least favourite thing to come out of a Mexican kitchen: potato tacos, invariably deep-fried to such hardness you could bludgeon someone to death with one and then eat the evidence. I know it's not just me; I see at least three people wince and wonder why they decided to fill their mouths with merciless shards. I opt for popcorn, since my teeth have done nothing wrong.

I take a seat and overhear someone say, 'Did you book a cemetery tour yet?' Shit. I pull out my phone, and put 'Book cemetery tour, idiot!' at the top of my to-do list. Much like Chris, I used to set alarms for everything. I would type every task with addresses and detailed instructions of what I needed to do, then set alerts to remind me to actually do them. But I haven't used my calendar for almost a year. Specifically, since my phone chirped 'Birthday dinner with Chris!' a week after he died. The atheist version of the old adage 'If you want to make God laugh, tell him your plans' is 'Don't put things in your calendar: it will only take the piss out of you later'. Like the atheist version of anything, it's uglier, less quotable, and true. Since I abandoned calendars, the notes app in my phone is a digital ream of last-minute to-do lists. It's not a brilliant system, but a haphazard list will never barge into my day to hurt my feelings.

Jaime welcomes us and the room hushes. He explains the history and mechanics of the Day of the Dead, that on 1 November, the souls of the *angelitos* come to visit, the 'little angels', meaning children and the unmarried (virgins, basically – you can just see a little bit of Cathol-icism peeping through, there). The second night sees visits from the souls of adults. As he speaks, Jaime cycles through a slideshow of images of the cemeteries in the area, dressed up for the occasion. It looks incredible – like the altar we built today, in the company of hundreds of others. Every grave is carpeted with marigolds, lit up by candles and watched over by families sitting up all night in the graveyard, wrapped in blankets.

'Do you really think the spirits of the dead come back? Literally?' asks one woman.

'I think they do,' says Jaime. 'In Michoacán we see an arrival of butterflies just before the Day of the Dead. They announce that the celebration is about to come, and many people believe they are the souls returning to us.

'It's solemn in the graveyard, but this is not a solemn occasion,' he continues. 'Outside the cemetery, it is a fiesta. This is the night our families come to visit after death. So we're not sad, or afraid. We are not mourning death. We're celebrating life.'

Some of the people need convincing that people aren't saddened by the memories of their dear departed. Jaime shows us photos of particularly creative efforts, such as a bike covered in marigolds, and insists it really is a celebration. And why wouldn't it be? Isn't death much less of a loss if you truly believe it's not the end, but just the start of an annual visit? Throughout history, religion, myth and ritual have conspired to convince us all that we're literally immortal – that the dead go to heaven, are reincarnated, or in this case, come back to visit every November. But none of this gives me the warm feeling I was expecting. I feel isolated and small, like I'm watching from behind a pane of glass. What are you supposed to do if you think death is the actual, definitive end? That death is nothingness? How do you deal with it if you have no ritual? I wish I could believe I was getting a visit. A ball of sadness and envy swells in my chest.

'The preparations begin in July with the planting of the marigolds,' says Jaime. 'Everything has to be perfect, because family members are visiting.'

My stomach goes cold. Family members. Not your old landlord, your partner's father. I wasn't even an in-law when Chris died. He wasn't my dad. I didn't find him in that bed. Do I even have a right to be here? Dion's the one with no parents left; I have both parents, a step-father and four living grandparents – two of whom I've stood up to be here.

As I sit and quietly panic, one of the retired American ladies raises her hand and asks, 'Are young people keeping up the traditions?'

'Sadly not,' says Jaime. 'For many young people, Day of the Dead has become more about partying than remembering the dead.'

'Oh, *tell* me about it!' barks one of the older women in the front. She's as American as cheese in a can, but is wearing a traditional indigenous dress and is draped in a shawl. 'I went to Janitzio Island for Day of the Dead forty years ago and it was one of the most beautiful, spiritual experiences of my life, but now – drunk people! Everywhere! That loud music, and all those neon lights! When I see drunken young people falling on the graves, I tell you I just cringe! It is *so* disrespectful!'

I want to ask a question, but I'm nervous to speak. I use the time Jaime spends trying to get a word in edgeways to get up the courage.

'Last year I went to a cemetery and they had a drone!' she says. 'In a cemetery!' She leans forward and groans again, 'A droooone!' sounding not unlike a drone.

Jaime looks at me. My hand must already be up.

'Yes?' says Jaime, smiling. My heart lurches. How can it be my turn to speak already? The drone lady must have needed to breathe.

'Um...' I say, and everyone falls silent and looks at me, the way they do in nightmares right before you realise you're naked. 'I...lost someone last year. My father-in-law, and we...we lived with him for two years but...I don't know if it's normal to...' My throat strains with the effort of not allowing my voice to crack. 'Is it normal to put down an *ofrenda* for someone who wasn't your immediate family?'

Everyone is looking at me with a mixture of kindness and pity. I fix my eyes on Jaime.

'I think it is normal,' says Jaime gently. 'When we put down *ofrendas*, we're inviting the dead to visit. You can invite anyone you're thinking of. They will come. And just remembering them is to ask them to come. People only really die when we forget them. And that's why, in the cemetery, we have an altar for all the people who have been forgotten.'

I nod and smile in a way I hope says, 'Thank you, sir, you have answered my question very thoughtfully and I do not now want to cry.' The talk finishes, and the guests disperse. Jaime makes a beeline for me and I do Cheerful Face, thank him for the talk, and confess I haven't managed to visit any cemeteries yet. He books me on a tour the next night, departing at 9 p.m. and returning at 5 a.m.

The other guests file past me to their rooms as I pack away my notebook. I hum cheerfully to myself in case anyone thinks I might need comforting.

'A drone,' the drone woman mutters, throwing me a look as she shuffles out of the room. 'Can you believe that?'

It's already lunchtime in Britain. I drink black coffee in the breakfast room, sitting strategically by the door to catch the very edge of the wifi – all the other guests seem to know each other, but I'm using my phone for company.

A message comes through from Dion: 'Hi honey, we missed you last night. Hope you're having a great time! Just a quick thing – before the party yesterday I got a call from the shop about Eric's present. I didn't realise you hadn't picked it up!' I wince, and look at my notes app. There it is, way down near the bottom. Cringing, I reply, 'I am SO SORRY, did you manage to get it before the party?' The word 'typing' fades onto the top of the screen, then stops. Stupid wifi. I hold my phone out towards the door in the hopes of a swift reconnect – and it buzzes. 'Yes, I picked it up, don't worry – just pleeeeeeeeaaase set a reminder next time! xxx' I haven't mentioned to him that I've replaced my calendar with this much poorer system, but he's clearly noticed.

At 8.50 p.m., I'm making my way through the plaza to the meeting point for the 9 p.m. cemetery tour. I don't know why I'm applying British rules of punctuality. Maybe if I'd lived here an extra year, I'd have got the hang of thinking half an hour late is entirely on time.

Pátzcuaro really isn't designed for numbers like these; the streets are heaving with people in Catrina make-up. The restaurants, all full to capacity, have queues snaking out of their doors. The sidewalks crumble under crowds shuffling at goose pace towards the plaza, where the light show must be visible from the next state over. I spot the tour group by their fluorescent coats and signs.

'*Inglés o Español?*' asks one of the tour guides.

'*Da igual*, either's fine,' I answer.

They give me a Spanish badge and make small talk as we wait half an hour for the inevitable latecomers – or as they might put it, 'everyone else'. I wave to Jaime, who is holding his own fluorescent sign on the other side of the plaza with a group of Americans from the hotel slowly gathering around him.

'*Vamos!*' shouts the tour guide finally, while an assistant does a frantic last-minute headcount. We follow the bobbing fluorescent signs, like baby ducks through swarming throngs of other tourists, to a coach waiting for us outside the town centre. A few of us make the ten-minute walk backwards, so we can watch the fireworks light up the night sky. We trip over cobblestones and children in scary face paint, who run up to us with little baskets shaped like pumpkins, asking for sweets and coins. It's their version of trick-or-treating; as the American influence tightens its grip on the country, Day of the Dead has Halloween nipping at its ankles. Victoria left an enormous bowl of hard-boiled sweets by the hotel breakfast room so we'd have something to give the trick-or-treaters – I thought two pocketfuls would be enough, but I'm tapped out by the time we reach the coach.

I plonk myself into a window seat near the back of the coach and realise with an embarrassed snort that at no point during my last-minute booking with Jaime did I think to ask where we're going. I could have wandered into a psychedelic death cult for all I know – though, looking around, it seems unlikely. I don't think members of psychedelic death cults wear Crocs.

I don't hear our guide's name because she introduces herself into a microphone that doesn't work. At all. She may as well be using a banana. One of the world's great mysteries is that when you tell someone their microphone doesn't work, they never quite believe you. Our guide is no exception, so I'll call her Silenciana. Someone shouts, 'We can't hear!' and she says, 'Oh,' gives it a shake and says, 'How about now?' and we all say, 'No.' That exchange repeats itself roughly seventeen times. Shaking and wishing fails to fix it, so Silenciana decides to just go ahead and pretend speaking into foam-topped plastic is preferable to raising her voice. I gather through straining and lip-reading that the first stop on the tour is a house for dinner.

The Day of the Dead traffic moves at the speed of treacle sliding off a spoon. The road is lit up by harsh orange street lamps and car headlights, and the mariachi music playing on the coach's stereo is drowned out by a cacophony of car horns – which, weirdly, do nothing to dislodge the traffic.

At 10.15 p.m. we stop in the middle of a stretch of dark highway. The traffic has disappeared, as has any trace of light. We're all told to get off the coach. If anyone else is thinking, *They could murder us in the woods and no one would ever know*, they don't show it. Silenciana sheepdogs all forty-five of us across the road and down a dirt path, then pushes open a pale blue gate. I'm one of the last people through; the others are already helping themselves to plastic chairs stacked against a little house with a wooden porch. Two señoras in Purépecha dress sit in the corner under a dim light, staring agape at the forty-five people who have just barged into the front garden of what is obviously the wrong house: there are no tables, no cooking smells, and the looks on the señoras' faces suggest they're searching for the polite way to ask Silenciana, 'Why are you, a stranger, here in the dead of night with forty-five of your friends?'

They clearly find the wording as they point us, with visible relief, in the direction of the next street. Silenciana blushes fiercely and tries to style it out: 'OK, *vamos* to the next street over, everybody...' Laughter snakes around the group, and people giggle, '*Perdón!*' as they leave.

'That was a close one!' an enormous guy chuckles to me as we slip through the gate.

'Yeah,' I say, 'except...well, not really. It was always going to be revealed pretty quickly that we weren't in the right place, wasn't it?'

'*De dónde eres?*'

'London.'

'Ah,' he says. 'So – part of Mexican culture is that if people come to your house, you must feed them. It's very rude not to.'

'Even if there's forty-five of them and they turn up unannounced?'

Three other people chime in, 'Oh yes, absolutely.'

The enormous man is Miguel. He's here with his son,

also called Miguel, who is filming everything – *everything* – on his SLR camera for a video blog. When we get to the right house, much like that of the two señoras we nearly ambushed, we sit together with a group of Argentinians at a long table with place mats, plates and cutlery.

The dinner is all the better for being served by willing chefs. Five people with enormous pots ladle out chicken breast with *mole rojo* (pronounced 'moh-leh roh-hoh'), a traditional Mexican sauce rarely seen outside Mexico, partly owing to the labour intensity of making it. It wouldn't be outlandish to list twenty or thirty ingredients, but the base of it is onion, garlic, tomatoes, chilli peppers, ground almonds, oils, spices and dark chocolate, which adds a rich sweetness that offsets the spice. Or something. Honestly, I'm just trying to sound cleverer than I do while I'm eating it. I mostly repeat variations on the theme, 'Oh my God, YUM.' I tell the other seven people at the table that I went to a work lunch in London, saw *mole* on the menu and raved about it to my boss. She ordered it, and when it came, it was just chicken in chocolate sauce. Not even DARK chocolate; it was as if they'd melted down a Dairy Milk and called it a day. My companions seem simultaneously horrified and proud that foreign attempts at their sauce are so dreadful.

The dinner is lovely. And it's just as well, because what follows is less a tour that affords peace and acceptance in the face of death, and more a series of absurd disasters.

*

Having narrowly escaped mugging two old women of dinner for forty-five people, we're taken to the edge of Lake Pátzcuaro, where we board a *lancha*, a long motor-boat with a roof. We all sit on benches running along the open sides. The driver stands at a wheel in the middle of the boat, facing forward, and we chat across him. He yanks on a line and a whiff of petrol bursts out as the engine springs to life. The open sides make for a chilly ride. We sit with crossed arms to keep warm.

Just as the boat reaches a section of the lake that could be described as 'the very middle of the dark, terrifying night', the engine conks out. Moonlight illuminates the horror-movie mist on the water. The *lancha* fills with the smell of gasoline as they poke around inside the engine for twenty-five minutes. They yank at the line, and the engine starts. Hooray!

It whimpers. And it's gone.

After three false starts, we stop cheering. After another twenty minutes, Silenciana is politely bullied into calling someone for help, and dials a number. We all lean forward to eavesdrop.

'Hello,' she starts, tentatively, 'we're a tour group and our *lancha* engine has broken down. Would it be possible, if you have one, to send another boat? If it's not too much trouble?'

Miguel and I look at each other and frown. Miguel Junior is filming this as well. I don't think he's looked at anything directly since dinner.

'She's being too polite, isn't she?' says Miguel Senior.

'Yes,' says Miguel Junior, 'we're stranded.'

'I'm English,' I say, 'and even I think she's being too polite.'

But the 'shake and wish' method that didn't work on the microphone eventually works on the engine. It sputters to life and we chug to tiny Uranden Island, where we disembark and make our way uphill along a cobbled street to a cemetery, the glow of candlelight visible even from behind the wall.

It's stunning. There must be over a hundred graves, every one lit by candles and covered in marigolds, photos, food, drink, love. The candlelight reflects off the marigolds and bathes the whole place in a rich, golden light. Families sit at the gravesides, solemn but not sad. Tourists pad around them, snapping pictures. The Night of the Dead is a ritual that promises a form of immortality, yet everyone seems to instinctively know this moment is about to escape; taking photo after photo, they snatch little bits of it as it rushes away.

A white church looms over the graveyard, and moments after we arrive and breathe in the aroma of the flowers and incense, the bells ring out at a startling volume. It's midnight. The spirits have arrived.

Inside the church, people climb a narrow wooden stairway that leads to a mezzanine, with a window above the entrance that overlooks the cemetery. This isn't the spiritual experience one might imagine when offered a high-up view of a candlelit graveyard. First, the creak of the stairway is alarming. I wonder if it will collapse before sunrise, or long before. Second, the window isn't exactly a seat of contemplation on the nature of mortality, with people leaning out of it trying to take a photo worthy of posting on Facebook. Peeking over their shoulders, I can see the photos are uniformly terrible, wobbly oblongs of orange in the darkness. I make a few rubbish attempts myself, before putting my camera away and trying the old-fashioned custom of looking with my eyes, so at least my memories will be in high definition.

Silenciana, a small figure by the gate, waves her sign, indicating that we should follow her back to our hit-and-miss *lancha*. On the way out we pass a tiny altar decorated with just a few flowers, with a sign written in Sharpie: 'For all the souls that have been forgotten.'

There are five cemeteries on the tour in total, but we skip Janitzio Island – the drone lady wasn't wrong. It's a beacon of loud music and neon lights, an incongruous backdrop to the group of fishermen with butterfly nets. They circle our *lancha*, lifting, waving and lowering their nets in a silent, beautiful performance. Or it would be beautiful if we weren't doing an amateurish job of lighting it with a continuous stutter of camera flashes. The harsh light illuminates the lines on their tired faces.

By the fourth cemetery, I'm starting to realise this is not the evening I had envisioned. The tourist activity could be called 'swarming'. Some twelve-year-old boys catcall me, and are only egged on when I confirm in

Spanish that no, I won't be taking off my top. It's when I walk past a tent that is quite clearly being used as some sort of Teenage Shag Palace that I start to lose faith in the whole exercise – would they be shagging in a tent if they really thought their grandmother was visiting? I trot back to the entrance, where several people on the tour have already given up and gone to sleep under their coats.

'We're going to crash!' yells Miguel over the growl of the *lancha* engine. 'Grab hold of something!'

Bleary-eyed and panicked, we brace ourselves for the collision. The thick green stalks trill fast past the open sides and flick harshly at our faces. Cries ring out, a smattering of '*Puta madre!*' I grab on to Miguel Senior, duck, tense every muscle and brace myself.

We hear a soft, muddy scrape and stop gently in the reeds. There is a silence. A collective breath. A burst of hysterical laughter.

Silenciana, ever embarrassed but always professional, ignores the laughter and the comparisons people are drawing with *Titanic* ('I'll never let go, Jack!' someone mock-wails), and calls another boat over to drag us out of the reeds. The spot at which we should have landed is only about thirty feet away, so the rescue *lancha* makes it to us in a couple of minutes. They attach a rope, kick it into reverse and rev the engine. We move precisely zero inches. We're sleep-deprived and practically sobbing with laughter, and don't stop as we clamber from

74

one *lancha* to the other for the thirty-foot trip to shore.

We step onto land, and look back at our poor boat, which somehow manages to look sheepish in the reeds. We laugh all the way to the graveyard.

If it's been difficult to spend the evening thinking about Chris, the final cemetery puts the nail in the coffin.

I understand why the Mexican government started promoting Day of the Dead in the 1970s. No one wants their ritual, especially one so beautiful, to live in the realm of NOGAS: No One Gives A Shit. But Day of the Dead has since been rehoused in a richer but slightly soulless neighbourhood called LEGAMS: Literally Everyone Gives A Massive Shit. The scenes before us take too much mental editing for comfort. A woman in a shawl nods off by a grave she's probably been working on for days; the candles throw a dancing light on to her face, shadows fold into her wrinkles. It's a beautiful sight. But a tourist with no-nonsense boots and a pony-tail leans towards her, hovers her SLR inches from her nose, and the CLICK startles the poor woman awake. A couple of rows over, a brash news crew shoves lights, cameras and microphones into the faces of the bleary-eyed graveside families.

I'm staring at what feels like the dregs of the night when I hear the weirdest sound; my brain conjures up an image of E.T., if E.T. had ever decided he'd had enough and shouted, 'EEEEEEEEEEEEEEEEEEEEEEEEEEE!' It's coming from above my head.

I look up. I don't believe it.
It's a drone.

'Thank you all for joining us on this Día de Muertos tour,' says Silenciana into the mic that, like the lancha engine, has sprung miraculously to life. The coach speeds along in the bluish light of dawn, an hour behind schedule. Everyone is trying to sleep but can't, because Silenciana is telling us to 'please try to remember the *bellas* things from the tour and not the problems'. The coach drops me off at the now-silent plaza and I climb the uphill cobblestones to my little apartment, and crawl into bed.

A fitful five hours of sleep is broken by rain drumming gently on the roof. I drag myself out to find coffee, my heart like a wet towel inside my chest. I am lonely and sad and, God, so stupid. I came here to look at mortal terror, how people deal with the knowledge that they're going to die, but clearly, I was harbouring some secret hope that I'd get healed along the way. Which was plainly idiotic. Going on a Day of the Dead tour as a way to feel closer to the dead is like going to Disneyland as a way to study mice. Did I really think I could just parachute into a death festival and have some Hollywood-movie epiphany that death is just part of life, actually, and fly home transformed? Did I seriously think I could Eat-Pray-Love my way out of the putrid anxiety of knowing that everyone I love is going to die, fragment, rot and disappear? I'm so stupid. I'm *so stupid*...

'Can I take this fork? I dropped mine.'

I lift my gaze and see a small, smiling lady in a crisp white jacket.

'Of course,' I say, imbuing my words with brightness, 'take whatever you need, no one's joining me.' Damn. That sounded sad. Maybe that's why she talks to me. Within three minutes I find out she's a retired American called Barbara, has two little dogs, lives in Jalisco, and is vacationing with her friend Mary Beth. She slips in the words, 'It's her last trip.'

'Her last trip?'

'Yes,' says Barbara, 'cancer— We had the most wonderful time in Capula at the Catrina festival – it had every type of Catrina you could imagine, painted figures, sugar skulls…'

She clearly doesn't want to dwell on her friend's illness, so I ask her more about Capula. Halfway through her description, a lady in sandals and an oversized red jacket opens the door. Barbara snaps her attention towards her dying friend so quickly and entirely that it's clear she mustn't have long. I open my laptop to give them space. They probably have a lot to get through.

I'm entirely engrossed in my notes when Barbara addresses me again, getting up from the table. 'It was nice meeting you, Erica.' She turns to Mary Beth. 'Are you ready?'

'Yep,' Mary Beth replies, 'ready.' She gets up, slowly, as if trying not to break anything, dumps her napkin and says, 'Let's go out and live a little.'

*

By the time night falls, I find myself in the crowded plaza, standing directly under the fireworks. They explode above our upturned faces and rain down in golden streaks, falling at our feet. Children run around laughing, dodging the cascading sparks. Light shows dance across the plaza's seventeenth-century facades as mariachi music blasts out of hidden speakers.

I stop at one of the stalls selling sugar skulls. Death, sweetened. What better way is there to say, 'You're going to die, but it's OK'? I never considered it, even in the two years I lived here, but maybe I should buy one and write my own name on it.

The upside of travelling alone is the freedom to slip away from the party whenever you want. No one detains you, shoves a drink in your hand with oppressive merriment while making exaggerated 'woohoo' faces you're expected to mirror. You can turn into a ghost, evaporate from the crowd and no one will ever know or care that you were there at all. By the time I arrive at the hotel, it's already approaching midnight, when the souls are supposed to visit.

The room is dark, but there's a flickering candle on the altar illuminating Chris's picture. The aroma of marigolds mingles with the smell of the gas fire. I feel tears prickle.

OK. I'm going to try this.

'Um...hi, Chris,' I say, with all the awkwardness of an English atheist talking to a photo. 'Oh, shit, I never put down an *ofrenda* for you. Hang on.'

I spin on the heel of my boot and scurry out to the bowl of sweets Victoria left for the trick-or-treaters, and sift through looking for the black wrapper that signifies liquorice. I return to the altar and place a sweet at the foot of his photo.

'I got you almond flavour. I couldn't find liquorice, sorry. Probably for the best. I tried to buy you some liquorice for Christmas once, but Dion wouldn't let me because of the time you ate a kilo of Allsorts and had to go to hospital. I know you hate it when I bring that up, but, you know ... it's funny.'

There is a silence, because I'm alone. There's just the hum of the water cooler, the hiss of the gas fire and the flicker of the candle.

'I know you're not really there,' I say, clearing my throat, imagining trying to explain any of this to him. He would scoff at this superstitious nonsense and pour me a glass of Vouvray. 'I just ... wanted to say goodbye.'

The silence is palpable. I could spread it on a cracker. If this were a movie, this would be a cue for A Sign. A draught would blow in from an unclear source and flutter his picture to my feet, or I'd swear I saw him wink at me from inside the photo. But of course, none of that happens. The water cooler hums, the gas fire hisses, the world carries on. I let out a breath and say, 'Bye.'

Feeling a little sheepish, I go back over to my bag and start to pack up my things. The sound of the midnight bells wafts in.

My phone buzzes. It's a text from Dion: 'Your birthday present is SORTED. Keep the 25th free. No googling.'

I sit down, take a long breath, and mark it in my calendar.

CHAPTER FOUR

A Boy Dressed as a Cow Will Do

The air smells of wet mud and exhaust fumes. Mopeds buzz around like giant mosquitoes, all but shaving me as they whip past, weaving between the potholes and pedestrians on the cracked, half-rubbled road to Patan Durbar Square. I try to walk like everyone else: cautious but casual, no flinching. Beeps shoot into the air like party poppers, and seem to simply mean 'here I am'; a rich cacophony of people announcing their presence.

It's a few days before the Kathmandu Valley's annual death festival, Gai Jatra, and I'm stumbling about in a jetlagged haze. I half-walk, half-slip down the muddy road, keeping my eye on the looming rain cloud – part of the Gai Jatra festival is to bid farewell to monsoon season, and I'm suspicious it'll want to wrap up with a big finish.

Patan Durbar Square is a concentrated cluster of

Hindu and Buddhist temples. Three years on from the 2015 earthquake, it's also littered with scaffolding. Huge tarpaulins flap in the breeze, monkeys leap from structure to structure and everyone raises their voices over the drilling, hammering, ting-ting-ting of the rebuild. I take shelter under the bottom tier of a wooden pagoda and stare up at the intricate carvings.

'You should go in, it's a great museum.'

I whirl round and see a man maybe an inch or two shorter than me. He has a sweet and welcoming smile, a well-groomed goatee, and shiny hair pulled back into a neat ponytail.

'I'm going to go tomorrow,' I say.

'Why not now?' he asks, and seems genuinely interested in why I would go as far as the door without going in.

'I'm jetlagged, I'd like to go when I can take it all in.'

He nods and we end up chatting for about half an hour. His name is Sandip Bhujel and he's a local tour guide. He's waiting, somewhat impatiently, for the start of hiking season so he can get back up to Everest. Since he's free this week and seems to be unstumpable when it comes to questions about the local area, he agrees to be my guide. We stroll around the square and I tell him about my visits to the festivals for the dead, and as he begins to suggest things to see, the rain arrives. We run and shelter under a temple that collapsed in 1934 and retreat closer to the wall to stay dry.

'So, tomorrow we should go to Pashupatinath,' says Sandip.

'OK, great. That's where they cremate bodies on the open-air funeral pyres, right?'

'Yes.'

'Will that be happening tomorrow while we're there?' I ask.

Sandip laughs and shakes his head. 'Tourists always ask this, "Will I be lucky to see the cremations?" It's such a silly question!'

'Right,' I laugh. 'I suppose Kathmandu is a big place and people die all the time. I don't know why we'd assume it only happens at four-thirty every other Wednesday.'

He nods and laughs again.

'Actually,' I say, 'now that I think about it, I do.'

He looks at me, interested in the seed of this stupid question weeding its way into all his tours.

'You know, I've never seen a dead body,' I say. 'Death is not something we look at, where I'm from. Not in conversation, and certainly not directly. We've managed to completely remove the corpse from view when someone dies. Well, in America they might embalm the body and have a viewing . . .'

He looks at me quizzically.

'Embalming is running chemicals through the corpse to delay decomposition. They put make-up and clothes on the body, they stuff their cheeks and eye sockets to make them look beautiful and alive, like they're sleeping.'

His eyes widen.

'But even that is pretty exotic to most Brits. Actually looking at a dead body, voluntarily, even if it has been made to look alive – it's really unusual. Nope, where I'm from, when someone dies the body is removed by professional body removers, burned by professional body burners, and handed back to you as ash in two stapled bags and a sealed box. So the idea of seeing a stranger's corpse is so bizarre I guess we assume it must be rare.'

He nods, no longer laughing. 'I think you will like Pashupatinath,' he says. 'It's a great honour to be cremated there.' He tells me his mother died six years ago, suddenly, of a heart attack, but she had already asked Sandip to make sure she would be cremated at Pashupatinath.

'I joked with her,' he says, 'like, "Oh shut up, I'll die before you, you can take *me* there!" You know, because she's only twenty years older than me. But I was happy to be able to cremate her there because it was her wish. I gave the first light, which is an honour as the oldest son. Most people walked away as she burned but I stood there for the full four hours, crying.'

I think of how I never saw Chris dead, how often I still double-take, thinking I've seen him riding past me on his bike, and ask Sandip if, by watching his mother's body burn, he thinks it gave him full knowledge, deep in his bones, that she was gone.

He doesn't. For months after, he would forget she was dead and go and ring her doorbell.

An impossibly cute baby monkey makes eye contact with me as he wobbles on a branch. We're ascending the stone hill behind Pashupatinath, and I've stopped to coo. Sandip hurries me along.

'You seem nervous, Sandip. Are they not friendly?'

They answer for him by breaking into a vicious, screaming brawl behind us, in exactly the spot I was cooing over the cutie. Big primates lumber past us to get involved, and mothers with babies hanging from their bellies canter to safety. We scurry away, up the stone steps and are greeted by a view of Kathmandu's rooftops, the gold of the temple flashing in the foreground, colourful blocks of flats fading into the distant trees and mountains. A thin layer of smoke hangs in the air like a morning mist. As we get closer to the vista, the smoke narrows into a tighter plume. I ask Sandip where it's coming from.

'A burning body,' he says, simply.

Pashupatinath sits on the bank of the Bagmati River, where, like the Ganges in Varanasi, people who are cremated are said to be fast-tracked to heaven without the need to be reincarnated – in fact, since the Bagmati flows to Varanasi, Sandip says, 'If the Bagmati isn't holy then neither is the Ganga.'

And like the Ganges, the Bagmati has had issues with pollution. The cognitive dissonance required to dump corporate and toilet waste directly into a goddess is hard to grasp, but Sandip says it's twofold: the belief that anything you dump in the river will just flow away, and because there was no other waste option. Now an alternative has been developed, and riverbank factories have been closed.

But the Ganges suffers another pollutant: uncremated corpses. In Hinduism it's believed that fire cleanses, so the bodies of children don't need to be cremated because their souls are still pure. In Varanasi, the bodies of children are taken in a boat to the centre of the river, attached to a rope and a boulder, and placed directly into the water. But much of the pollution from corpses is an issue of funeral poverty; not everyone can afford the costs of cremation. The poor have limited firewood with which to cremate their dead, so uncremated and partly cremated bodies are floated into the river. In early 2015, in Uttar Pradesh's Unnao district, a canal that connects to the Ganges dried up and over a hundred bodies were found in various stages of decay.

We make our way to a stone platform, and to my left the source of the smoke comes into view. It is, as he said, a burning body. That's absolutely, stunningly clear. The sight and smell hit me at once; a brief terror wave flashes and my breath whips itself into me as I detect something familiar in the aroma, mixed though it is with wood and flowers and ghee. The dank, dark hallway of Chris's house flashes through my mind; the moment the stench enveloped us, thickly, like chocolate enrobing nougat, the moment I felt a thudding wet crack somewhere deep behind my eye sockets, the moment barely manageable terror began to pour in.

And then it's gone, as quickly as it arrived. The smell becomes one of sandalwood and smoke and spice.

Ahead of us, below the platform and across the river, stands the golden temple gleaming proudly before the dirty stone steps leading down to the Bagmati River. There, on the bank, three men stand before a body wrapped in an orange sheet, lying on a *chita*, a kind of wooden stretcher for the dead. A crowd of people stand behind them, many of them in white, the colour of mourning: a sad colour, the absence of colour. Monkeys leap from roof to roof.

A woman is wailing.

'"Bring him back,"' translates Sandip. 'In the Newari community, if you don't want to cry, you have to make yourself. If you can't, you take water and put it in your eyes.' Since the cremations tend to happen the same day the person died, sometimes three or four hours later, I see no reason to doubt the sincerity of the woman's wails.

Sandip points across the river to where another body is on a *chita*, covered in a white sheet, the family crowding around. 'That place is called Brahmanal, and there we put the pure water from the holy river in their mouth.' It's as if he's a narrator to this extraordinary scene, as no sooner does he say it do they start doing it. 'And then we clean their feet in the river.'

'Why are all the women off to the side?' They're sitting in a line along the river, looking sombre.

'Women are not allowed to do this type of thing.'

'Because it's an honour of which women aren't worthy, or because they think it's too hard for them?'

'The latter. Women are more sensitive. When some-one dies, they cry so much, and it will be harder for them to see the body.'

'What if there are no men in the family?'

'Then they'll get his brother's son, whatever, to do it.'

'So even the most distant man is preferable to a woman?'

'Yes.'

'And if there really are no men, what then? The priest does it?'

'Exactly.'

The men drape strings of marigolds across the body – carefully, as if they might wake him up. I think of how we treated Chris's body. Like a problem to be solved. I realise eight days is much too long – marigolds wouldn't have cut it – but I doubt we'd have behaved much differently if it had been eight minutes.

Another body is being crowded around by a group of men holding up a sheet. They look as if they're shielding the body from public view.

'Actually they are,' says Sandip, 'but because they're taking off the clothes they're wearing, since you're cremated without your clothes.'

A cultural lens is tricky to remove, which is why I'm asking Sandip to confirm every little thing I'm seeing. My assumption was that they were shielding the body to protect us, the people who might catch a glimpse of dead flesh. But they're protecting the dead person's dignity – and given that we're gathered here uninvited to watch someone else's death ritual, it would be a bit rich to demand protection for our delicate sensibilities. Similarly, moments later, I notice the body draped in marigolds is surrounded by burning incense. I ask why, expecting to be told it masks the smell of the body, but Sandip says, 'It's to give the dead person the scent. It's a way of saying: you're dead but we still care about you.' I shake my head, almost laughing with how wrong I am every time I guess. Time and again, I see fear where there is only love.

We climb to a lower platform to get a closer look. We're not the only ones; there's a surprising number of spectators. Tourists, mostly from other parts of Nepal – even couples on dates.

'Ah, look.' Sandip indicates the body that was obscured for dignity. 'He is naked now, only wearing a sheet, so now they will put him on the *chita* and take him to be cremated.' The men of the family, themselves swathed in white sheets, transfer the body ever so gently to the stretcher. They scatter poinsettia leaves, which flutter down with grace and rest among the marigolds. I wasn't expecting a ritual as visceral as open-air cremation to be so gentle, to have so much beauty and care injected into it. Perhaps balance is the key to a better relationship with death; something between the horror of finding the decomposing corpse of a loved one and a sanitised, soulless goodbye.

A woman walks back and forth across the bridge,

crying and wailing. My eyes well up in sympathy immediately. A friend hooks her arm around her as the wailing gets louder and higher pitched.

'I was the only one who cried so much when my mother died,' says Sandip, 'and my younger brothers still feel sad and depressed if we talk about her, but I feel OK. If you don't cry then your emotions are, like, stuck.' I think of the days I spent in my flat convinced I was frantic, abuzz, dashing about and busy – when in reality only my eyes were moving, my fingers flicking from one open internet window to another, as life moved on around me. A fly in amber.

We step down to the riverbank, directly across from the pyres. We stroll along the bank, looking for a place to sit among the many people who have chosen this as a way to spend their Saturday.

'Is this really not disrespectful, Sandip? To watch someone's cremation like it's entertainment?'

'From here, it's fine. This is life, you know? But over there' – he points to a couple who are standing amongst the family members – 'you can see some Chinese tourists who've joined the family. In my opinion, keeping your distance is far better.'

'Right, so…' I say, trying to locate the line of offensiveness, which my instincts insist was about half a kilometre ago, 'from this side we're watching the reality of life and death, but getting up close is like saying, "I want to see the flesh bubble." And I suppose their feeling might be, "My mum is not your day trip."'

'Right,' Sandip nods. 'Also, they're wearing masks. That's also disrespectful: "I'll look, but I don't want the smell." Ugh – now he's taking a picture.'

The man has his camera poised and is leaning close to the body, taking a photograph of the woman's exposed head. Thankfully, by the time the body is ready to be set alight, the couple have wandered away.

The body is laid out on the *chita*, with a few salt-and-pepper strands of hair visible from under the sheet that's draped and decorated with flowers and offerings of money. The priest carefully places wood and straw on the body, and empties out a jar of ghee onto it. 'Ghee causes a smooth burn,' says Sandip. 'Also, when you burn yourself, you put ghee on it for relief, so it's like: we're burning you, but we're putting on ghee to soothe it.' The priest puts some sandalwood at the foot of the pile, for fragrance.

From the gathered family, the son emerges, bent double under the weight of his loss. His white shroud is wrapped across him, like a sling for a broken arm. An older man, perhaps the uncle, holds him around the waist, tight, as if letting go would release him to the floor like water. The son touches his head to the dead woman's feet, sobs visibly rippling through him. Monkeys clang their way across the rooftops and scuttle over the pavement. The family members drip water in her mouth. A bull behind us moos with fury. The son circles the body three times, clutching a flame, and his cries travel across the river to the people watching, to the angry bull, the oblivious monkeys. As he starts to howl, a relative rushes to his other side, and they lead him away.

The priest lights some incense, drips a little more ghee, and lights the pyre under the body. He removes the scattered offerings of money as the flames begin to catch.

The son quakes. He is led even further away than the women. The priest adds barley to the fire and it crescendos. The smoke is dark as it emerges from the pyre, turning white as it billows into the sky.

The funeral pyres used to be separated by caste, but in 2011 Nepal brought in laws forbidding caste-based discrimination or untouchability practices. Of course it hasn't erased the caste system entirely, and can only do so much to curb people's internal revulsions. Further down the river in Varanasi, India, the men who man the funeral pyres – heaven's gatekeepers – are from the lowest, untouchable caste: the Dom Raja. In the mid-nineties, the right-wing Hindu Bharatiya Janata Party pulled a publicity stunt in a drive to demonstrate solidarity with the lowest castes: the leaders of the party would have breakfast with the Dom Raja. Even that was too big an ask for a few of them, who waved away the food for fear of being 'polluted'. Given the love and care that goes into saying goodbye to a loved one, it seems odd that you would want the person who sees them off to be someone for whom you have no respect.

A flash of orange skims past my face. I gasp at the

realisation that it was a stretcher with a dead person on it.

'Sorry,' I whisper to Sandip, 'I'm not past the shock of it yet.' They walk past the pyres – they're headed for a building entrance. 'Where are they going?'

Sandip looks confused, then his face brightens. 'Ah, they're taking this body to do it electronically.'

'You mean a crematorium?' In January 2016, the Pashupati Area Development Trust installed the first functioning modern electric crematorium in Nepal, in an attempt to diminish carbon emissions, river pollution and deforestation. I ask Sandip what's different about this family that they're choosing the crematorium – do they want to get it over with quickly? He says it must be a sign of wealth. I look into it, and it's the opposite: aside from being faster and more environmentally friendly, burning a body in a crematorium is considerably cheaper than in the open air. It's likely that it will catch on; the traditional method has led to substantial deforestation around the Kathmandu Valley, with a huge increase in population over the past fifteen years and each cremation using between 350–500 kgs of wood.

As we discuss whether or not being removed from the process of the burning body will lead to less acceptance of death, the ramp leading away from the pyres becomes crowded by a procession of old women in the wake of a *chita* on the shoulders of two young men in t-shirts. The body is a wisp, with white hair peeking out from under an orange sheet. We move aside to let them pass.

'I'm quite sure this party is from an old orphanage,' says Sandip.

'You mean an old people's home?'

'I call it an old orphanage.'

He goes to investigate. There is one old man and at least thirty old women. Sandip chats to them as the body is set before the pyre. People mill around. No one seems to be mourning, or even considering the body.

'I was right,' says Sandip, coming back over. 'She's from the old orphanage. They said she died one hour ago. She wanted to drink some hot water, drank it, lay down and died a few minutes later. She had been in the old orphanage for eight years. She used to say she had four sons, but they never came to visit her. They don't know if it was true.'

'Maybe they died, and she doesn't know because she has dementia or something?'

'Or maybe her children don't like her.'

You can never assume someone was loved. Poor Sandip stood on this very riverbank crying for his mother for hours, and here this woman is, about to burn alone.

The women file back to the old orphanage. The one man hobbles over to the bench to sit.

'I'm glad the man is staying,' I say. 'I was sad no one was going to be with her.'

'Me too,' says Sandip. 'I feel kind of sad.'

We step away and leave the old orphan to her lonely exit.

*

The story of Nepal's death festival starts, of course, with a man being trampled to death by an elephant. King Pratap Malla, who ruled Nepal from 1641–74, had a unique system of rule: he wanted his sons to each take a turn running the kingdom while he was alive.* His second son, Chakrabartendra Malla, was killed in the unfortunate elephant incident the day after he took over as king. His mother, the queen, was inconsolable. She wouldn't eat or sleep and wouldn't stop crying. No matter what Pratap did to cheer her up, nothing worked. In desperation, he turned to his kingdom, and announced that anyone who could make her smile would be richly rewarded.

Gai Jatra was already an annual festival, literally translating as 'cow festival', a procession of people led by a cow. The procession was brought before the queen, and people performed comedy skits for her – or, by the sound of it, *at* her. Anyone who's ever been inconsolably sad and had well-meaning idiots dance around them vomiting glee will be sceptical about this approach, but eventually she cracked a smile. The successful skit was one that mocked the obscene wealth of the country's high society. Some sources claim she burst out laughing. Whatever the reaction, Pratap jumped on it. He decreed that henceforth, Gai Jatra would feature jokes, mockery and satire – even during the oppressive Shah regime, which was eventually toppled in 2008, it remained the

---

* I'm going to go out on a limb here and just guess: micromanager.

only day people were allowed to criticise the government – and that it would become a death festival; every family who had lost someone that year would take part in the procession.

'So is it a festival for the people who are grieving,' I ask Sandip, 'or a festival for the dead?'

'It's a festival for the people who died,' Sandip says, 'but it's also a festival for the people who were really close to them. To remind them that life and death is a natural thing. We believe that after a person dies, they become a spirit, so if their spirit can see their people crying all the time, they'll think, "How can I leave them?" They will be stuck. Stuck by your sadness. So to make them happy, to make their spirit go on to heaven, we have this festival.'

Whenever anyone suggests the dead are in attendance, gifts and sugar always seem to follow. As Sandip tells me stories of the Gai Jatras of his childhood, my mind conjures up images of trick-or-treating. 'Everyone receives and everyone gives,' he says. 'They used to give coins before inflation, when it was worth it. I remember hearing the ching-ching-ching in my pockets; my pants used to come down with the weight of them. People also gave packs of sweets made from different types of flour, cooked in oil or butter. I used to carry them in plastic bags and when they became too heavy I'd drop them off somewhere and go out again. I couldn't eat it all, so I'd go to school the next day with my tiffin box big and full, and pass them out – enjoy, enjoy, enjoy.'

*

The traffic moves at festival speed, like honey through an hourglass. The taxi is old, rattly, filled with the smell of exhaust fumes. But the time passes easily with my companion for the day, Junu Shrestha, a tour guide from the medieval city of Bhaktapur.

'In this celebration people are more happy than sad,' says Junu. 'It's a festival for dead people, but it's also for all of society. Because it's not only *your* family members who died: everybody dies, so why should we be sad? If everybody dies and we have to accept those deaths, let's celebrate it in a nice way.'

Even though we're discussing it in these terms of radical acceptance, talk of death in Nepal always leads back to the earthquake in 2015, in which 9,000 people died and many more were injured. Death seems to hang around, ready to drop in at any moment, like an overbearing neighbour. Junu was lucky; she used to live in Bhaktapur's central medieval square but had moved to the hillside for more reliable access to water. She was watching a movie with her sister on the ground floor of her earthquake-proof house when the ground started to shake. She stares into the distance as she tells me, 'From the hillside I looked down to Bhaktapur. The sky was full of dust and helicopters. It was devastating. Lots of houses from the sixteenth and seventeenth centuries – and even the eleventh and twelfth centuries – collapsed. Dead people are dead, they have no problem; it's the people left alive who suffer.'

Hinduism and Buddhism, the two major religions of Nepal, both emphasise sharing and helping others. But when food sources were threatened in the wake of the devastation, many did not come through. 'There was no food, and people were afraid that no food would be provided, so even the shopkeepers and wholesalers were storing it for themselves, and not selling it.'

'Did people come out for Gai Jatra that year?'

'Yes, but they did it in a small way. The government provided some money to the families to celebrate Gai Jatra.' Sandip told me a similar story of Patan's festivities, that despite the many deaths, participation was lower than usual. The earthquake on 29 April had been swiftly followed by another on 12 May. Even by the time the festival rolled around in August, areas of the city were still under restricted access, and many people were still afraid to go out.

We arrive, finally, in Bhaktapur, jump out of the car and make our way to the centre, an as yet sparsely populated square. The sounds of drums waft through the air like bonfire smoke. From around a corner, a line of people file into the square holding an enormous bamboo structure hoisted on their shoulders. It towers at about ten or twelve feet; at the very top sits an umbrella over a thick wig of hair. The rest is dressed in white and orange silk sheets, and draped in a pashmina. There's a handbag hanging off the side of it.

'Is that supposed to be … a person?' I ask Junu.

'Yes,' she says, 'we call this a *Taha-Macha*. It's a

representation of the person they're remembering. We can see this was a woman because she is wearing a sari. You see there is an umbrella on top to protect them, and also hair and clothes.'

'Who are the people following it?'

'These are the people who knew the person, the friends and family. They will spend all day giving food, fruits, juice, biscuits, anything they can to other families who have lost someone.'

'Where are they off to?' I ask, watching them round the corner.

'They will walk all around the city, and come back to the same place they started.' She laughs. 'It's a strange festival!'

We walk around the back streets, and come across a static Taha-Macha, waiting for the festivities to start. The 'skirt' is black with red and gold pendants, and it's topped with a bright pink-and-yellow umbrella. Underneath, instead of a wig for hair, there are bunches of flowers. A long black-and-white 'scarf' frames a picture of the woman the Taha-Macha represents: an old Newari woman with black-and-white hair and a bindi – a red dot on the centre of her forehead. Junu translates the caption: she was born in 1999 and died two months ago, in 2075 – which, using the Western calendar, means she was born in 1942 and died this year, 2018, aged seventy-six.

Turning the corner, we come to what feels like a makeshift backstage area full of children, around three to five years old, dressed as little Vishnus. The boys have thick moustaches painted on their chubby faces, and some are clutching deep-pink incense sticks as thick as cigars. Junu explains children dress as Vishnu for Gai Jatra when a grandparent has died. Behind us a group of little girls start a chant.

'Do the children understand that somebody has died?' I ask.

'No, they just love dressing up and being beautiful; they don't understand what's going on. In later years they'll see it and understand what it meant.'

'It must be great to have such good memories of the Gai Jatras of your youth, so when you lose someone, you know you'll have this support waiting.'

'Exactly – people want to do Gai Jatra in a big way for the person who is gone, but also for society,' Junu says. The constant debate of 'who is a funeral for, the dead or the bereaved?' rages on in the West, but when it comes to Gai Jatra, the aim appears to be balance.

More and more people are starting to filter in, building into a crowd. As in Pashupatinath, the people who've suffered a loss are distinguished by white clothes, and they're joined by friends and relatives. Next to the little Vishnus a few slightly older children are standing in two lines facing each other, rehearsing a dance in which they each hold a hollow stick and knock them against each other rhythmically. Junu comments, 'The sticks used to be just for the boys.'

'How come?'

'Because men dominated society before,' she says simply, 'and nowadays girls say: no, we need a place in this space.'

I tell her I was quite surprised at Pashupatinath that women were cut out of the experience of preparing bodies for cremation because of their supposed fragility. Especially after seeing the son practically collapse under the weight of his grief; that reaction is seen in women as frailty, something from which they should be protected, yet he was simply supported and led away.

Junu says, 'My neighbour gave fire to her husband, so I think if we want, we can do it now. For years it was just for boys, but now the girls are asking for this right – why not us?'

Somewhere behind us, some drums whip up a catchy beat. The air thrums with sound. Thick wisps of incense rise from the clutched fists of the little gods.

We duck down an alleyway and Junu tells me she wants to show me where some people are now living after the earthquake. We stop by a building site.

'People are still living in houses that aren't fit to be lived in. Some houses have huge cracks – some have even fallen down, but they have to live there. They have no other option.'

'Is that safe?' I ask.

'No, not at all,' she says, waving her hand. 'If there is another earthquake they'll die. But this is where some people live now.'

It takes me a moment to realise the rusty, corrugated-iron half-cylinder we've been standing next to isn't a storage space for a building site; it's the government's solution to a collapsed house. The top of the door doesn't reach the curved roof. Flaps of tarpaulin poke out from inside it, presumably to keep the rain out. The wooden door is splintered, with a flimsy lock on the front, smaller than one you'd use for a bike.

'My uncle's house was destroyed in the earthquake,' says Junu. 'He got some money from the government to build a new one, but it was not enough.'

'What percentage of what he needed did he get?'

'He got twenty-five thousand rupees.'

I do a quick calculation. Twenty-five thousand rupees, that's . . .

'Wait . . . wait, that's *nothing*.'

Junu nods. 'Nothing.'

It's £165. It's 250 plates of fried vegetable momos. It's about eighty-five beers – sixty-five if you want the imported stuff. It's six nights in my Airbnb. A quarter of an iPhone 8.

'How much would it cost to build a house?'

'More, more! And the money comes in instalments.'

'So they give not enough, in small bursts. So whoever lives here might live here the rest of their life.'

'Yes.'

'This doesn't look like it protects from the rain. And it must be so hot in there!'

'And in the winter, it's very, very cold,' she says, 'and there are rats.'

There's something scrawled on the door in large orange letters. Since I'm illiterate here, I ask Junu what it says.

'"Welcome."'

I follow Junu up a set of stairs and we emerge in a café. We take a seat by the balcony overlooking the square, order coffee and wait for the procession to start.

'So tell me about this book you're writing,' she says, so I tell her about the Worst Tuesday and how I got interested in the ways others deal with the certainty that death is coming.

'Are you afraid of death?' she asks.

'God, yes,' I say. 'There's this perception that we're "more afraid" of death in the West. But I don't think it's true. I think we all have the exact same fear instilled in us just by being human, but some people are dealing with it well and others are dealing with it badly. And I think where I'm from, we deal with it badly. *So* badly. The death culture where I'm from couldn't be more opposite to what you said happens here, Junu. That today is about people coming together to be reminded that you're not alone, that death is normal. When I think about what happened after Chris died – where I'm from, instead of coming together, people disappear. Because they "don't know what to say". Instead of saying it's natural and a part of life, they say they can't believe it happened, even though it happens to everyone. When someone dies, there is a sense that something has gone horribly wrong. It's almost always a shock.'

'Was it a shock for you?'

'Yes, completely. But Chris wasn't sick, so we weren't expecting to lose him so soon, or so suddenly, or at all. You expect a decline. It was strange, because I looked at his calendar to see what he was doing the day he died, to see if anything he did that day could give us a clue. He'd been at the lawyer's office. I called the lawyer and told him Chris had died, and he immediately asked, "Was he murdered?" And I said, "What? No, of course not, he was attacked by his own heart like everyone else." The lawyer thought he might have been murdered by another family member, because when he went to see him it was to change his will to leave Dion his house.'

This all spills out of me without my express permission, but Junu doesn't seem shocked.

'He changed his will the same day he died?' she says.
'Yes.'

'I think he knew he was going to die.'

As if on cue, music pours into the square. Loud drums, cymbals, maracas, trumpets, a beat so solid you could climb onto it like a table. We lean over the balcony and see the procession creeping into the square. It's thin at first, a Taha-Macha followed by some people, then another, then another, and soon the procession thickens with decorated wheeled chariots and teenagers with face paint. The ting-ting-ting of cymbals gets louder and the sticks come into view. Two endless lines of children, jumping and chanting and hitting their sticks with one rhythmic 'HEY!' after another.

The beat backs off and is replaced with a tinkling, and lines of teenage girls in matching black, white and red saris and golden hair pieces, necklaces and anklets sidle along, doing a gentle stick dance. They're then obscured by some younger boys doing the same dance but with the kind of head-banging enthusiasm usually found in a mosh pit. One boy holds his denim jacket in the air, screaming a chant and jumping up and down. It's a chant we'll hear throughout the day. I can't make out the words, of course, but the rhythm is burned into my brain:

Da-da-DA!

Da-da-DA!

DA-da-DA-da-DA!

Some of the dancers are young and bang their sticks with little rhythm or skill. But before long, we find ourselves looking down on a group of men in their twenties, all dressed casually in jeans and t-shirts, doing complex choreography in their two lines, involving spins, skips and sidesteps.

Sometimes the beat slows down, and the people walk a little slower, savouring the atmosphere, hitting their sticks languidly like a friendly high five, grinning at the face paints and Taha-Machas wavering in the sunshine...then the beat speeds up, and the line starts bobbing up and down and the cries of 'HEY!' get louder, the thwacks of the sticks get harder. The entire city crackles with electric energy.

*

Junu and I pay for our coffee and dive into the crowd, let ourselves be carried along by it, the beat of the drums and cymbals. We follow a red umbrella sheltering a Taha-Macha. Plumes of incense whirl above us and the sun beats down. Junu is hard to follow; she's not tall and she's better at navigating the crowds than me, but I focus on her green t-shirt and follow her down a quiet side street.

'Just for a break from the crowd!' she says. We walk past shops selling postcards and pashminas towards a green mountain looming in the distance, framed in the narrow space between red-brick walls. We emerge into Taumadhi Square and take in Kathmandu's tallest temple. The stairs leading to the bottom storey are steep and blanketed with Gai Jatra spectators.

'Let's go up,' says Junu.

From across the square, you might not think of Nyatapola (which means 'five storeys') as something to be avoided if you're afraid of heights. But standing at the foot of the stairs, I look up and gulp. The five roofs of the temple stand thirty metres tall and sit on a five-tiered staircase. A steep one. And there are people crammed on every single step. The colours of their outfits and parasols look beautiful against the darkness of the looming wood, the flash of green grass growing out over the edges of the roofs, the shock of blue sky behind. But to be part of the colourful crowd, we must climb – in an uncomfortably true sense. I feel like an upright baby goat. The temple itself is solid enough; it was built in 1702 and survived both the 1934 and the 2015 earthquakes. When we find a tight space and turn to look at the view, I wobble, struggling to hold myself so as not to tip backwards (annoying) or forwards (domino effect down five flights of stairs, leading to many more Taha-Machas at next year's festival). Junu reaches over a short woman standing between us and takes my backpack, presumably to minimise the chances of a tragic topple.

With proper footing, the view is sensational. Bhairabnath Temple stands proud to our left, a three-storey pagoda, against a backdrop of lush green mountains, fluffy clouds and blue skies. On the ground the procession gathers momentum, that same beat wafting through the air.

We get reacquainted with the ground, bones intact, and squeeze ourselves onto a shopfront step to watch the procession file past. Teenage boys do the stick dance with empty water bottles, grinning as they sweat in their sunglasses and wet shirts. A cross-dresser in a black skirt, neon green shirt and a straw hat hams up a jig for my cameraphone, behind a fat man in a t-shirt with the belly and nipples cut out. What a strange and delightful way to face your mortality.

But it's working. Just like it worked for the queen all those centuries ago, when Pratap summoned everyone who'd lost someone that year to the palace, and she watched as it became crammed with people. Grief is like drowning. It's gnawing absence, and a threat. It's raw terror, it's bargaining for extra time, it's your heart outside your body in a hailstorm, it's nothing mattering any more. But suddenly I'm seeing, as if for the first time, that it isn't unusual. And that's all I can think about as the joyous crowd passes, bouncing and singing and dancing and chanting. This obvious thing I feel I'm learning for the first time.

It's normal, it's normal, it's normal.

Later, back in my room and far above the continuing beat of the drums, I look up the stick song, 'Ghintang Kishee Twaak', and email Junu and Sandip for their best translations. They come back with completely different versions of it, probably owing to their different backgrounds. Junu says 'ghintang kishee' is the stick dance, and 'twaak' is the sound of sticks hitting each other.

Sandip's translation hits closer to home:

People die, but this is not the same as mourning.
We will leave that in the past.
We need to move on,
And not feel sorry any more.
This is nature.
Let's celebrate while we're alive.

CHAPTER FIVE

Equal in Death

*We're all going to die, all of us, what a circus! That alone should
make us love each other but it doesn't. We are terrorized and flat-
tened by trivialities, we are eaten up by nothing.*

– Charles Bukowski

'Of course you're afraid of it,' said the taxi driver, 'everyone's afraid of death.'

He was driving me to the Templo de Santa Muerte,
just outside of Pátzcuaro. After the Day of the Dead
celebrations, I decided to go and be among people who
don't just celebrate the dead during one annual festival,
but pray to death herself, year-round.

'Mexicans are constantly claiming death doesn't scare
them, though,' I said.

'Yes, but it's nonsense. Of course we're afraid.'

'What scares you about it?'

'I'd be afraid for my wife and children,' he said thoughtfully, 'of how they would survive without the money I earn.'

'OK,' I said, 'but what about you?'

'Well, I'd be worried about my family being sad that I'm gone,' he said again.

'These are totally rational reasons to be afraid,' I said, 'but, where I'm from, we're afraid of *being* dead.'

'Right, because of how your families will cope, what will happen after you've gone. That's normal.'

'No. I mean, yes, but aside from that – look, if you knew your family would definitely be fine when you were gone, protected, happy, with everything they'll ever need, would you be afraid of death?'

'Well, I don't want to die in a horrible way.'

'OK, done. You'll die peacefully in your sleep, you won't know it's happening, and your family will be fine. Where I'm from, this might remove a lot of the stress, but we would remain essentially terrified.'

I didn't tell him how this thought plagued me as a little girl, how I used to crawl into the cupboard under the stairs, clamp my eyes and ears shut, and try to imagine that this is what death would be like, then crawl out shivering from the boredom, knowing even then how stupid it was to imagine I'd be present for any of it.

Instead I asked, 'Don't you feel that way?'

He gave me a sideways glance.

'No. That's dumb.'

*

Until March 2009, the Mexican border had a collection of shrines to the saint of death, many of them elaborate, marble, with electric lighting. Then Mexican army troops teamed up with workers and used backhoes to topple and crush them. Over thirty Santa Muerte shrines were demolished just across the border from Laredo, Texas. In the Mexican government's war against the narcos (short for *narcotraficantes*, or drug traffickers), Santa Muerte had become spiritual enemy number one.

President Calderón, in office 2006–12, was part of the conservative PAN party, which has close ties to the Catholic Church, so it's likely the government's efforts to crush Santa Muerte's influence was a result of lobbying by Catholic bishops. Or at least that's what Andrew Chesnut, the leading expert on the folk saint, suspects.

'Catholic Church rejection [of Santa Muerte] is twofold,' says Andrew, Skyping me from his home in Virginia, where he works as a religious studies professor. 'On the theological plane, Christians believe that Jesus gave his life on the Cross to give Christians the opportunity of eternal life, and in that way really defeats the last enemy, which is death. So if you're venerating death, then in a way that's antithetical to what you should be doing as a Christian, if death is the enemy of Christ. On probably an even more important plane, Santa Muerte is religious competition. Religion in Latin America and Mexico already felt besieged by Pentecostal competition [a form of evangelical Protestantism imported from the USA]; now this heretical folk saint emerges

111

on the scene, and by my estimates has some ten million followers.'

Most of the Santa Muerte devotees in Mexico still consider themselves Catholic, whether or not they are practising. As a saint very much rejected by the Catholic Church, Santa Muerte has no annual feast day, but 2 November (the second Day of the Dead) is emerging as the unofficial date, as *santamuerteros* have started incorporating her into the festivities. 'So now, every week before Day of the Dead, the Catholic Church in Mexico goes ballistic, warning parishioners not to traffic with Santa Muerte during Day of the Dead, that those two things are separate.'

The Catholic Church certainly has a history of telling people what to celebrate and when, the original Aztec festival for the dead having now been shrunk down and made inextricable from the Catholic celebration with which it was forcibly blended.

Though it wouldn't be true to say every Mexican *narcotraficante* is a Santa Muerte devotee, there's no doubt that she is the pre-eminent spiritual figure among narcos today. Why?

'Because if you're looking to bring death upon your enemies, be they rival narcos or law enforcement, who better to ask for that than death herself?' says Andrew. 'She's also prayed to for protection from those rivals who might be coming against you. She's a folk saint, not a Catholic canonised saint, so in theory it's easier to ask her for dark deeds.'

The taxi driver drops me off at the *templo*, about four miles west of Pátzcuaro in Santa Ana Chapitiro. It's a courtyard on the front of what is clearly a family home. To the left of the entrance there's a small room with an altar, steadied with models of Santa Muerte. The image is what I grew up calling the Grim Reaper: an enrobed skeleton holding a scythe in one bony hand and a globe in the other. A young man in a baseball cap and a black t-shirt with a skull on it is bent over the altar, lighting a bowl of incense and letting the smoke fill the room. 'For atmosphere,' he says. He clearly runs the place and moves through the multiple images of death with easy grace, as if he and Santa Muerte have their own handshake. Front and centre of the altar sits a skull, also wearing a baseball cap. It's got a cigar dangling from its mouth above an ashtray with two cigarettes, extinguished after a single drag.

'Sorry, Andrew, did you say she has *ten million* followers?'

'Unfortunately, we don't have any systematic surveys,' says Andrew, 'but yes, ten million is my best estimate, with probably seventy to seventy-five per cent in Mexico, fifteen per cent in the US and ten to fifteen per cent in Central America. And this is only in the past fifteen years, since devotion only went public in 2001. To put this in perspective, after thousands of years of existence, there are only fourteen million Jews in the entire world – obviously the Holocaust eliminated half of them, but still, there's probably almost as many Santa Muerte devotees as there are Jews in the world. So it is not hyperbole to say that in the past couple of decades there's no faster-growing new religious movement in the entire West, including Europe. Most new religious movements are born and die within a few years, just like businesses.'

Though Santa Muerte is now gaining followers from all walks of life, her followers are still disproportionately working class, those who feel that death could be around the corner, which for Mexicans is more the case than almost any other country in the world; in the last decade, only Syria has surpassed Mexico in violent deaths. But finding someone who's willing to talk about it is like finding someone who's happy to chat about their haemorrhoids – not impossible, but tricky, with a lot of polite batting away.

Here in the *templo*, the death discussion is less about the nation's violence and more the simple, repeated reminder that death is coming. The walls are covered in framed pictures of La Flaquita (a nickname for Santa Muerte, meaning 'the skinny one'). She peers out of her hollow eye sockets under billowing robes. One particularly terrifying image has death emerging from the blackness wielding a glinting scythe, grinning, pointing right at me.

'So, what do you think is causing this unbelievable explosion in popularity of this one saint?' I ask Andrew.

'One really important engine of her growth is her reputation for being very efficacious and speedy in delivering miracles. I don't know how many devotees I've interviewed in Mexico who say, "I was asking San Judas to get me a new job for three months, he was ignoring me, then my aunt said 'go try La Flaquita' and then within a week I had a new job." You hear all these stories about how she comes through much faster than her rivals, and most of the miracles have to do with health, wealth and love. She's a major love doctor as well, and still her number-one-selling votive candle is the red candle of love magic.'

From the 1940s to the 1980s, when devotion to Santa Muerte was still somewhat cultish, American and Mexican anthropologists reported her only performing one type of miracle: love magic. 'Her oldest known prayer is a love prayer for women asking for their cheating husband or boyfriend to come back humbled at their knees, and to take that scythe and take out the other woman from their path.'

A woman in her early forties enters the *templo*. She is wearing a body warmer, leggings and trainers, a big silk red bow on her head that reminds me of Minnie Mouse, with multiple silver piercings around her mouth like glinting cold sores. She's holding a shot of tequila, a cigar and a candle. She approaches a skeleton in a sequinned wedding dress, white veil and tiara, with a huge, gaudy ring on its left hand. She sets down the tequila (Santa Muerte loves a drink – the Greek etymology of skeleton goes back to meaning 'parched'), and then she lights the cigar and candle. She kneels and bows her head. Her silk bow shines as the shadows move with the sun. She stands, her head still bowed in silence. She lifts her head and with arms crossed, she smokes the cigar, not moving her eyes from the skeleton bride's skull.

'What is the most common misconception about Santa Muerte?'

'That she's exclusively a satanic narco saint,' says Andrew, 'because the lion's share of the press in the US, Mexico and the UK has been on Santa Muerte as the patron saint of the cartels – also propagated because the Catholic Church rebukes her as satanic as well. The truth is she's the patron saint of the Mexican drug war writ large, because she also has significant following among Mexican law enforcement – especially the municipal police, who are on the front lines against the narcos.'

Contrary to the idea of a sinister, satanic narco saint, people go to these shrines for healing. 'That might seem odd,' Andrew continues, 'but who better to ask to grant you more life, to heal you, than death herself?'

Behind the woman smoking a cigar arrives a young couple with a little girl in tow. She's about six, clutching a candle and a cigarette in her little fists. After a while, the cigar woman sits next to me on the metal bench, which also depicts multiple visions of hooded death. She looks tired, and sad, but smiles from inside her cloud of smoke as the couple and child pass to take their turn with the skeleton bride.

'Devotion has proliferated at a time of Mexico becoming vast killing fields,' says Andrew. 'A lot of those folks who feel like death could be imminent feel that she's the right saint for them. I think her cult would be booming anyway, but it can't be ignored that the time she has mushroomed is one of great, bad death. One of the translations of Santa Muerte in English is "Holy Death". This bold Catholic concept of having a holier, good death, where you die at home surrounded by your family members – hopefully a priest is there to adminis-ter the last rites – becomes, I think, desired and appealing in Mexico, in these days of so much bad death: the desire to die naturally and in a good way, as opposed to gunned down in the street like a dog.'

Tracey Rollin's book *Santa Muerte: The History, Rituals and Magic of Our Lady of the Holy Death* details the history and cultural influences of the folk saint and says she is associated with 'safe passage to the afterlife', so I put it to Andrew that perhaps Santa Muerte is the bouncer, someone to pull back the velvet rope and say, 'I'll vouch for this one.'

'Actually, I'd say that's kind of minor,' says Andrew. 'I think concerns about the afterlife are less important for most Santa Muerte devotees; wondering where you're going to go in the afterlife is a luxury. It's more about a few more years, weeks or days. Those of us who are well heeled and have all our needs satisfied can sit around and contemplate these things, but when someone's coming after you with an M16, your afflictions are way more immediate.' As Santa Muerte expands rapidly beyond her Mexican base to devotees with what we might term 'first-world problems', the emphasis also seems to shift to reflect more middle-class concerns. Less 'please let me live another day', and more 'please let my check-in to heaven go smoothly'.

I tell Andrew I think I've been guilty of letting cultural bias cloud my understanding of what I was looking at when it came to Day of the Dead. 'While I was in a cemetery in Mexico, I noticed there were some teenagers making out in a tent. And I surmised that they didn't really believe it, because there's no way they'd be shagging in a tent if they thought their grandmother was visiting. Am I wrong about that?'

Andrew laughs. 'I think what you're describing in the cemetery is classic Mexican working class, where the sacred and the profane mix together; you have some people reciting the prayers and looking lost in their devotion, while other people are on their cell phones, drinking, changing diapers. I think that kind of carnivalesque mix is par for the course with Mexican working-class religiosity. I think just because they're "shagging in a tent" doesn't necessarily mean they don't believe their ancestors are coming back to suck the nutrients out of the food. They don't have to be mutually exclusive, right?'

'Maybe this is my Englishness. What I interpreted was a lack of reverence: if you think of reverence as a mixture of love and fear, here we've got much, much more fear than love when we talk about death and our dead – in fact I'd say our version of "reverence" and "respect" for death are just academic terms for "shitting our pants".'

Andrew laughs, and says, 'Mexico is unique in the world in that no other country in history has ever had a death figure like La Catrina as a kind of totemic figure of its national identity. I think it goes along with the whole death-positive movement, in which Mexico becomes a model for a more holistic view of death as a natural part of life – as it always was historically in Europe anyway. It's really just in the last century that Europeans and Americans started to remove and sanitise death.'

The mother and young daughter approach the skeleton bride and gently touch the dress, her bony hand. The mother holds and caresses the hand as if it's someone she knows, as if she's saying, 'You'll get through this.' But judging by the messages scrawled all over the pictures of death, she's probably saying thank you.

The father stands in solemn silence and holds death's gaze.

Santa Muerte devotees are, as Andrew pointed out, overwhelmingly working class. Even as her popularity explodes beyond Mexico, her devotees are primarily those who have very little choice about how they might die. As such, the movement has attracted a lot of trans women, who go through life with a much higher risk of violence and murder. The American Civil Liberties Union reports that, according to one survey, one in four transgender people have been assaulted because they are trans, and in recent years the number of murdered transgender and non-binary people has hit record highs;

2017–18 was the deadliest year on record for the transgender population – both in the US and the rest of the world – and as the numbers peak and trough, the trend shows no signs of letting up.*

But if there were a community living without fear of a 'bad death', how might their mortal terror manifest? Let's start an imaginary road trip in Tijuana – where people used to go to pray at the foot of Santa Muerte shrines, before they, too, were demolished – and drive north for eight hours. We'll arrive in the quaint neighbourhood of Mill Valley, just north of San Francisco. This is the home of a large, friendly, extremely blond man who doesn't carry house keys because he has a door-opening chip implanted in his hand.

I first saw the name Zoltan Istvan in a tweet from an angry young man. Furious that a group of (mostly) women were meeting in Winchester, England, to share ideas about death acceptance, he tweeted, 'I'm seriously pissed off ... these people are openly celebrating death as a good thing – fuck off deathists' (and yes, 'Fuck off, Deathists' was an alternative title for this chapter). After a torrent of tweets in which he argued that death should never be accepted, he tweeted, '@zoltan_istvan, we have a lot of work to do.'

Zoltan Istvan is the face of transhumanism, an anti-death movement that proposes technology as the answer:

---

* Rosa Furneaux, 'Ten facts on trans murders as world marks second deadliest year', *Reuters*, 20 November 2019, available at www.reuters. com/article/lgbt-crime-rights-idUSL8N2804FQ humans will inevitably, they believe, become cyborgs who never have to die. While statistics on how many people identify as transhumanist aren't available, Zoltan believes anti-ageing and life-extension research is up 1,000 per cent in the past eighteen months. Since I'm in California, spending two weeks holed up at a writers' residency in Santa Cruz, I email Zoltan and ask if he'd be happy to meet me for an interview. He sends a pleasant response, so I hop on a Greyhound to San Francisco and a bus to Mill Valley.

Zoltan is the American dream incarnate: his parents came over from Hungary to escape communism. Zoltan had a successful career in journalism, presenting TV spots for National Geographic, saved enough to buy a property, then made himself a millionaire by flipping houses. And he's not short on confidence: when his wife told him to get a job, he left her a Post-it note on the fridge letting her know he was running for president. Let me repeat that: when Zoltan was left to ponder what job he'd like to do, the answer he came up with is 'I'd like to run the whole damn country'. His main policy? Eradicate death.

I'm sitting in Zoltan's living room, a square room with a window overlooking the garden. With one eye on the clock so we don't forget to walk round the corner to pick up his young daughter from school, he explains the thrust of the transhumanist argument when it comes to politics, which briefly put, is: if I want to modify my body to avoid dying, no one should stop me.

'We would consider that a civil rights issue,' says Zoltan.

The privilege in this sentiment stops me, momentarily, in my tracks. This is a statement he's happy to make shortly after a white supremacist in Charlottesville drove his car into a crowd of people who were peacefully protesting against white supremacy. In the US, black Americans are on average eight times more likely than white Americans to be killed by firearms, and black men are more likely to die by guns in homicides than white men (who, when they die by guns, more often die in suicides).* To frame dying of natural causes as a civil rights issue when the world still shrugs at black and trans people living with such a higher likelihood of violence and murder – well, Zoltan's timing is, putting it kindly, off.

Zoltan's concerns about death don't involve his enemies coming after him with an M16. He doesn't lie awake at night worrying about being killed in the street for some minor infraction, like Eric Garner (who was killed by police in 2014, who held him in an illegal chokehold while arresting him for selling loose cigarettes), or for nothing at all, like Philando Castile (who was shot in the front seat of his car in 2016 by the police officer who'd asked him to reach for his driver's licence). The death Zoltan worries about – the death many of us

---

* According to the Centers for Disease Control and Prevention, in its 2017 report 'Age-Adjusted Rates for Homicides, by Race/Ethnicity—United States, 1999–2015', available at www.cdc.gov/mmwr/volumes/66/wr/mm6631a9.htm

worry about in the affluent West – is deemed a privilege elsewhere: death by ageing.

I ask Zoltan why transhumanism is so overwhelmingly white and male. He says there has been interest from a few people of colour, but transhumanists continue to be confounded by women's apparent lack of interest in immortality.

'I can tell you that the single largest dilemma we've had is getting women into it,' says Zoltan. He publicised the movement by touring the country in a bus shaped like a giant coffin, and complains, 'I could barely get any girls on my bus. We had an open invitation for anyone to travel with us. We had a constant influx of guys, but it looks terrible when you only have guys travelling around on a coffin bus.' Is it unprofessional to guffaw? Because I do. His eyes widen with interest. 'If you have ideas, tell me. We are all at a loss.'

Where to start with why the ladies aren't forming an orderly queue for the coffin bus? How do you explain to a rich white man the various ways that death hovers over women? How do you explain the psychological effect of being taught, repeatedly and from a young age, that you're constantly in danger? That you could be raped and murdered, and even blamed for it afterwards? That in much of the world – including parts of America – you can be denied a life-saving abortion because your life is still less important than the collection of cells that are threatening it? How to reveal that we walk home at night fashioning pitiful shivs with our front-door keys between our fingers to a man who's had a key chip implanted in his hand for pure convenience? There's a reason why only society's most privileged see death as something to be cured. They have food, water, shelter; the cops aren't shooting them; no one's threatening to rape them – death is a problem to the most privileged because 'this sweet deal has an expiry date' is the gravest of very few problems. I don't wish to devalue the transhumanists' mortal terror: we all have it. Reaching old age is a privilege, but it's also no picnic.

Still, Zoltan has asked me why women don't want to get on his coffin bus and ride to immortality.

'I suppose it's that we don't believe you.'

When it comes to immortality, there's no way to slice it that isn't awkward. Is it only for people rich enough to afford it? Awkward: that would create a two-tier society of superbeings being supported by a mortal underclass. That's a wealth divide that goes far beyond rich and poor.

No, says Zoltan, because the first principle of transhumanism is that it would have to be available to everyone.

The American medical system is not known for its wide or affordable coverage, but let's skip over that for a moment and assume that it works: everyone gets immortality. Awkward: do we stop people having children, so it doesn't get too crowded? If so, does that mean we're going to stick with this generation? The generation that elected Trump and had a resurgence of Nazism seventy years after it had been killed off? If we do still let people have children, awkward: how will we cope with a rapidly expanding population and no extra resources?

A common answer is that we'll go and live in space. But, I ask Zoltan, can we be honest for a moment? Space looks rubbish. What about the beach, the wind in your face, a liberal supply of oxygen, culture, the Grand Canyon, chocolate, or, you know, sound? I ask Zoltan if he would really consider moving out of this lovely neighbourhood to go and live in space.

'Well,' he says, 'one thing that's going to happen is soon we're all going to be so tied into virtual reality, even if you're in space you're still going to be experiencing the beach – in fact, probably better beaches than you've ever come across in your life.'

'You studied philosophy though, you know the Robert Nozick thought experiment, where you have the choice of a real life with all its problems or a simulated one that's perfect.'

'It's true, if you can be sent to a box in space but you know you're going to be perfectly happy for ever, would you do it? And nobody says yes,' he agrees.

'Right. So why would we be plugged into VR all the time? Especially if we've got a broadly lovely life. Why would you want to be plugged into virtual reality? What would you want it to give you?'

His answer is essentially that 'we would make a virtual reality that's as exciting as the real reality', which misses the point entirely: people don't want a real life because it's more exciting than fantasy. It definitely isn't. People want a real life because it's real. Transhumanists answer 'Technology!' to every question, and even suggest humans and robots will one day become indistinguishable (which they call 'the Singularity' – and as Zoltan tells me about this exciting moment that we're all waiting for, he reminds me of a preacher talking about the Second Coming). But every advance relies on us losing pieces of our humanity. Nature seems to have put everything in place to make bargaining for extra life rather expensive. The real sticking point with living for ever is the brain: neurons do not regenerate in the same way as other cells. They could be made to, but they would then lose their connections with other neurons – namely, our experience, our memories, our very selves. As a price for immortality, it's hardly a bargain.

'If you had that choice,' I ask, 'if you got to reboot every hundred years or so but you would forget everything – you wouldn't know or love your wife, wouldn't remember your children – would you take that deal?'

'Well, I would take that,' he says, 'though I wouldn't be thrilled, just so you know.'

It was on Twitter, while following the hashtag of the 2017 Death & the Maiden conference in Winchester, which I couldn't attend in person, that I first became acquainted with transhumanism. The event was organised by death studies scholar Lucy Talbot. I refreshed the search for #deathmaidenconf, to see what people were saying about the event.

The 'fuck off deathists' tweet from the angry young man appeared at the top of my feed. Two hours and ten minutes later, the conference's keynote speaker, Caitlin Doughty, celebrity mortician and author of the memoir *Smoke Gets in Your Eyes*, responded '...you need a hug, bro?' and a Twitter storm erupted. Her many fans jumped to tell the tweeter, 'Might as well accept it, it's going to happen!' The young man replied to almost every tweet, replied and replied and replied, arguing that death is a blight on mankind, that it should never be tolerated. He seemed to take 'death positive' to mean that loss is good, that these people gathering in Winchester were glad his grandmother died and thought she 'deserved' it. They protested to the contrary, that death is not good or bad, it just is. He accused them of being 'sick individuals' and told more than one person, 'If you really want to die, I invite you to do so.'

Lucy Talbot had a bad cold and had barely slept in the run-up to the conference. She was panicking that no one was having a good time. Then attendees came up to her to excitedly tell her that #deathmaidenconf was trending. She checked Twitter, and the first thing she saw was the 'fuck off deathists' tweet.

'I would have liked to have directed people to the hashtag to show what the weekend was all about,' Lucy told me over a plate of chips in a Winchester pub, 'but that guy's repeated use of it completely drowned out the incredible voices we had there that weekend. That's my issue with it, selfishly. It was an event upholding equal rights, giving voices to people from minorities, speaking about social issues around death such as funeral poverty, violent death, grief, denial, repression...'

'And they were all drowned out by one angry white man.'

'One really angry white man who wasn't even there, and who completely missed the point.'

The 'one really angry white man' turned out to be a self-declared 'DIY cyborg' and transhumanist. One of his many, increasingly wild claims against the death-positivity movement was that encouraging death accept-ance is dangerous, because it discourages life-saving medical research into ageing. This is, to put it mildly, a leap. Organisations such as Caitlin Doughty's Order of the Good Death – a group of funeral industry profession-als, artists and academics trying to get a death-phobic society to become more accepting of their own mortality – are hardly mainstream, arguing as they are for us all to talk about something we've been taught not to men-tion, and at no point have they ever protested medical research or petitioned for it not to happen. I check with Sarah Chavez, director of the Order, who emails:

Oh my. I have never heard or read anything stated that could be construed this way and I'm sad and dis-appointed if someone (mis)understood this. Anyone I know or have worked with within the movement is very much in favour of medical research that will help save lives and improve quality of life. That's what the movement is about – in the end it really isn't about death, but about improving the quality of all our lives.

It seems we've reached the point at which the transhumanist ideology that death shouldn't be accepted morphs into wordplay and fearmongering; just as the term 'feminism' has been mistaken to mean 'amateur castrations on innocent men', some think the term 'death positive' means 'cheering when people flatline'.

In fact, the ideology behind 'death positive' is closer to body positivity: just as in recent years we've been hearing that we should 'embrace our curves', we can embrace the fact of our mortality, and in doing so, our lives become richer, more mindful and less anxious. It isn't just an analogy; body positivity and death positivity come from a similar place. We live in a society that pegs a woman's worth to her beauty and her beauty to her youth. This goes some way to explaining why, in the death-denying West, the duty to deny ageing sits much more heavily on women's shoulders: North Americans buy 25 per cent of all the world's cosmetics, and American women spend more annually on make-up and skincare than the US government spends on all its federal agencies. In a society that values women only as objects of youthful beauty or baby-making, older women become devalued. In the face of this, to undercut the patriarchy by accepting your body is undoubtedly a feminist act; to accept its eventual decay is a step further.

Sarah believes Western women are trying to take back what was lost when women were cut out of deathcare, towards the end of the nineteenth century. 'Men weren't interested in deathcare until they thought they could make money from it,' she says. It's often true that society fobs off its deathcare onto those it doesn't like; deathcare is one of the many jobs that myriad societies have dubbed 'women's work'. It's not as if men haven't had to do uncomfortable or frightening jobs – but hunting and going to war have glory attached to them, which can't be said for housework, childcare or dealing with corpses.

'When death and dying became professionalised by the medical and funeral industries, women had to figure out different ways to grapple with their relationship with mortality,' Sarah says. 'We still live in a society that bases a woman's value on their youthful, beautiful body, or their childbearing body – as soon as those aren't applicable, they have limited places of value in our culture. So I think a lot of these women who are joining the death-positive movement are striving to reclaim and imbue ageing and death with meaning and value. That's their way of resisting patriarchal ideas.'

I'm talking to Sarah at the height of the Trump/ Pence administration, which has been a hideous festival of regulation over the bodies of women. Reproductive justice has been under fire with the government restricting the already scant access to abortion, defunding Planned Parenthood, which includes abortion provision among its services, and talk of forcing women to have burials or cremations for aborted or miscarried foetuses. In 2019 Texas state legislators considered a bill that would have allowed state execution for women who have abortions (with no exceptions for rape or incest – the bill failed at the committee stage), and an Ohio bill has instructed doctors to 'reimplant ectopic pregnancy' or face 'abortion murder charges' (Ohio is apparently undeterred by the fact that ectopic pregnancies are death sentences for both mother and foetus, nor are they put off by the fact that such a medical procedure doesn't exist).

You'd think, if nothing else, that death would be a sweet release from it all, but even corpses are regulated by men: the male-dominated Catholic Church, which still has a ban on female priests, has condemned aquamation (a more eco-friendly alternative to cremation, which dissolves the corpse in a mixture of water and lye, heated to about 160°C/320°F), just as they condemned cremation until 1963.

'It seems we have these three death movements booming at once,' I say, 'and the societal divisions reflected are really stark. The Santa Muerte movement is overwhelmingly working class, transhumanism is overwhelmingly white and male, and death positivity is overwhelmingly female. But you have a huge following of trans people in the death-positive movement, right?'

'Oh my gosh, yes,' says Sarah, 'because again, people in those communities have the experience of something that a lot of us don't think about: how we appear gender-wise, and protecting that in death. There are horror stories. If, for example, a trans woman dies without an advance directive or plans, and her parents then have legal rights over her body, they can dress her as a man and call her by her old, male name. These are real acts of violence against these bodies that follow them from life into death.'

'You don't think of death as a privilege, do you? And yet getting to choose it and plan it has become part of privilege.'

'Absolutely,' says Sarah. 'We are not equal in death. Those inequalities follow the bodies of marginalised people into death as well; they don't just end.'

It's clear why women, trans and non-binary people would be attracted to a movement that encourages agency over one's own corpse. What's not clear is why the death-positive movement seems to attract white women in particular. 'I think people of colour are going to be less focused on issues like green burial than what the urgent needs of the community are,' says Sarah. Much like those who choose to pray to Santa Muerte for a little extra time rather than pontificate on whether they'll have a king-size bed in heaven, even the way we deal with mortal terror eventually comes back to privilege.

We need only open a newspaper to see how inequality follows us to the grave. The first white victim of Ebola had a huge amount of coverage that wasn't afforded the black victims who'd gone before, who were reported on as an amorphous mass. Black victims of murder, such as those shot by police, are always subjected to a discussion of what they might have done to deserve or cause it. Twelve-year-old Tamir Rice caused his own death in 2014, argued the city of Cleveland, because he was holding a pellet gun. 'Blame only the man who tragically decided to resist' said the headline in the *New York Post* about Eric Garner, who during his arrest for selling loose cigarettes gasped the words 'I can't breathe' no less than eleven times, while the police held him in an illegal chokehold, on camera. Philando Castile made the poor cop nervous, people reasoned – apparently police training doesn't cover staying calm while holding a gun in the face of a citizen, and it's unclear where citizens can go for their training in how to soothe a jumpy cop. 'Trayvon…' – said one headline, of Trayvon Martin, a seventeen-year-old unarmed black teen with no criminal record who was shot in 2012 by a Neighbourhood Watch coordinator, a man who regularly called the police to report 'suspicious' individuals, all of whom were black males – '…typical teen or troublemaker?'

Meanwhile, Dylann Roof, a twenty-one-year-old white man with a criminal record, murdered nine people at a historic African-American church in Charleston in 2015 and admitted he did it because he wanted to start a race war; he was described as 'disturbed'. In 2017, sixty-four-year-old Stephen Paddock opened fire on an outdoor country-music festival on the Las Vegas Strip. He murdered fifty-nine people, injured around 500, and killed himself. He was described as 'sick'. Black murder victims brought it on themselves; white murderers are afflicted. White people can't control their circumstances, black people should have.

Last year, I passed a subway station in Bushwick, New York, and saw a sepia-tinted poster of a pile of skulls, with the word 'EQUALITY' emblazoned underneath it. It's a neat sentiment, that we're all equal in death, a reminder not to get too pompous and caught up with status, material possessions or ambition because ultimately, they will be meaningless. But it's also a way to sidestep two uncomfortable truths: firstly, that while we're all at the same level when our skulls are skinless, that level is a low one. Worm-level. It's a demotion. Our projects are over, our power is gone. Hence our aversion to speaking ill of the dead: you don't kick a man when he's six feet down.

Secondly, it sidesteps the fact that such 'equality' is woefully – and literally – skin-deep. Yes, we're all as gone as each other and yes, it's hard to tell skulls apart. But when the corpses of some are being controlled more than others, if people are becoming skeletons early because of the tint of the skin that was stretched over them or because their gender and sex didn't match, the notion that we're equal in death is as absurdly short-sighted as suggesting a slum and a mansion are the same because they're both places to live.

Society's divisions are reflected more by our fear of death than perhaps any other metric. None of us feels we have enough control over how we will die. In a much-improved world, we'd all get to live the anxiety of the privileged white man. Zoltan, who has the options so many others lack, feels oppressed by the very fact of a mortal body. 'I just want the choice,' he says, in his safe neighbourhood, to a straight, white, cis woman with access to free healthcare. 'This is the "I'm privileged" statement, but we suffer under the spectre of death, we have to worry "I could die from a heart attack" or "I might get cancer". I don't like that idea at all. If I'm going to die, I want to choose how to die.'

Don't we all?

CHAPTER SIX

Not Haunted

It is indeed impossible to imagine our own death; and whenever we attempt to do so, we can perceive that we are in fact still present as spectators.

– Sigmund Freud

It's always lovely to see my friend Arin, but we're together for barely an hour before I'm yelling at him for putting my brain in a bin.

He and I met in Thailand, where we worked together for two strange months, making films at a flailing tech start-up. We never lost touch, and when he saw I was going to be in San Francisco, he invited me to stay with him and his girlfriend, Hillary. I drag my suitcase up two flights of stairs into their baked Alaska of an apartment – freezing on the inside thanks to an enthusiastic air conditioner, and scorched on the outside under the midday sun – all ready to tell them about the bizarre interview I've just had with the transhumanist who reckons he can eradicate death. They bring me into their living room and my eye falls on a decorative mini sign that says: THE FUTURE IS TRANSHUMAN.

Dear God. They're everywhere.

We spend a weekend in a tech haze. We drive down Lombard Street in a car hired for an hour via an app, we eat ice cream that's been frozen with liquid nitrogen, and (as is generally the way with Arin) we have conversations that might kindly be described as 'batshit'.

'What if you could take out a part of your brain,' asks Arin, trying in his methodical way to convince me that transhumanism is the route to a better world, 'and replace it with a machine that can do the same job?'

'OK,' I say, 'go on.'

'And then you could do the same thing to another part of your brain.'

'Right, so you've removed the part of my brain which controls, for example, walking, and put in a machine which does the same thing?'

'Right.'

'OK, yes, fine, go on.'

He does go on. He hypothetically removes every bit of my brain from my skull, and hypothetically stuffs it with hypothetical machines.

'So eventually, your *entire brain* is a machine!' He beams at me, his hands outstretched as if to say, 'Ta-da!'

'OK, I've just got one question, one I don't think we touched on.'

'Go ahead.'

'Why?'

'*Why*?' he says, then cocks his head to the side and says, thoughtfully, 'Huh. Why...?'

'Arin! You've just put my entire brain in a bin! It was a perfectly good brain. I was planning on using it until I was eighty. There is no machine yet that even has a comparable shelf life. Get it out of the bin, now.'

I told you. Batshit.

I want the polar opposite of the anti-death sentiment I've been immersed in with the transhumanists, somewhere people accept death as a part of life. If I'm going to find that anywhere in the US, it's in a city where funerals involve an upbeat procession of people dancing their way to the cemetery. Perhaps a place where every funeral is its own mini death festival can reveal something about the human capacity to cope with mortal terror.

After a four-hour flight to New Orleans and a taxi to the French Quarter, I couldn't feel further from the high-tech, chrome-edged world of San Francisco. It's machines vs dusty history books. The Singularity vs the Second Coming. Robots coding us into the future vs spectres endlessly playing out scenes from the past. The blazing swamp heat peels the paint on muggy, fairy-lit porches, and gently smothers me as I blink up at a real-estate sign that reads: NOT HAUNTED.

I wonder how they verified that.

It turns out to be a 'joke to drum up business' dreamed up by local real-estate broker Finis Shelnutt – although when the signs first went up in 2014, he told *USA Today* that he believed the eight properties he had on the market were indeed haunted.

The belief that the dead walk among us lends humans a kind of supremacy; it suggests our deaths are so important that they imprint the very air. (That said, the cuteness hierarchy has allowed a couple of man's favourite animals into our ghostly chronicles – dogs, cats, a few cows. But to my knowledge, no one has ever reported ghostly activity following a rat or cockroach extermination.)

For once, I'm not travelling alone. My friend Steph has flown in from New York to meet me. Even taking into account the Western reluctance to discuss death, it would be unfair to describe Steph without using the word 'anxious'; I have spent roughly 4 per cent of our entire friendship reassuring her that she doesn't have rabies. So she's not keen to join me at the Museum of Death.

I do, however, convince her to join me on a ceme-tery tour.

You're a French prisoner in the 1700s, and someone gives you the choice of staying in prison or going to a swamp across the world to help build a new city. You'll be released from prison with a new life and a new job – but it's a swamp. There's no getting around it. It has a

tropical climate, and on a cooler day in August temperatures might, if you're lucky, drop to only 100°F/38°C
with 100 per cent humidity. Ah, you're a tough guy – you
can handle it. Now, do you like alligators? What about
poisonous snakes? You worry, but it's the mosquitoes
you've got to watch out for: they carry yellow fever, which
in 1853 will kill 10,000 people in one summer alone. It'll
take until 1905 for anybody to realise it's the mosquitoes;
they'll assume it's being caused by all the decaying bodies.
Oh, I almost forgot – the dead bodies absolutely refuse
to stay in the ground. Now, do you want the job or not?

As New Orleans was a Catholic colony when it
was founded in the early 1700s, bodies had to be buried; it would be another couple of centuries before the
Catholic Church withdrew its condemnation of cremation, and even today it maintains that it doesn't 'hold the
same value' as burial. But New Orleans is a terrible place
to bury the dead. Firstly, they believed (as many still do)
that bodies had to be buried at six feet, which is tricky to
do when you hit water after four. So, since bodies were
being interred in what amounted to an underground
river, there was no guarantee your grandmother would
stay in the spot where she'd been buried. She could have
floated all the way back into town by the time you came
to put flowers down.

Secondly, the dead didn't just move sideways, but
upwards – when it rained, rising water levels would bring
coffins back to the surface.

The solution left a lot to be desired, particularly for

the ones who had to carry it out. Let us spare a thought for the poor guy whose job it was to drill holes in the coffin so water would get in and weigh it down. Then he'd dig to four feet, put the coffin in the ground, jump up and down on it until it equalled six feet, then cover it with dirt. Job done – until it rained. The rising water levels would *still* bring the coffins closer to the surface; only by now, the body would be producing gas. In a coffin full of holes. Scientists among you will have worked out what's coming: the dead were popping out of the ground like horrible champagne corks, all over the city. They built a gate to contain the leaping corpses to the cemetery, where our poor friend with the Worst Job in the World would find the remains, have no idea whom they belonged to, and simply dig a hole and rebury them. So, to recap life in early New Orleans: it was a blazing, humid, disease-soaked swamp; the cemeteries were disgusting and overflowing with surprise cadavers leaping out of the ground – and to top it off, no one even had any idea whose remains they were visiting.

In 1789, they opened Saint Louis Cemetery with an ingenious and 100 per cent green solution to the problem of their city's reappearing dead. As of today, Saint Louis has around 700 tombs housing approximately 100,000 bodies. The tombs are all above ground, like stone morgues, one on top of the other. The body is placed inside, where, under the Louisiana sun, temperatures can get up to 350°F/180°C, the temperature at which you'd roast a turkey. Over a year this causes a natural cremation, leaving nothing but ash, maybe a few teeth. After leaving the body for a year and a day, they take a ten-foot push broom and sweep the remains to the back of the tomb, where they fall through an opening into a pit. The Catholics of early New Orleans reasoned that this form of cremation was acceptable because Jesus was also buried in an above-ground tomb – plus *they* weren't cremating the dead: nature was.

When the Americans arrived, they didn't take kindly to being told what to do by the French Catholics, so they went ahead and buried their dead and put down a slab to stop the bodies popping out of the ground. The practice didn't catch on. Our cemetery guide, Dartanya, tells us, 'You wanna hear that coffin hitting that big heavy slab all the time. And this is where French parenting comes into play: a child would say, "Mama, what's all that tapping?" And the mother would say, "Well, honey, when they were alive, they were very wicked Protestants, so they're trying to break out of hell. So, honey, you be a good Catholic and that will not happen to you."'

The dead outnumber the living in New Orleans ten to one: there are around 4 million corpses in a city of fewer than 400,000 living people. There are a number of reasons for this: by American standards it's a very old city, founded in 1718, decades before the USA declared its nationhood. There were also two major fires, including one that burned down over 1,000 of the 1,100 buildings in the French Quarter – not to mention cholera, malaria, yellow fever, hurricanes and a consistently high murder rate. Essentially, though death comes for us all, it doesn't have to commute very far to get to New Orleans. People who are drawn to death are drawn here. Nicolas Cage built his tomb here in Saint Louis Cemetery in 2010: a huge white pyramid, smooth aside from two cracks where it's been struck by lightning three times – despite being nowhere near the highest point of the cemetery. 'What that says for Nic and the actor life,' says Dartanya, 'we do not know.'

If any tomb was going to be struck by lightning, you'd expect it to be the tallest, a stunning monument that looks like a giant marble jewellery box: the Italian Benevolent Society tomb. Immigrants in New Orleans would often pool funds for society tombs to lower individual burial costs, creating a kind of tribal effect in the cemetery. The architect Pietro Gualdi came over and designed it in 1857, but finished three weeks early because he despised New Orleans and couldn't wait to get home. Unfortunately, the society didn't have even half of his money ready, so they told him to get an apartment and sit tight.

But the mosquitoes got him.

He caught yellow fever.

He was the first to be entombed in his creation.

I give Steph one last chance to come to the Museum of Death with me, but she instead chooses walking around, taking photos, and declining the many offers of two-for-one drinks being yelled about in the street at 11.07 a.m. (I give it two hours before she caves). She wanders off down Decatur Street, and I follow my map, stopping three or four times to listen to street jazz.

I hate the Museum of Death with some energy. The outside is whimsical enough, with cabaret-style lights spelling out 'Museum of Death' and pictures of skeletons in jaunty hats. I'm hoping it might offer some insight into how we see death, fear it, live with it. The notes I emerge with show how rapidly that delusion deserts me, beginning:

> Skeletons: a goat, a horse, an alligator looking like it's attacking a human skeleton. Mummified cat, rat and mouse. Pig foetuses at different weeks. A neck brace on a skeleton – why? Sheep brains in a jar. Skulls, jars of teeth. Taxidermy birds, mice, dogs, squirrels, fur-bearing trout. A dog's head mounted on a wall with a poem by the owner. Wtf is the point of any of this?!

I realise how absurdly quickly I've built myself an echo chamber when it comes to death and the idea that everyone is working towards either fighting it or accepting it, rather than continuing the cycle of denial and terror. A city where funerals entail dancing in the streets seems like a place where a death museum might tend more towards acceptance, but the Museum of Death is a bog-standard scare-fest. In the 'serial-killer room' they have mounted 'facts' such as: 'Fun Fact: Experts estimate that between 0.5 and 5 per cent of Americans are psychopaths or sociopaths. That's 1.5–15 million people.'

This seems largely irrelevant to death, unless the erroneous suggestion is that all psychopaths and sociopaths are murderers rather than, I don't know, bankers? There's also: 'Fun Fact: A 2005 *Journal of Forensic Sciences* article estimates that women are responsible for four to fourteen serial killings a year.' What does that mean? Is that supposed to be few, or a lot? I'm not having fun learning any of these facts.

There's an entire section dedicated to Charles Manson, the cult leader who persuaded his followers to kill nine people in 1969, with graphic crime-scene photos of actress Sharon Tate's murdered body mounted right next to a *Playboy* pictorial of her from 1967. Aside from being cartoonishly sensationalist, it's hideously tasteless, like a still form of a clichéd slasher movie in which a woman has sex then immediately gets stalked and murdered.

I'm going to take a minute here to tell you about the practice of embalming in America. It's still very common for funerals in the US to include an open casket and a viewing of the deceased. The process of decay is forestalled with an injection of around eleven litres of embalming fluid – typically a mixture of formaldehyde, methanol, glutaraldehyde and various other solvents – into the carotid artery. They also arrange the features, which may include applying make-up, wiring the jaw shut and stuffing the eye sockets so they don't appear sunken, all to make the body seem palatable, more 'asleep' than dead. The practice began largely owing to America's size – when soldiers died in the Civil War (1861–5), they were embalmed so they wouldn't deteriorate as much while they were being shipped back up north to their families for the funeral. But, this being America, it wasn't long before it was seen as a business opportunity. It was sold as a procedure that would stop decomposition entirely, rather than simply forestalling it. People were fed the idea that their loved ones would lie in their underground vault, like a subterranean Sleeping Beauty, for all eternity. They were later labelled as 'hygiene services'; it's still common for people to think embalming is a legal requirement, and to shell out for it, only to have the body cremated the next day. What started as a procedure performed purely for love, to give people one last chance to see their relatives before their funerals, has become a slightly scuzzy money-spinner.

I learned none of this at the Museum of Death. The embalming section is basically just an ad for embalming fluid and some old bottles, with no further explanation, followed by some black-and-white photos of car accidents taken by Florida Highway Patrol, and, directly beneath, pictures of people who died from auto-erotic asphyxiation. There follows a film of randomly spliced images of death (corpses; people being shot; a man shooting himself in the mouth) next to a Día de Muertos display that looks like it was assembled by someone who couldn't point to Mexico on a map. I won't take you through the whole museum – you've done nothing wrong.

I march out into the street, shaking my head. I have learned nothing about death, except that the taboo is still strong enough that someone thinks this stuff is edgy. That wasn't a museum, it was word association; it was like google-imaging 'death' and scrolling for pages and pages. I've learned so little I think I may have left some knowledge in there. Like the answer to the question, 'Why did I come here?' Actually, I know why I came here. I thought I'd find out something about mortal terror, how people live alongside it. And outside of comforting movements like death positivity, where mortality is to be accepted, or transhumanism, where mortality is to be cured, or Santa Muerte, where mortality is to be delayed at the behest of a mother figure, the answer turns out to be: by sensationalising it until it doesn't feel real. By reaching into the deepest caverns of our mortal terror and plucking out that kernel that tingles when we read about a death that isn't our own. The haunted-house feeling, the bed sheet with eye sockets cut out and the ghostly 'woooo!', the spook factor. People will, it's clear, pay good money to get that tingle.

I get a text from Steph. 'I'm in Pat O'Brien's. You're coming at 2 p.m., right? Shall I order you a Hurricane?'

Yes, Steph. You can order me two.*

---

* Hurricanes have alcohol in them. Lots. This is a thing you should know. The first sip does not make much of this. Ah, juice, you'll think. They've skimped on the alcohol and put in mostly lovely juice. That's fine. You stand up. Ah, your legs have news: it wasn't just juice. It was four shots of rum disguised *amongst* the juice. Wait, your legs have more to say: someone is playing a trumpet outside so you should probably dance a bit. Go on, have a dance. To go with those beads the barman put on you at 3 p.m. on this fine weekday. No one will mind. And no one did.

*

I open my eyes and look over at the twin bed. Steph is sitting up, looking surprisingly sprightly. She says, 'Hey! Why is there a fry in this water?'

I grin, cross my legs and proceed to explain, for perhaps the third time in our six years of friendship, why she should never have a third drink.

'We took the fries to go, and then I was trying to make you eat one to sober you up and you didn't want to, so you dropped it in the glass of water.' She laughs and covers her face. 'Then you cried because one of the bedside tissues was blue. You were really concerned about it.'

'Yes! I remember! Why was it blue?!'

'Because not all tissues are white, you tissue racist.'

'Oh!' she says, hit by a memory, somehow brought to the forefront of her mind by being called a tissue racist. 'Something crazy happened in the middle of the night!'

'What?' I ask, already giggling. I have a spidey sense that tingles when Steph is about to say something ridiculous.

'I woke up and I was definitely still drunk, but feeling a little better—'

'So you were over the horrific tissue incident?'

'I still think blue tissues are weird – anyway, I got up and thought I saw something on the wall, right there.' She points to the wall directly in front of her bed. 'It looked like a baby on the wall.'

I laugh. 'Like in *Trainspotting*? You had three drinks!'

'No, like a *ghost* baby! So I got my iPad and I, like,

creeped towards it...' – she mimes creeping along the floor with her iPad outstretched, as if simultaneously using it as a torch and a shield – 'and then when I lit it up there was nothing there.'

'Right. I'm going to go on the record here: there was no ghost baby; it was a dream, or a Hurricane-induced hallucination – but I'll ask the front desk if anyone else has seen it.'

After a quick shower, I make my way downstairs to the lobby. I stop at reception and, feeling a bit sheepish, say, 'Hi, um... so my friend thinks she might have seen a ghost.'

'Ah, a man in a top hat and trench coat?' says the receptionist, smiling.

'Er, no,' I say, already wishing I hadn't started the conversation, 'um, it was probably just the light playing tricks on her but, er, she thought she saw, on the wall, a ghost... baby?'

'Nope,' she says immediately, shaking her head. 'No babies.'

Of course, no babies, I think, trying not to roll my eyes. *No one wants a ghost baby – that implies a dead baby, and a dead baby is not going to convert to room bookings, is it?* I wave it off as a trick of the light and go out in search of coffee.

On a bench on Rampart Street, outside a bar called the Voodoo Lounge, Cindi Richardson and I watch the traffic and chat about ghosts. A local in her fifties, Cindi runs the bar and a tour company called French Quarter

Phantoms. She's not alone: in the one and a half square miles that make up the French Quarter there are currently fifty-two ghost-tour companies, the majority of them under three years old. She started her company in the aftermath of Katrina. The city was devastated, and it took about three years for tourism to pick up in New Orleans. In the interim, while people did what they could to save and revive the cultural aspects of the city that were in danger of being lost – the jazz scene, the history – Cindi ran ghost tours for rescue workers. 'We wanted to help answer that question, "Why should we save New Orleans?"'

'What a horrible question,' I say.

'It was a very common question,' says Cindi. '"It's below sea level, it's just gonna happen again, why are y'all bothering?" So we did a lot of free and five-dollar tours just to keep morale up and hopefully show people why it was worth saving.' After the unthinkable wave of death that swept through the city, it seems astonishing that people could have their morale boosted by ghost stories. Perhaps it demonstrates how utterly detached ghost stories are from our genuine concept of death, grief and loss. Or perhaps it's a way of processing it that the brain likes: a story arc, where the point of the story is that death isn't the total disappearance we all fear. I'm starting to see why this part of New Orleans has settled on ghosts and spookiness as one of its draws – it's not death acceptance at all. It's death repackaging. It's the spook tingle, that lucrative glimpse through the mortality peephole.

'Just walking around New Orleans there's images of death everywhere,' I say.

'It's a very spiritual city,' says Cindi.

The night before, our ghost-tour guide, Luke – who is originally from Texas – asked the group, 'How many absolute believers do we have, by show of hands? Three people. OK. Now: total sceptics, just here to be a good sport, drinking and walking sounded fun, six thousand years of evidence is meaningless to me?' I put up my hand. 'Four or five. No problem. Not trying to convince you. The rest of you are on the fence; you're curious, you suspect. When I started as a ghost-tour guide, I was on the fence too. It was doing the tours that convinced me once and for all.' (I wonder if they're all required to have a 'the moment I started to believe' story? If I ran a ghost-tour company, I'd probably want them to have one.) 'I was just a few weeks into the gig, telling a story about five little boys who died in a fire. Everybody was taking pictures of the hotel where it happened. Then a girl squealed, showed me the picture on her phone, and I squealed. It was five little boys staring out of the hotel window, plain as day – grey, transparent, one had his head on the other one's shoulder. It was cute and terrifying. I know it's not Photoshop: I can see the timestamp. And it exactly matches a story that has been told for two hundred years. It was the right number of boys: five died. They were the right age: between eight and eleven. And they were wearing night-gowns; they died in their beds in their dormitory in the middle of the night. How do you explain that? I could not.'

I tell Cindi, 'I just flew in from San Francisco where a common attitude to death seems to be "No thank you! I'm going to be a robot and live for ever!"' Cindi cackles. 'And they thought I was really negative for being sceptical about that.'

'Wow,' she says. 'We all think we're going to die and we're looking forward to it because there's something else to move on to. No matter whether you're Protestant or Catholic or a voodoo practitioner, we all think we're going somewhere else.'

'So you're not going to die, really.'

'Well, we're not going to cease to exist.'

'So where do you think you're going?'

'I think I'm going to heaven. I'm about the one Baptist in a Catholic city. Ultimately, we all believe in the same thing, we just pray a little differently.'

'So once again I'm in a city where no one thinks they're going to stop existing.'

'Yes. I think whether people are sceptics or believers in ghosts or an afterlife, they want to believe, because even an atheist doesn't really want to believe that this is all there is, if a car hits me this afternoon I'm just done, there's nothing to me for ever and ever and ever.'

'Do you feel like people believe in ghosts because it almost feels like proof that death isn't the end?'

Cindi doesn't really answer this. She's a business-woman selling the spook tingle; I'm going to be hard-pressed to get her to philosophise that it's all an adult game of 'let's pretend' with invoicing. Instead, she guesses, 'I think about sixty-five per cent of people really believe in ghosts, I think another twenty per cent are kind of on the fence about it, and then there's that small margin that are just like, "Nah you're full of it, that didn't happen," but they enjoy the story anyway.'

'This is the Andrew Jackson Hotel,' Luke said as we stopped in front of a brightly lit-up yellow building with blue shutters and hanging plants. 'It's not the scariest or the most violent haunting, but it's creepy because it's haunted by little kids.' As he mentioned in his intro speech, the five little boys were trapped on the second floor of their Catholic boys' boarding school when it burned down in the 1790s. The second floor of the hotel is not the original building, but supposedly the little-boy ghosts are still drawn to those bedrooms that are roughly where their bedrooms would have been, and are said to play pranks on hotel guests.

'They're not good pranks,' Luke said, 'they're little-kid pranks: your toilet's going to flush all night long and drive you nuts, girls have come back to the room to find their undergarments strewn around, and the front desk says they get calls pretty regularly saying, "We have been kept up all night by some kids running and laughing in the halls, banging on our doors and running away – would you please tell their parents to shut them up?" Front desk says, "We'd love to, if there were any kids staying at the hotel."'

'Why are we afraid of ghosts, Cindi?'

'It's the unknown.' She shrugs, then explains what is even meant by the term 'ghost' here. 'There are different types of hauntings. Most are residual, a spirit or entity that repeats the same motion over and over; they're never going to be able to do anything different. Then there's a malevolent spirit that can actually affect things around it, and those would come from somebody that died a violent death; they're much harder to get rid of. So when you're afraid of ghosts, you are afraid of the malevolent spirit, which is a very small number of what hauntings are.'

The fact that a violent demise is seen to lead to a malevolent spirit transfers some kind of unassailable meaning onto our pain and our deaths. It gives credence to the idea that a violent human death is objectively bad, in the way a violent spider death is not. Isn't that what we'd all like to believe?

'This big grey mansion here on the corner is called the LaLaurie mansion,' said Luke. 'It's not just the most haunted but supposedly most *evil* haunted house in the US. Honest to God, you could offer me a thousand bucks right now to go in this house and spend the night, I would tell you absolutely not. You could offer me a hundred thousand dollars to go in this house and I would tell you absolutely, yes – but if it's not a life-changing amount of money, really not interested.'

Luke's first words, that this building is 'called' the LaLaurie mansion, are crucial. Because the building we're regarding isn't strictly the one occupied by Madame Delphine LaLaurie, 'the evil Paris Hilton of the 1820s'; it was rebuilt after a fire in 1838, and the top floor wasn't added until later in the nineteenth century. But the building still holds a powerful 'spook status' in the French Quarter, after the notorious torture of slaves that went on within its walls. LaLaurie was the heiress of the McCarty family fortune, one of the largest plantation fortunes in history. She and her third husband, Parisian physician Leonard Louis Nicolas LaLaurie, held extravagant parties most weekends. During the last party they threw – on 10 April 1834 – a fire broke out in the kitchen. The firefighters arrived, put out the fire, and were shocked to find an old enslaved woman, unconscious, shackled to the stove by her ankle – Louisiana was brutal to its slaves, but there was a French law in effect called the Code Noir that demanded that on the surface, slaves had to be properly clothed, fed and housed. They broke her shackles, brought her outside and revived her. 'She told them, "I started the fire. I would rather burn to death than spend another night in this house,"' Luke said.

Some accounts of what they found when they searched the house come from the 11 April 1834 edition of the *New Orleans Bee*; others have been passed down – and, it must be said, rather embellished over time. 'First they see two metal tables,' said Luke, 'on top of which are a male and a female, victims of what today we would call a crude gender reassignment. In addition, each person has had their arms and legs amputated and surgically reattached to the other person, we assume to see if the limbs and organs would heal and become functional. Both those people are, blessedly, deceased.' He goes on to describe crude amputations, strips of skin peeled off in patterns, and bones broken and reset upside down. The LaLauries escaped in the confusion as the party raged on outside, and later turned up in Paris, where they lived out the rest of their lives and were never charged with their crimes.

The house's reputation for being haunted began the very next day. The screams that no one heard from the living victims were now supposedly audible from their ghosts. People started crossing the road to avoid walking under any part of the mansion – a practice many locals keep up today. Luke tells us that a friend of his, another ghost-tour guide, spent his childhood in New Orleans under strict parental instructions to never walk under the gallery of the house, and even tried to convince his bosses to omit it from the tour. I'm not surprised that request was denied. This is clearly the tour's big-ticket item: we are currently one of at least seven tour groups gathered, phones poised, around the 'cursed' mansion.

I'm sitting at a table in the brand new Haunted Museum across from the owner, a voodoo priestess known as Bloody Mary. When I told Steph the name of my interviewee, she told me about the tween superstition that if you say 'Bloody Mary' three times into a mirror, she will appear.

'Now that I'm in New Orleans I want to do it, but what if she really does appear?' Steph said.

'Steph, she was one of our queens,' I scoffed. 'They called her Bloody Mary because she had hundreds of Protestants burned at the stake. Even if she did appear, I don't think she'd have any beef with New York Jews. Also, she isn't in charge any more, so she couldn't do anything to you.'

I spent the afternoon here yesterday with Mary's son, Jagger, who gave me a tour. As I switch on my dictaphone I vow to be gentler than I was yesterday – Jagger was incredibly friendly and polite, and dealt well with my slightly grumpy questions, such as, 'What's the significance of this terrifying-looking figurine? This is just to look spooky, isn't it?'

I don't know what I expected when I turned up to interview Mary, but this isn't it. She looks so… normal. She's blonde, about fifty, wears red lipstick, jeans and a pink top. Just someone you'd find queuing in front of you at the grocery store. But she has a no-fucking-nonsense-whatsoever manner, and a deep, resonating voice that sounds like paraffin catching fire, and she wastes no time sizing me up as the death-phobic European.

'We don't have a fear of death here as much,' she says, with a hint of something hovering near disdain. 'When I was a kid we had a great respect for death but not as much fear as I'd say the rest of the country has. Here we sit down, light a candle and break bread with the dead.

We picnic in our cemeteries, we played hide and seek as kids in them.'

She breaks off and picks up a rag doll that's sitting on the table. 'Hold on, just checking on this doll's legs. What is in there?'

I pause, and watch her fiddle with the doll.

'What's wrong with the doll's legs?' I say.

'Nothing, it was just donated as a haunted doll. But there's obviously something in there...'

I ask in my politest voice, without wanting a hint of scepticism to bleed through this early in the interview, 'Do you think it's haunted?'

She responds as if she's dealing with an idiot: 'It just got here, I haven't got to talk to it yet.' She turns to the doll and asks, 'What is your status, my dear?' I have a moment of intense self-reflection, whereby the Worst Tuesday flashes into my mind and I wonder how that led to me sitting at a table 4,500 miles from home, watching a woman talk to a doll.

I snap out of it just as she puts aside the doll, and says, 'The concept of death shouldn't be feared like a disease. Forty or fifty years ago children ran around in cemeteries and visiting them on the weekends was very popular. Now the families are almost gone. In a relatively short time period, that has changed.'

'And what caused that change do you think?'

'It is theorised that it's the fear of death,' says Bloody Mary.

'But fearing death isn't new, surely?'

'In some ways it is, because less than a century ago death was a way of life. People were dying left and right – plagues, infant mortality – there were piles of bodies outside; you couldn't escape death. And in New Orleans we had the highest mortality rate in North America. But as time went on it was like, let's shield the children, let children be children. So that's changed.'

Similarly to Cindi, Bloody Mary describes the mind and body as separate, that the body is just a shell that will wither and that 'we' will continue on. When faced with someone who boldly claims they do not fear death, it's somehow less impressive when you learn that they essentially don't believe in it – at least not the cold, athe-ist non-existence I was raised to fear. Moreover, we're sitting in a room that, if you were to imagine the brief given to the interior designer, would simply be 'spooky'. Dusty swathes of fabric, old furniture, 'haunted' dolls and low lighting. It seems like voodoo as imagined by the artistic team at Disney, an Americanised repackaging of an imported religion. But just as I'm ready to dismiss the whole thing as a white, cynical, showbiz-sheened capi-talist interpretation of life beyond death, Mary goes on to talk more appreciatively about symbolic immortality than anyone I've ever heard.

'I think the ancestors have a lot to teach us,' she says. 'The things that our ancestors have built are all around us; the things that they have taught have shaped us. Their echo is still there, teaching and talking and letting you know that *they're not dead*.' Of course a city where the dead so drastically outnumber the living will be said to contain multitudes of ghosts, but Bloody Mary claims it *attracts* ghosts. 'Because we're inviting to it, because we haven't denied it as much as the other places, we're kind of a beacon that attracts them.' It never occurred to me that a country that's big on death denial would feel unwelcoming to the dead, and in spite of myself, I love the idea of them congregating where belief in them is strongest.

I want to hear more about her relationship with ghosts. So I ask, 'Which is the ghost that's pissed you off the most?'

'That thing after Katrina that was just going around sucking everybody's energy and vitality when there wasn't any to give,' she says. 'It was like a mass entity of negativity that was just hungry and on a mission to feed.'

'It sounds like depression or sadness or something?' I say, in an effort not to ask if she's deliberately describing the Dementors from Harry Potter.

'But it wasn't anthropomorphic. It was alive but amoral,' she says. 'For three years all I did was banishings and cleansings of people, places and things. There was nothing left of goodness here after Katrina. Everybody's darkness coagulated. Most of the people left, and everybody was afraid, and everybody had PTSD, and everybody was drinking, and everybody was mad, and the government was screwing us. We had looters – and this was kind of like a looter on the spiritual plane. It was the bursting of the primordial energy from deep underneath the sea, unleashing some ancient creatures, if you will. It was not a normal aftermath of a hurricane, which I've lived through before. It was interesting to watch the city turn right back into a swamp; nature took it back so quickly. The hollow eyes of tens of thousands of houses staring back at you. It seemed like all our ghosts left with the families. It was the death of a whole city, a whole lifestyle, plus there were people who had been here for generations like me and they did not make it back.'

It's true; while New Orleans is now close to its original population, over 50 per cent of its inhabitants are new.

'So, the revival hasn't been . . .?'

'Oh no, it sucks,' she says, anticipating my question. '*Sucks*. It's good financially, but no, we've lost too much of our heritage. We're trying to hang on to it, but while the newcomers love what we had, they bitch and holler about music in the streets and the very things that New Orleans is known for, so to grasp our original spirit, to keep some of it alive, it's a struggle right now. Because the new people that came here want to whitewash it.' I think of the fifty-two ghost-tour companies that have sprung up in the last few years, and wonder what percentage of them are run by newcomers, capitalising on the most gruesome aspects of the city's history.

I feel bad for dragging up memories of Katrina, so I ask, 'Is there a spirit you're fond of?'

She tells me she's good friends with a ghost known as Julie the Octoroon Mistress – 'Octoroon' meaning one eighth black – so, despite being beautiful and highly educated, Julie wasn't permitted to marry a white man. Nevertheless, in the 1850s she was a mistress to a Frenchman, who refused to destroy his social status by marrying her. In the middle of an argument in which she begged him to propose, he said in jest that she could 'prove' her love to him by waiting for him naked on the roof. He spent the evening drinking with his friends, and Julie, taking the suggestion seriously, took off her clothes and waited for him on the roof on an incredibly cold, wet December night. Some stories say he found her later that night, others say he passed out and didn't find her until morning. What all the stories agree on is that when he did find her, she was curled up, dead.

'Oh, I remember this story!' I say. And before I can think, I've already said, 'Her boyfriend was a *prick*.'

Bloody Mary laughs and says defensively but sweetly, as if Julie's on her way over and she wouldn't want me to put my foot in it, 'She doesn't like to hear that; she just kind of looked at it as a sign of the times, she's not even resentful about that. They're not all so sweet. I've got an understanding with Madame LaLaurie.' My eyes widen as I remember the horrific details of her crimes. 'I am not afraid of her, but I can set the boundaries with her. I've done a couple of exorcisms to pull her out of people.' I ask what she's doing here when she lived out her days in Paris, and she looks at me like I've asked why sheep exist and says she doesn't know.

Bloody Mary sees herself as an advocate for spirit

rights – their oppressors being those who believe 'anything that's not the Holy Spirit is evil' – and believes they should be able to live in the houses they built. She says she also teaches people how to have a relationship with the dead. That wording, the concept of continuing a relationship with someone who can never, ever come back, cracks through my cynicism. I realise I've been focusing on my non-belief in literal ghosts, just as in Mexico I became distracted by the question of whether the teenagers shagging in a tent really thought their grandmother was visiting. Suddenly, the value of these stories, this manner of talking about people as if they're still here, begins to bleed through for me. Because some small part of my brain still doesn't understand that Chris is dead. The double takes when I think I've seen him on the street are still happening more often than I'd like to admit. Perhaps if I knew how to have a relationship with the dead, that small part of my brain would understand that he's somewhere else – because the message that he's nowhere clearly does not compute.

'We help people build ancestral altars and to feed the dead, and write letters, and know they're still part of your family whether they're there in the flesh or not,' she says. 'It's just a totally different relationship you have to have with them. To salute them on holidays, to still buy them a gift at Christmas, to visit them now and then: these are healing and important rituals, traditions that are all over the world. You have to find the one that sits right with you. But denial is not a good ritual. It does not work.'

My face grants onlookers access to my every thought. It's probably what made her spiky at the start of the interview, my total lack of ability to hide my cynicism. But it's probably also what changes her demeanour now, as her comments on continuing a relationship with the dead – which entirely tracks with everything I've been told about the death festivals – get in. As I think about how awkwardly I spoke to Chris that one time, how suddenly I began to use calendars again, she meets my gaze with the grip of a hundred eyes. 'You want to say those last words? Well, you go back and you do it. Because they're still their echo, their ghost, their memory flows through you.'

Then she leans forward, and in her lit-paraffin voice, says, 'We've got it all, and we've just got to face it, never deny it, and never fear death. Dance with the dead. Dance with death, and it'll teach you the right steps.'

I feel elated, and small, and like I could cry, or dance right here. Before I even realise what I'm saying, the words come out: 'I will. I promise.'

Right. That's it, I think, *that was my very last Hurricane.* Or this is, I should say, since I'm carrying it, and there's half left. It's our last night in New Orleans. I can't account for the entire night, but I know there was music played by people so talented I'm certain they're aliens, I know we went back to Pat O'Brien's, I know it's later than 2 a.m., and I know I'm feeling excellent. I don't think I've ever felt this excellent at such an ungodly hour. I am buoyed by music and laughter and expertly mixed cocktails. I weigh nothing.

Steph and I have turned off Bourbon Street onto a quiet, residential road. As I talk, the sober part of my brain listens in near fascination at how incredibly clichéd drunk me sounds. If an actor were to do it I'd say it was overdone – slurring, implausible enthusiasm, the sense that I'd probably hug a mugger.

'Ooh, look!' says Steph, pointing. I follow her gaze, and gasp. It's just a porch with a disco ball, but it's lit beautifully and the effect is quite magical; the paint is cracked and faded and scrubbed by the heat, with pins of light dancing across it in the dead of night, presumably for the delight of we drunk passers-by. Steph insists on photographing me underneath it. I spin my head left and right to check no one is around, and see the street stretching out either side of me. I imagine how nice it would feel to sense the presence of the New Orleanians of centuries past, the millions who walked and drank and danced and died on the surface of this bizarre and beautiful swamp. And the most optimistic, suggestible and – yes – drunk part of me whispers, *What do I know, anyway? Maybe the dead do hang around. Maybe we're surrounded.*

I remember Bloody Mary's instructions. Well, I did promise.

I stand underneath the disco ball, and, with the sober part of my brain rolling its eyes, do a little dance under the sweeping, star-like pins of light. No one shows me any steps, but I think of the city's ghosts, I think of death hovering unseen next to the warmth of my rum-flushed skin. I hold my plastic cup aloft, let my hair fall in my face. Steph laughs at the glittering snippet of footage she's taken and says, 'That's awesome!'

I laugh. It's documented. That moment is mine now. The night I danced with the dead on a quiet, dusty street, thousands of miles from home.

CHAPTER SEVEN

Sweets in Shoes

Autru è parrai di morti, autru è muriri.
— Sicilian proverb, meaning, 'It's one thing
to talk about death, it's another to die.'

'*Io no. Oggi no.*'

It's an old language-learning trick, speaking to your-self when you're alone. The trick, really, is to name whatever you see, or describe your actions to practise your verbs. Instead, in my bedroom in Sicily, I'm trans-lating famous death quotes. I've started with an easy one, one I can't find a reliable source for, about the 'only thing' we say to death: 'Not me, not today.'

This isn't quite what I'd planned to be doing here.

I arrived two days ago, dragged my suitcase three flights up a narrow spiral staircase, past curt nods and *buongiornos* from gruff neighbours, and knocked on my host's door. I knew little about her; just that she's Brazilian, married a Sicilian and stayed here in Palermo. Adriana opened the door, all smiles and curly hair and flowing skirts, and wrapped me up in the warmest hug, as if we'd been friends for years and it had been much too long since we'd seen each other. She brought me upstairs to her dining-room table, where she was having a coffee morning with a group of women – Italian, Russian, Brazilian, English – who all welcomed me with similar warmth. They asked what brought me to Sicily, and their eyes widened at the answer, 'I'm writing a book about death festivals, so I'm here to talk to the people who are reviving the Festa dei Morti, and learning Italian so I can understand them when they talk back.'

Being English in Europe requires that you explain yourself if you can speak more than a few words of any other language, so I told them, in 95 per cent Italian and 5 per cent accidental Spanish, that I used to live in Mexico and that Italian was a sideways step. They practically applauded, even though they probably had similar stories. This suggests nothing good about the perception of the language-learning abilities of the English.

Adriana passed around a basket of figs that she'd brought back from Morocco, warning that they were 'very organic' – which, she explained, meant there might be worms in them. I tore one tentatively apart, extremely grateful I had already learned the word for 'worm' and not just nodded and bitten right in. The mercifully worm-free flesh was sweet, restorative. I nibbled and listened to the women's stories, feeling immediately warm, safe, at home.

But something's happened to me since. I'm going to class in the mornings, but as I walk around town, I have the overwhelming urge to go back and hide in my room. It feels like agoraphobia is trying to poke its ugly rat head into my life again. So I'm here, in my room, jittery from copious espresso, translating quotes about death into Italian out loud like a madwoman in an attic.

Adriana knocks on my door and I jump out of bed, and assume the posture of someone who hasn't been hiding under a duvet. I open the door with a sunny, '*Ciao!*'

'*Ciao, tesoro,* I haven't seen you for days!'

'Oh, I've been busy,' I lie.

'Of course – how are the classes going? Are you enjoying the city?'

'It's gorgeous,' I say, which is true, and, 'I'm planning to go and find granita later,' which isn't.

'Good idea!' she says, and gives a detailed description of where to get the best pomegranate granita. It seems a fitting suggestion: in ancient Greece, pomegranates were offered to the gods for the spirits of the dead.

'Also,' she continues, 'if you have time tomorrow, shall we go to the *biscottificio*?'

'Is that…where they make biscotti?'

'*Sì*! It's like a bakery but only for biscotti – we can find you the *ossa dei morti* and ask them if they will teach you how to make them.'

Ossa dei morti, or bones of the dead, are a traditional Festa dei Morti treat. It's a hard, golden-brown cookie that has a white 'bone' on top, and the recipe calls for more sugar than flour. I love the combination of confrontation and denial – here's a cookie designed to make you imagine you're eating a dead person's bones, but don't worry: this contemplation of mortality will be literally sugar-coated. Not that literal sugar-coating is unusual in Sicily – if the Festa dei Morti-themed sweets on display here are any indication, come 2 November I can only expect the people of Palermo to be spinning across town like the Tasmanian devil. Baskets of *frutta martorana* – marzipan painted to look exactly like fruit – adorn practically every bakery window as the go-to festival treat. But the *ossa dei morti* seem like treats I could actually make.

'I'd love to go to the *biscottificio*, thank you!'

'*Prego*, my dear. I'll knock on your door tomorrow after I get back from work.'

She goes, taking my desire to hide under the covers with her. I put my shoes on before it can come back, grab my notebook, and sail out of the front door, in search of semi-frozen pomegranate.

Adriana and I wrap ourselves up in coats and scarves. I'm surprised the place is still open as it's already dusk, but damn it, people need their biscotti. We dodge puddles of piss and jump over roadworks railings on pavements. While Palermo is definitely 'grittier' than some of Italy's more gilded cities, it's come an extraordinarily long way from its years at the mercy of the criminal organisation Cosa Nostra. In a 2017 *Guardian* article, *la Repubblica* journalist Attilio Bolzoni (who lived in Palermo for twenty-five years) said:

> I had been in Afghanistan, the Balkans, Iraq, but I had never felt so afraid as I did in Palermo during those years. I had to watch my back all the time. You found the *mafiosi* everywhere, on the streets, in the shops, in the banks. It felt like a curfew was in place, there wasn't a single café where you could sit at a table in the evening. Every time the phone rang at my desk, I was afraid they had killed the umpteenth journalist, police-man or judge.[*]

The high-profile bombings, killings and drug traf-ficking have diminished since legislation was passed to remove the bosses. Penalties and prison conditions were made harsher, so the prospect of lighter sentences in exchange for giving up associates to the police became more attractive, which led to more arrests. Now the city has been regenerated to the point where it became Italy's 2018 culture capital. That's not to say that the mafia have disappeared: the intimidation of businesses to pay

---

[*] Lorenzo Tondo, 'The resurrection of Palermo: from mafia battlefield to cultural capital', *Guardian*, 27 March 2017, available at www.theguardian.com/cities/2017/mar/27/resurrection-palermo-mafia-battlefield-culture-capital

a *pizzo* (which could mean a regular payment, a tax on the promise of peace; perhaps agreeing to hire someone the mafiosi 'suggest'; or allowing mafiosi to do business on the premises) continues. Those who refuse to pay can expect trouble, though these days they tend to receive silent but frightening threats to their livelihood rather than high-profile, bloody revenge: for example, after the first refusal, a business owner might come to work the next day to find the lock on the door has been filled with superglue. The grassroots movement Addiopizzo has built a community of businesses with a policy of refusing to pay *pizzo*, and their stickers adorn the windows of shops all over the city, a subtle detail of resistance in the background of people's holiday snaps.

Adriana and I arrive at a slim shopfront, with a sign above the door reading 'Biscottificio'. The walls are stacked floor to ceiling with biscotti. A woman who I immediately cast as a no-nonsense Sicilian matriarch is buying two packs of *ossa dei morti* that she's plucked from an enormous pile. They are bagged in the stiffest, loudest kind of plastic, as if to turn off the midnight sneakers who in daylight hours swore the diet started today.

Adriana gets the attention of the tiny baker behind the counter, who seems to be even less nonsense than the woman she's just served, and asks if they would allow me into the kitchen one day to teach me how to make them.

'We really can't,' she says. 'For this quantity we have to use a machine. But you can make them at home — they're easy.'

'But you have to make two types of dough, right?'

'No,' says the biscuit boss, 'it's one dough. It needs five hundred millilitres of water, five hundred grams of flour and six hundred grams of sugar. And a little cinnamon. You cook it until it's thick, cool it, shape it into bones, and leave them to harden.'

'For three days, right?' I offer.

'Meh – two should be fine. They will be hard like bones, like' – she knocks on the counter – 'then when you bake them, the sugar leaks out and caramelises, and leaves a hard bone on top. See?'

She reaches into the glass cabinet where the biscotti are displayed, and hands us each one. We inspect it, and it's true, they're one mass of sugar and flour, separated by the science of time and heat.

'*È un biscotto magico,*' she says.

I buy a packet, and the next afternoon we sit at the kitchen table and watch a YouTube video about how to make them.

'It really is magical!' says Adriana, delighted. We each take a biscotto, and knock them on the table. Hardly appetising, I think – but I'm an idiot. How could something so sugary be anything but delicious? As the sweet shards dissolve on my tongue, I forget it represents the bones of the dead; I forget deciding sugar would stop Dion's heart if I let it into the house. Adriana savours every bite, with one arm resting across her front. She stares into the distance, utterly content with her thoughts, the quiet, this biscuit. She takes a deep breath and lets out a vocal sigh. I've never seen anyone eat with such quiet, uncomplicated joy. How did I turn food into such a blunt, cartoonish bargaining situation after Chris died, whereby I agreed to eat overpriced, bullshit 'health' foods encased in plastic, and even then, only after a series of calculations and concessions?

Adriana has clearly never been told that baking is science, not art. Following the YouTube video, I painstakingly measure out the flour, water and sugar, and then grab the cinnamon. The recipe calls for a few shakes, a big old pinch. Adriana upturns the shaker, and shakes. And shakes. And shakes and shakes, for several minutes, until the entire mixture is dark brown.

'This will really make the difference,' she says.

'Won't it change the scientific make-up of dough, though?' I say.

'No, it'll just make it nicer,' she says, still shaking.

We simmer the mixture and stir. It thickens a little, and Adriana suggests it might be done.

'I don't think it's thick enough,' I say. 'The video mixture looks thicker.'

'It'll be all right,' she says, switching off the stove.

'I don't know,' I say, though not stopping her – it's her kitchen, after all. 'I think it has to be thicker to be able to harden. Because ... science.'

I think about the time I bought Dion a salad because he was coming home early but had had to skip lunch. I'd pored over the nutritional information in the same crowded supermarket where I would later throw a sandwich, and concluded that as long as he had no other sugar at all that day, this wouldn't be too much (he would still be coming in a good 12 g under the daily limit for men, but I'd lowered it just to be safe). He enjoyed it, but something was niggling me. I took a sharp intake of breath and ran to the bin, dug out the packet and confirmed my suspicion: I hadn't been looking at the 'per pack' side, but the 'per 100 g'. I started breathing heavily and shouting, 'Why would they do this?! Who eats a *third of a salad*?' The next thing I remember is being on the floor sobbing, with Dion's chest pressed against my back and his arms around me, his voice whispering, 'It's OK, it's OK...' as I gasped, 'No, it was too much...it's *science*...'

The sugary dough thickens a little as it cools, but shaping it into bones is tricky.

'This is why they're bones of the dead,' I say, laughing at the wobbly wet oblongs on the baking sheet. 'No one could survive with bones shaped like this.'

The dough hardens a bit over the next two days, but not much. On the third day, having disobeyed some element of almost every stage of the process, we put the first batch in the oven and decide to spend the fifteen-minute baking time looking at our phones.

After just a few minutes, Adriana cries, 'Oh my God!' I look up. Black smoke is pouring out of the sides of the oven door. She rushes to switch it off, pulls the tray out and dumps it in the sink, and then turns to me sheepishly: 'I had it on the grill setting.' I crack a smile, and then a giggle, and then we weep with laughter at the sight of the black blobs on the baking tray.

The second batch is perfectly tasty, matching the flavour of the professional biscotti almost exactly, but abandoning the science cost us the bone-on-top effect. They are brown, sugary oblongs.

Later, I sneak into the kitchen and hold one of the perfect golden-brown-and-white *biscottificio* bones of the dead over the black blobs, snap a picture of the comparison and text it to Adriana with the message, 'Nailed it.' I hear her phone ping and then wonderful, shrieking laughter. From different ends of the house, we laugh together at our gloriously botched attempt at this long-held tradition.

If you're lazy, don't die in Italy. The dead have a lot on their plate.

Take the Fontanelle Cemetery in Naples, a network of natural caves and ancient Greek and Roman tunnels that was turned into an ossuary when the cemeteries ran out of space. The bones of around 40,000 people are in meticulously arranged piles, creeping up the walls, hundreds of skulls staring and grinning to the sounds of echoes and drips. Many are victims of World War II bombings, though most are from the plague of 1656, which eradicated half the city's population.

But having the dead simply placed there rather than buried out of sight caused a fascinating relationship to bloom between the dead and the Neapolitans. It grew organically: the workers responsible for stacking and arranging the bones began praying for the anonymous dead. People started 'choosing' a skull to 'own'; they would name it, care for it, and then ask it for favours and prophecies – revealing next week's lottery numbers was a particularly popular ask. They would scrawl a wish on a scrap of paper and place it in the eye socket. Once the favour was granted, devotees would reward the skull with trinkets, jewellery or even housing, in a wooden box with a little roof.

The Cardinal of Naples was no fan of this practice of keeping skulls as good-luck charms and closed the cemetery in 1969 in a bid to end it. It's now open to tourists. When Dion and I walked in he said, 'Hang on, is this why you brought me outside the town centre? Is this why I'm not eating pizza? Oh my God, is *this* why you chose Naples for our trip?!' And I said, 'Shh, dead people trying to sleep here.' We saw a basket of offerings on a dusty little coffin by the entrance. I'm no historian but I'm confident the doll, the collapsible cup, the Magic Marker, the Chupa Chups lollipop and the (euro) coins aren't from before 1969. I later checked in with Andrew Chesnut, the Santa Muerte expert, who confirmed that Fontanelle is 'the coolest cemetery in Italy' because devotion is ongoing.

The reason anyone thinks these skulls are in a position to grant favours is because of the anonymity of their owners' deaths: by dying in a plague epidemic or in the violence of war, their burials would have been hasty, chaotic or non-existent. It's likely they were given no last rites or grave markers, which means they wouldn't have been granted entry to heaven or hell.

'We call people who died in violence the *decollati*,' says Silvia, my Italian teacher in Palermo. I take two hours of conversation class with her every afternoon. She's about my age, always wearing a different pair of fabulous earrings, and because she's been landed with me as a student, she's telling me everything she knows about Sicilian death culture.

'Does *decollati* mean . . . the beheaded?' I say, drawing my finger across my neck.

'Exactly,' she says. 'Without the last rites, they go to a form of purgatory. This means while they aren't in heaven or hell, they know things the living don't, and they can still affect life on earth. Because of the way they died they *hate* murder and crime, so they take it upon themselves to protect the living.'

Silvia tells me about her grandmother and her frequent visits to the church of the *decollati*, to ask the dead about her husband, who was away fighting in the war. She would pray for his protection and then listen, for the next hour or so, for a response to interpret. A barking dog, the crow of a rooster? That must mean good news. Water spilled on the floor? Clearly that represents tears, and means he is hurt or dead. A door creaks open in the breeze? He's alive. Slams shut? Dead.

The dead in Sicily aren't even let off the hook when it comes to gift-giving. Up until a few decades ago, Sicilian children didn't receive gifts on Christmas morning, but rather on 2 November – and the gifts were left by their dead relatives. On the morning of the Festival of the Dead, children wake up and commence a treasure hunt to find what's been left for them by their dead. Older Sicilians recall finding a pear or a chocolate, but over the years the toys got bigger and more numerous – these days they might get a bicycle, as well as sweets hidden all over the house. The excitement isn't only in the presents, but in finding them. Children would leave pairs of shoes outside their bedroom doors in the hope of finding them filled with sweets. Smart children set out their father's shoes, the biggest in the house, to maximise the haul. The day I threw the sandwich, I read about Sicily's Festa dei Morti with amazement and envy as I imagined growing up associating the dead with a treasure hunt, a sugar hit and a gift, instead of an awkward silence, averted gazes and the obligatory muttering of 'very sad'.

One thing the death festivals have taught me thus far is, of course, that where there is contemplation of death, there is sugar. Mexico has sugar skulls, Nepal has treats changing hands and filling children's tiffin boxes – but this is Sicily, and when it comes to sugar, they don't mess around. This is already an island of desserts – cannoli, delicious pastry tubes filled with sweet ricotta and topped with a candied strip of orange, are ubiquitous, as is cassata, a liqueur-heavy sponge cake, granita, every kind of biscotti worth chewing...but in the run-up to the *festa*, wares in shop windows are flanked by the ultimate sugary treat: the *pupi di zucchero*, or 'sugar puppets', a traditional centrepiece made of the same kind of smooth compacted sugar as Mexico's sugar skulls, traditionally in the form of a knight and a horse. Puppetry has always been a strong part of the Sicilian tradition, and medieval knights are part of its iconography, so disgruntled purists aren't happy with the emergence of sugar puppets in the shape of Mickey Mouse and characters from *Frozen*.

'Ugh!' says Giusi Cataldo, who is definitely a purist. 'No, no, a Mickey Mouse *pupo di zucchero* – this is not traditional. It *has* to be a knight.' Giusi is the artistic director of the Notte di Zucchero – the night of sugar – an annual event in Catania and Palermo, which she started with the express aim of reviving the dwindling traditions of the Festa dei Morti. We're sitting at a table outside a café in Palermo's Piazza San Domenico, sipping espresso while we chat and I fiddle with my dictaphone and consult my illegible notes. She's so stylish and perfectly manicured, I must look like I'm interning as her assistant.

'So, tell me about the Festa dei Morti,' I say. 'Why is it dying?'

'Because Halloween has taken hold,' she says without hesitation. 'On TV, in fact across all media, they don't talk about the Festa dei Morti, they talk about Halloween and pumpkins.' On the surface, Halloween and the Festa dei Morti might not seem drastically different – they happen around the same time, they're both based on the idea that the veil between the worlds of the living and the dead become thin, and both give the pancreas a lot to do. But a fundamental difference is in the emotion that's being brought to the forefront: Halloween is about fear and that strange, exquisite enjoyment of it. But the Festa dei Morti is about love, memory, and *vanquishing* the fear of death. From what little I've caught of the news here, Halloween has definitely been mentioned – Silvia showed me one segment about the death of the Festa dei Morti, which opened with the line, 'Every time a child says "trick or treat", a sugar puppet dies.' As a journalist, I can see how Halloween gets the airtime the Festa dei Morti doesn't: for the short attention spans that light-hearted news segments are tailored to, fear is a better story than love, and spookiness is easier to revel in than a sense of fondness for our dead, whose absence is old news to us. Plus, a grinning pumpkin is a more striking image than a sugary knight.

Giusi continues, 'My son asked me, "Mum, what is it, this Festa dei Morti?" I realised we're losing this festival for our own children, so I decided to get it back in the game.'

So in 2013, Giusi teamed up with a costume and production designer and organised a three-day event in a huge, empty furniture factory. Thirty thousand people showed up. They've since held the event in theatres, and last year in Palermo's historic centre. This year they're holding part of the festival in the Cimitero degli Inglesi, a cemetery that's been abandoned for 200 years. Giusi and her team have cleaned it up for the *festa*, after which it will be reopened to the public.

'Why do you think it's important that children have this connection to the dead?' I ask.

'Because when you think about the grandparents who don't exist any more, it's better to think of them in a way that's cheerful, not sad. It's a way of remembering them. We ask children, "What did your dead bring you?" and they can say, "My dead brought me a doll!"'

'I love the phrase "my dead"!' I say. 'In life, people are yours. My mother, my sister, my husband, my dog. Why shouldn't they be your dead too?'

'Exactly!'

'Do you have nice memories of the Festa dei Morti of your childhood?'

'*Sì, certo*,' says Giusi with enthusiasm. 'The traditions were so much fun: you had to go to bed early, because if not the dead would scratch your feet with cheese graters. So you had to hide your feet from the dead.' She laughs at the memory.

'They'd grate your feet?!' I gasp, laughing. 'That's *terrifying*!'

'It was!' she says. 'You'd lie there all night like this' – she mimes curling her feet under her in bed – 'just waiting. We interviewed people on camera about their memories of it. There was an old man who said he remembered he didn't sleep, because he'd asked his mother how the dead get in, and she'd told him they enter through the door lock, and he thought... *but how will they get the toys through*?!' We laugh.

'Do you think that having this link to the dead

changes our attitude to death?' I ask. 'Perhaps makes us less fearful of it?'

'Yes, I think so,' says Giusi. 'It's always been this way in Sicily. When I was little, my aunt died, and it happened in a room in the house. Everyone came to say goodbye. Even us kids. And, of course, it's a little scary, but it's also a way to *remove* the fear. It's strange, but it's like . . .' She hesitates.

I offer, 'A normal thing?'

'A normal thing, yes. But you know, it's not really about the toys. It's about the memory of the person. It's a way of bringing them back to life.'

I shelter from the rain under a tiny awning with the other weirdos who are here to spend the afternoon looking at corpses. We huddle closer as the wind agitates the puddles, splashing drops up to our feet and legs, as if trying to hitch a ride inside. With audible relief, we hear the lock turn. The door is opened by a monk. I'm surprised – not to see a monk: this is a monastery, after all – that this monk is wearing a brown robe cinched at the waist with a rope, exactly like Friar Tuck in Robin Hood. He also looks startlingly like my father: round, with a bald head and white hair.

In the late sixteenth century, Palermo's Capuchin monastery ran into a common problem that has historically come with Catholicism's insistence on burial: the cemetery ran out of space. They excavated crypts beneath it, and in 1599 they mummified the recently deceased Friar Silvestro da Gubbio and placed him into the catacombs. Originally only for the Capuchin monks, the practice of mummifying and displaying bodies was a type of burial that later became available to Palermitanos who could afford the costly status symbol. The process of mummification was fairly simple: the bodies were laid out on ceramic pipe racks, washed in a vinegar solution, some even stuffed with hay. But the real cost came with the upkeep of the bodies, for which relatives were responsible. Sometimes the deceased would stipulate that they wanted regular changes of clothes in a bid for barely diluted death denial: the toil of bodily upkeep that mortals are saddled with in life, but without any of the payback of actually living.

I buy a three-euro ticket from Friar Dad, go down a spiral stone staircase and emerge into an underground room with a glass floor suspended above flat tombstones. A hallway stretches out ahead, and another one to my left and right. The walls are strung with corpses. They're in two rows; one at eye level and the other above. They seem to be hanging on hooks. They slouch, shoulders hunched up around where their ears used to be, arms tied together at the waist, heads lolling down towards the floor. They look absolutely sick of it.

I stand dumbfounded at the foot of the stairs for a moment, then turn left and see Friar Silvestro da Gubbio. He is still chubby. It makes me feel a little better to see names and death dates, to know that P. Gregoria da Salemi died in 1878. It feels somehow less rude to be staring at him, knowing he retains his identity in this corridor of horrors. I know that objectively I have no real reason to be horrified – death isn't cured by an averted gaze – but between the skeletons and the dry air I find myself needing to sit down on a step and sip some water.

I stand back up, deciding to focus less on my own kneejerk horror, and more on the incredible historical record this place is – and to think more about how these people *wanted* to be seen. They're dressed in their best: hats, ties, coats, cravats, bow ties; it's as if I've arrived hundreds of years late to a fashion show. One wears a skinny black tie that would look fabulous today on a live Sicilian, after a thorough dry-clean. If it weren't for the fact that his jacket and trousers are utterly moth-eaten, or that it's all a bit ill-fitting now he's a skeleton, he'd be able to walk down the street today looking pretty sharp. I feel bad for two particularly gruesome skeletons, one of them with the bottom-right side of his skull missing, because they're positioned either side of a 'no smoking' sign like a graphic health warning. It's a perfect visual joke.

Whoever originally took care of their beloved relatives eventually wouldn't have been able to any more, and it shows. I don't have a ton of experience to draw on, but it doesn't feel controversial to say that these fellas are in bad condition. Many of them have parts missing, broken fingers, spiders' webs visible through the sides of their necks. One female has lost most of the middle section of her skull; it's as if there's a scream stretching from her lower jaw to the top of her right eye socket. Relatives would donate money to have their dead kept in a certain place, but when donations stopped, the body would be moved to a shelf, and presumably all maintenance would cease. And sure enough, the shelves are mostly filled with piles of disintegrating bones and rags. That said, I wasn't expecting any of them to have skin, dry as parchment paper though it is, but many have retained their wrinkles, eyelids, eyelashes, teeth and facial hair. I start to feel rude again, scrutinising the wrinkles of a dead person – then a godlike voice booms over the tannoy to let us know it's forbidden to take photos. Right, I think, staring into the eye sockets of a skeleton hanging above me on the wall, hunched over as if exhausted after a one-hundred-year shift, because *that* would be disrespectful.

Everyone is whispering; everyone, that is, except the many young children whose parents implore them to be quiet. Nothing would have convinced my medic parents to bring me here, but the children seem unfazed by the corpses surrounding them.

I start to feel strangely ill, a mixture of still air, heat and unease. The hooded skeletons look the way Death was depicted in films I watched as a child. One of them looks like it's going to lift its head and tell me something terrifying about my future. But when I walk into the Cappella Bambini, the children's chapel, I let out an audible, 'Oh no, oh dear.' The wall is covered in dead children in dresses, with bonnets on their tiny, exposed skulls. Every single person who rounds the corner exclaims some variation of 'Oh my goodness' and 'Oh dear, dear, dear'. I stand there for around fifteen minutes and watch almost everyone – particularly the Brits – do the same thing I did: exclaim something suggesting that what they're seeing is terrible, then approach, getting almost as close as they possibly can, the peering equivalent of taking all but the last cookie on the communal plate. I wonder if we're all filling in the gaps in our curiosity left by a culture and education that told us to look away.

Whenever you mention to a Palermitano that you're going to visit the catacombs, they mention Rosalia, the mummy toddler famous for being *bene conservata* – well preserved. At just two years old, she was one of the very last to be interred in the catacombs, in 1920, after dying from complications of pneumonia. The preservation is, indeed, startlingly good. Her face is still plump. She has a yellow ribbon in her shiny blonde hair, and her eyes are slightly open. Just as everyone said, she looks for all the world like a sleeping child. Her embalmer, Alfredo Salafia, took the formula to his grave, but his notes were discovered in 2009 by Dario Piombino-Mascali, anthropologist and curator of the catacombs, and in them the list of ingredients: glycerin to prevent her from desiccating in the dry air, formalin to kill bacteria, zinc salts to petrify her, and salicylic acid to get rid of fungi in the flesh. They haven't added that information to her spot in the catacombs. Somehow the romance of the perfectly preserved child, frozen in time in her crib like Sleeping Beauty, is lost at the mention of the chemical solution that achieved it.

As I walk down the Corridoio Donne (the women's corridor) towards the exit, I stop to send Dion a message, because I have an overwhelming urge to check if he's OK. I realise I am standing close enough to a skeleton, lying down on a shelf, to stare into the caverns of her hollow eyes, which are turned towards me. Something makes me lift my face to the ceiling and there, high up on a shelf, is a long-dead toddler. She still has full lips and chubby cheeks, and her eyelids are half open, revealing nothing behind. Her left hand hangs by her side, and her right hand is stretched forward.

She's pointing right at me.

I zero in on her fingers, and note with an absurd measure of relief that the digits are all curled into her palm. She's not pointing at me, obviously: of course this mummified child isn't foreshadowing my imminent death. I take a step back. Her 'gaze' stays fixed on the spot where I was standing.

Not me. Not today.

I do feel like a nosy weirdo. I mean, I'm here for research, but they don't know that. As far as these people are concerned, I'm some creepy voyeur looking at strangers cleaning the graves of their dead relatives. Not that I'm what they're focusing on at the moment.

The graveyard above the Capuchin Catacombs is

slick with last night's rain. It is arranged into corridors lined with tall trees and mausoleums, and the graves have elaborate marble and stone decorations; books open on a page with a profile of the deceased, a picture and a quote. Many of them are a declaration that their dead are, in some way, not dead, such as, 'Nothing dies. Everything is energy, constantly changing.' It's true, but I wonder if anyone is truly comforted by such a technicality. It certainly wouldn't get you off a murder charge.

There is a huge flower stall outside that is steadily being emptied into the cemetery. The place is alive with petals, and people have strung decorations across some of the graves, with red hearts and messages such as 'We still love you, Victoria' in bright, shiny letters, as if it's her birthday. The elaborateness of the decorations seems to correlate with how young the person was when they died. There are far more children buried here than I would have imagined; many of the trees have plush teddy bears tied to them. A Winnie-the-Pooh and a Bart Simpson smile out from the same trunk, their arms outstretched, soaked in rain.

An old man with a blue bucket chucks water on the floor in front of a grave and hobbles to get his broom, and a woman three graves down is sweeping wet leaves. Across the way, a woman uses a white rag to wipe raindrops from a gold-trimmed tombstone. I find myself, not for the first time on this journey, feeling envious of their tasks. For me, grief was like drowning without arms, no way of getting through it except by getting through it.

These people have something to do, someone to care for, somewhere for their love to go.

I don't know why I expected the taxi driver to know the whereabouts of a cemetery that's been closed for 200 years. We find it with help from Google Maps and the unmistakable sign of the Notte di Zucchero – a smiling, skeletal knight on puppet strings against a starry night sky, with the words in white: '*Notte di Zucchero; Festa di morti, pupi e grattugie*' ('night of sugar; festival of the dead, puppets and graters'). The taxi driver tells me to have fun, in a way that sounds like he's omitting the words 'in a cemetery at nine o'clock on a Friday morning, you unfathomable freak'.

The turnout is bad. There's no way around it. Giusi greets me from under a black umbrella and grimaces at the rain, saying people probably won't show up now. As a Brit I can't say I'd describe this gentle misting as 'rain', but I reassure her that there are a few people gathering at the entrance. She introduces me to Sandro Dieli, a man with a trim white beard and a firm handshake, who says the Festa dei Morti was an important part of his childhood and that he's delighted it's being revived.

While things warm up, I take a stroll around the cemetery. The 200 years of abandonment are not invisible. It's incredible to see how quickly things break down without human intervention. I stop and take a picture of one of the graves, once a proud block of stone, now claimed by moss and overshadowed by bushes and crumbling underneath – and realise with horror that I'm standing right in the background of Giusi's TV news interview. I freeze, and tell myself to walk casually out of shot, *not* to rush and trip over a rock and break a tooth on a tombstone on Italian TV, like some kind of *Bridget Jones* Halloween Special. (I make it out of the shot, but I later check the footage on *Giornale di Sicilia*. Yep, there I am, and it's exactly as embarrassing as I imagined. I look like I'm doing an impression of a ditzy millennial viewing the world through her phone's camera. A flawless impression.)

The actors are dotted around the cemetery. Some are professionals, in costumes; there's a woman in a white dress with a halo of red flowers playing the patron saint of Palermo, Santa Rosalia. A middle-aged woman is dressed in a blue dress with a yellow ribbon in her hair, talking in dialect (it's not hard to understand; it's like hearing Italian and Spanish swing dancing in my brain). She's speaking like a small child. It takes me a moment to realise she's playing the other Rosalia: the well-preserved toddler in the catacombs. I approach her when the beautifully acted monologue is light and sweet, with her calling, 'Papa! Papa! It's me, Rosalia!' and singing a haunting lullaby, but it takes a dark turn into the horror of being mummified, neither alive nor dead.

A flurry of excitement ripples through the crowd when the mayor, Leoluca Orlando, turns up. A starry-eyed Giusi introduces us and we have a brief chat about sugar puppets before the cameras swarm towards him.

With dictaphones and microphones and iPhones open on the voice notes app hovering in his face, he gives an eloquent description of why the festival needs this revival, and why we need it: 'The games, the gifts, even the sugar puppets that characterise this festival – they're a way of accepting death as a part of life.'

After the mayor leaves, orbited by a cloud of his people, I notice Sandro standing alone, so I decide to go and chat to him. I get to about five feet away before he starts speaking, in the kind of raised voice only actors use.

'Children ask each other one question as the November and December festivals approach: "In your house … does she visit, or not?"'

I stop in my tracks, relieved I didn't scupper the opening. A crowd draws in like iron filings on a magnet. 'It's an important question,' he continues, 'because if she did come, there would be toys and festivities, and if she didn't, it was a really sad thing.' He's talking about La Befana, a figure in Italian folklore – an old woman, often depicted as a kind witch on a broomstick, who delivers presents to Italian children on the eve of Epiphany, like a January Santa Claus.

'La Befana didn't come to my house,' says Sandro, and continues with some indignation, 'but she went to my cousins' house. How could La Befana, with all her technical means, like a flying broomstick, not manage to come to our house? But my father stated categorically that no, La Befana does not come to our house.'

'But,' he smiles, 'at our house, the dead visited.'

And as he speaks, I forget where I am; I see the world from the perspective of a small boy excited by a visit from ghosts bearing gifts.

'And during that night, when the dead visited,' he continues, 'they came to my house and flew around, or at least that's how I imagined it, flying all around the house to leave us our gifts. In fact, that day, and that day in particular I'll never forget, I woke up with the excitement of the Day of the Dead and I started to search and search and search – until I found a box, a big one. And I ripped the paper off and' – he gasps, and brings his hands together in front of him as if the joy of it is all too much – 'what an incredible surprise!' He starts laughing in disbelief, 'How did the dead do it? How did my grand-parents know just what I wanted – a tricycle – and that I wanted a *red* one? It was really an incredible thing. So I started playing with it for days on end, and I needed a runway, so I used the corridor that went like this...' He indicates that it went straight, and then bent sharply to the right. 'Then one afternoon, my father went for a nap and, unexpectedly, closed the glass door to the hall. And I went down my runway, not noticing the door was shut, and I crashed into the door. The glass smashed into pieces and I remember how, in slow motion, the shards of glass passed beside me, behind me ... and didn't touch me! I'm sure it was because my grandparents were there, moving aside the shards as they fell.' He mimes their hands, gently moving fragments of glass away from their little grandson's face, these ghosts who seemed even in death to need something to do, someone to care for, somewhere for their love to go.

'When my father arrived he got very angry with me,' Sandro continues, 'and I remember thinking, "Why is he angry with me? He's the one who blocked the runway!"' The crowd laughs.

'Anyway,' he says, bringing his hands together in front of him, 'since I was a child, even after the cynicism of maturity took hold, even now I can say: that day, yes, *i miei morti*, my dead – they came. They came.'

Filled with the excitement of the Day of the Dead, I jump in a taxi and manage to squeeze in one last conversation class with Silvia, where she presents me with a certificate that states my language level (which I'm delighted with, and I tell her so, in almost-advanced-level Italian). Hugs are exchanged, class photos are taken and by the time I turn the key in Adriana's front door I'm grateful for the solitude that greets me.

I climb the stairs to the kitchen. The light filters through the curtains. Through the window, left ajar, I can hear neighbours chatting in dialect.

I take the moka from the drying rack and brew some coffee. It's time for an *ossa di morto*. I know I left them on the table but I don't see them. My eyes dart around and then I'm opening cupboards, looking behind cereal boxes, wondering where they can be – then I spot the fruit bowl covered with a tea towel. I pull it back, see the biscotti and realise, with a giggle, that I just had my own little treasure hunt on the day of the *festa*. Under a tea towel is probably exactly where Chris would have hidden them, as well.

I bite into the biscotto. It snaps loudly. I sigh like Adriana and close my eyes as the sugar dissolves on my tongue.

CHAPTER EIGHT

RIP (For a Bit)

I'm teetering on the roof edge of a concrete tomb. The air is filled with the smells of sweat and rum, and I'm being jostled from all sides by excitable dancing men, hollering announcements in Malagasy to the surrounding crowd of thousands. They wave their arms, swaying to the upbeat trumpets of the brass band. I grip the concrete Cross, inhaling plumes of dust as below us men in baseball caps drive shovels into the dry, compacted earth. The crowd waits eagerly, many of them clutching rolled-up straw mats, demanding they dig faster and bring out their dead.

So, basically, a typical Friday.

I emerge from Antananarivo airport on a chilly night in late July and see my name on a sign held by my Madagascar guide, fifty-one-year-old Eric. He's a kind, six-foot

smile of a man, and shakes my hand warmly. I greet him
in French, and he tells me, somewhat relieved, that it's
been a while since he spoke English and he'd been nervous about having to rely on it.

'Don't worry,' I say in French as we walk to the Jeep,
'I've been practising. I didn't think English would be that
common here.' At which point Eric reveals he speaks
fantastic Italian, so we quickly settle into an absurd mix
of all three.

At my hotel, I confirm to my family on WhatsApp
that I've landed safely and promptly collapse on the
bed. In the morning, Eric rolls up in the Jeep and we set
off into the highlands, where around this time of year
people exhume their dead in a ceremony called Famadihana, the Turning of the Bones. It's a raucous party
with rum and dancing around the opening of the family
tomb.

As we drive out of the city, Eric teaches me a few useful terms to know in Malagasy. 'The first you need to
know is "*mora mora*",' he says, 'slowly, slowly. In Madagascar, we take our time. No rush, no hurry. Like tomorrow,
we will leave early so we can get there *mora mora*, stop for
coffee, stop for lunch, see the views. Not rushing. Never
rushing. *Mora mora.*'

'*Mora mora*,' I repeat. 'Got it.' Eric is married to a
Dutch woman. For a while they lived in Switzerland,
where his daughter still lives, but he and his wife moved
to eastern Madagascar because Eric was so homesick he
could barely see straight. I'm guessing his affection for

doing things *mora mora* was part of his desire to get away from the home of the psychotically correct clock.

'Also you are going to hear the word "*vazaha*" a *lot*.' I repeat it (pronounced 'vazza'). 'It means "white person",' he says. 'It's not pejorative, it's just the word.' He teaches me how to say 'hello' – *salama*, 'sorry' – *azafady*, 'thank you' – *misaotra*, and 'thank you very much' – *misaotra betsaka*.

'What about "*fady*"?' I ask. I've done enough research to know that when something is *fady* it's taboo, or bad luck, which Eric confirms. 'It's *fady* to wear red at Fama-dihana, right?'

Eric waves his hand, 'Not so much any more. Where we are going they are quite relaxed about the *fady*. But some are still important – for example, it is *fady* to point your finger at a tomb. It's too direct, like you're invit-ing death.' As if on cue, Eric spots a tomb on a hill and pulls over the car. 'You see up there, on the hill? That's a family tomb.'

I lean forward and, completely forgetting what he told me about eight bloody seconds ago, I point, 'That square concrete thing up there?'

'Don't point,' he says quickly, 'do it like this.' He curls his fingertip towards his palm and indicates with his knuckle.

The importance of the ancestors in Madagascar is visible to the naked eye – from its position on the hill, the tomb overlooks a village of little huts constructed from mud, sticks and straw, some with deep, sun-dried cracks etched into them like wrinkles. But the tomb itself is much more durable and decorated: it's made of concrete and granite, topped with a Cross, and painted dusty shades of pink and blue.

I turn to Eric and say, 'I heard that in the eighties, an aid organisation donated concrete to Madagascar. It was for people to upgrade their houses, so they'd be less vulnerable to cyclones, but instead they upgraded the tombs. Is that true?'

'Yes,' said Eric. 'People are happy to live in mud huts they have to rebuild over and over, but tombs have to last *for ever.*'

We're only 29 km outside of Antananarivo when Eric pulls over the Jeep and says, 'Shall we get a pineapple? They grow just over there.' There are a few wooden stalls stacked high with bright, vibrant pineapples before a lush valley and blue skies.

He signals to an old lady behind the stall. She stands, takes a pineapple and a knife, and walks right over to the Jeep where we're checking out the view. She suspends the pineapple by its spiky stalk and uses the knife to carve off the skin, letting the strips fall to the ground. Her knife glints as she cuts thick strands of pineapple lengthways off the core for us to pull away and eat. The juice glistens in the sun and drips off our fingers into the red dust. Madagascar is often referred to as the eighth continent, and people insist it's nothing like the rest of Africa. I have to admit, everything does taste subtly different here: the pineapple, the honey, the coffee; it's like hearing a familiar song played on another instrument. We finish the last bites and wipe off the juice on our clothes. Eric flashes a wide grin and says, 'Now you are in the heart of Madagascar!'

Fortified, we drive on, and begin to swerve around increasingly numerous potholes.

'We are beginning to dance with the road,' says Eric, and continues, 'I think the road is like the system in Madagascar.' Clearly given to philosophical musings, he says that since earnings here are so low, people have to dance around doing fancy footwork just to find a way to live. As we drive on, I fall silent, taking in the scenery as the road winds into the highlands. It's like nowhere else I've seen. The red soil is topped with sun-faded grass. Clothes are laid out flat to dry on hay bales, on the ground, in trees. We pass valleys of precisely divided rice fields. People walk along the edge of the road in the sunshine, waving as we pass.

In the early evening, Eric knocks on the door of my room. We're in the town of Antsirabe, in a functional hotel owned by a gruff Frenchman. I open the door.

'Hello!' Eric says cheerfully. 'Lala and her father are here.'

It's been over a year since I first started emailing Rojo, a woman who owns a travel company in Madagascar, in hopes of securing an invite to Famadihana. Just two months ago, I received the email: Rojo's own employee Lala had invited me to attend her family's ceremony in the village of Ambatomiady, around seventy miles from Antananarivo.

I thank Eric, and grab an envelope of money for them to buy a *lamba* (a shroud to rewrap the body) as a thank you for inviting me to the ceremony. I come outside and join them at a table under the cold blue porch lights. Lala is thirty-four, lives in northern Madagascar and regularly makes the long and arduous journey to visit her family. She's little, wears a pink fleece, has her hair tied back in a ponytail and her hands crossed over her front to protect from the chill in the air. She smiles and nods in greeting. Her father, Edmond, wears a brimmed hat and a coat, and clasps his hands formally on the table. They speak in Malagasy and Eric translates.

When I ask if Edmond and Lala would like the envelope now, Edmond makes a long speech. I wonder what he can be saying. Eric translates that there have been a lot of unanticipated things and that they're organising the finishing touches of the ceremony now – which turns out to be a delicate, sweetly diplomatic way of saying 'yes'. I pass the envelope and Eric says, 'In our culture it's traditional to give a speech at this moment.'

Eric translates as I say, 'I appreciate the invite so much. You don't know me at all, so it's really kind of you, and I feel really privileged. Rojo said you could use this for the *lamba* but I realise you may have bought one already; obviously you can use it for whatever's needed for the day. Where I'm from, we don't really have a relationship with the dead and I'm not sure it's doing us any

favours. So I'm really delighted to get to see this ceremony I've read so much about, and talked to Eric about.
I'm very honoured to get to come and celebrate with you
and your family. *Misaotra*.' Their eyes brighten in recog-
nition at the sound of the word for 'thank you'.

Edmond speaks, and Eric grins.

'He said you're welcome to take pictures of everything
you see, and also that there's going to be music and
drums and dancing, and he said to tell you you'll *definitely*
be expected to dance.'

I grin at Edmond and Lala, and nod. 'Deal.'

Barely fifteen minutes into our drive to Ambatomiady,
I stumble into a *fady*. I ask Edmond, who is in the back
seat with Lala, exactly how many bodies there are in the
family tomb. Edmond says he's not quite sure, and when
I probe – are we talking tens, hundreds? – Eric tells me
it's *fady* to get too precise about numbers of corpses in
tombs. That explains the delicate atmosphere in the car,
as if I've just asked Edmond about his prostate. I'm fascinated to find a reluctance to discuss numbers of corpses
when we're on our way to literally exhume them. But
Edmond happily confirms that the tomb is seventy years
old, and that fourteen bodies are being exhumed and
rewrapped tomorrow – including Edmond's grandfather, who died before Lala was born.

Fear of corpses seems to abound most in cultures
where death is associated with a loss of power. When
death means becoming a demigod, the person to whom

the living now turn for favours – such as here and in Tana Toraja, where I'll be going in a few weeks – the corpse seems more likely to be invited to the party. A van overtakes us, with a coffin wrapped in a sheet on the roof. It's flying a small Malagasy flag, a legal requirement when transporting a dead body. It's a common sight during the months of Famadihana, as people who have died in the past few years are transported to the family tomb so they can be placed inside when it's opened.

'Are you afraid when you see a dead body?' I ask.

'The main feeling is sadness,' says Edmond, via Eric. 'We're not afraid because when people die, we have a wake, so we get used to seeing a dead body. You have that last image before you wrap them and place them in the tomb. You have a mourning period, and then you accept it. Then after five to seven years we accept that the person has become an ancestor. The separation is painful and sorrowful, but when time has passed, we accept it and have a party.'

We pass a house with a band that's firing up the trumpets – another family's Famadihana kicking off.

'We have a saying,' Edmond continues. '"At death we cry, at Famadihana we dance."'

The road betrays us more and more the closer we get to the village. In one pothole the Jeep tilts so alarmingly to the left I have to hold on to the handle to prevent myself from toppling onto Eric, who could practically elbow the ground through the open window. The last eleven miles of the drive takes around two hours, since the road morphs into a dirt track so drastically potholed it resembles the surface of the moon – if the surface of the moon had a bus resolutely stuck in the mud on a sharp corner, inclining at a dangerous angle.

We get out of the car and take a look, along with about five other people who stand around discussing what ransom to pay the mud to get their bus back. Eric wonders aloud if it will claim us too. We look into the logistics of abandoning the Jeep and walking five hours or so the rest of the way, but no one wants to be left responsible for Eric's car.

Then an older Jeep comes along and manages to tear down into the hole and up the other side without getting stuck or shattering to pieces, so we decide to follow suit. Eric revs the engine, and we all mutter some version of, 'Come on, come on...' in our respective languages.

Eric turns to me and says, *'Andiamo!'*

'Let's go!' I repeat.

He floors it. We clamber into the pothole and climb out the other side without breaking a sweat. We cheer, and look back at the poor, stuck bus, wondering if it will have moved an inch by the time we make our way back.

Eric parks the car next to a wooden plough and a hay bale. This grassy ledge on the side of a hill winds down to Edmond's mud-and-brick house. Under the thatched roof there's a wooden picket balcony painted those same shades of dusty pink and blue. The house has no stairs;

the upper floor is reachable only by a wooden ladder. A long stick of bamboo leans out of a high-up window bearing the Malagasy flag, a sign that Famadihana is in progress. The flag flaps gently against the cloudless afternoon sky. The view beyond the house is a valley of rice fields, and houses dotted across farms on the hillside opposite. Below the balcony four enormous speakers have been set up for the party.

We get out of the car, and I step over a patch of pig's blood to greet the family members. Edmond's aunt Janet greets us with a firm handshake, and a woman swaddling a baby gives us a welcoming smile. A dead pig, which has been drained and sliced in two, lies atop some tree branches. Two men are crouched over it in the final stages of the butchering. One of them turns, smiles and approaches, goes to shake my hand, and hesitates. He turns to Eric and shows his hands are covered in dried pig's blood. 'Does she mind?'

'It's fine.' I smile, sticking out my hand. 'I'm Erica, nice to meet you.'

He seems surprised, and pleased, and shakes my hand warmly. He turns to Eric and speaks.

'This is Henri,' says Eric. 'He said you're very welcome, that you can take pictures of everything you like and when you get home, please tell everyone what you saw.'

Famadihana is not simple or quick to organise. For one, you need legal permission to open a tomb. The family

decide on a rough date – usually five to seven years since
the last, or an odd number in any case, as it's *fady* to turn
the bones on an even year. Then, three to six months
beforehand, they must visit a local astrologer and ask
which date would be safe to open the tomb. Some dates
are, everyone knows, off limits – it's *fady* to open a tomb
on a Tuesday or Wednesday, for example. The astrologer
asks when the tomb was constructed, and issues a selection of dates between June and September, when it's dry
– getting here today was tricky enough, but during wet-
ter months many villages in the highlands are impossible
to reach. Once they have a date, the family must then
apply for permission from the state to open the tomb.

Thirty years ago a typical Famadihana ceremony
lasted a week and attendance was mandatory. Now
that the cost of living has risen, most only last two or
three days. But even a short Famadihana remains eye-
wateringly expensive. 'You're feeding an entire village for
two or three days,' Eric explains. 'You're hiring a band,
maybe paying for transportation for families who live
far away. Some families save money by doing small, simple celebrations – but for others that's not acceptable.'

Often people get a bank loan to pay for it and fall into
cycles of debt; it might take three or four years to pay
off, at which point the next ceremony is just a year or
two away.

'I made a terrible faux pas at a Famadihana once,
when I was younger,' Eric told me while slowing down to
drive through a pothole the size of Cardiff. 'I said, "Why

do we spend all this money on the dead? Life is expensive. We should spend it on the living."'

'Were they offended?'

'Yes, terribly. I had to apologise.'

Eric isn't a Christian, but this sentiment of prioritising the needs of the living is often echoed by the Church. Like many African nations, Madagascar had an influx of Christian missionaries – white saviours of the soul – beginning in the 1800s. Now, while around half the population maintain traditional religious practices, around 41 per cent practise Christianity.* Eric says many Christians question the value of spending money on the dead, even condemn it, as life for the living becomes ever more costly.

That is, of course, easy for them to say.

'In the Malagasy tradition, we don't have Jesus or Buddha or Muhammad,' Eric explained. 'The ancestors are our prophets, our intermediary, the link between us and God. That's why it's important to take care of them.' When Christians – or a young Eric – suggest Malagasy people stop venerating their ancestors, they're essentially recommending they abandon their prophet, their advocate, their protection against mortal terror.

We all find ways, regardless of our beliefs, to believe in our own immortality. Some of us follow religions that tell us our souls are immortal, that we'll be reincarnated

---

* US Department of State, *2016 Report on International Religious Freedom: Madagascar*, available at www.state.gov/reports/2016-report-on-international-religious-freedom/madagascar

or go to heaven. Non-believers might find symbolic immortality in naming children, stars or hospital wings after themselves. Some of us, ahem, write books.

But some methods of keeping death anxiety at bay are pricier than others. At Edmond's house, watching the preparations, I wonder if the debt people go into for Famadihana is almost like a tax on living without terror.

It's dark by 6.30 p.m. Everyone dances in front of the giant speakers, which vibrate with the volume. A few of the younger guys set about finding and hanging a light bulb, since right now the lighting is being provided solely by the stars – and the orange glow of cigarettes, which bob up and down in the darkness.

Eric and I break away from the party and find ourselves standing in a huddled circle under the stars with 'Big Uncle' Rafaely (at seventy-two years old, he is the oldest member of the family and therefore the boss, the closest to ancestor status), Henri, and several children who come over to listen to the conversation and, according to Eric, to have a closer look at me, their first *vazaha* guest. I roll my dictaphone and ask every question a journalist is supposed to ask – name spellings, ages, the system of opening a tomb – as well as some philosophical questions they raise about why Malagasy people venerate the ancestors. Eric translates whole debates and discussions had by the group in answer to my questions, the longest of which is about where their love intersects with their fear.

'Listening to you all talk about the ancestors, their power to make good or bad things happen to you – is this ceremony more about love for the people you lost, or fear of what they might do? You mentioned how expensive it is, how people go into cycles of debt – are you doing all this so you can live with less fear?'

Eric puts this to the group, and they discuss it. It seems they only partly agree with the idea that Famadihana is a tax on living without terror.

'Honouring the ancestors in this way, it's a duty, but also a pleasure,' Eric says. 'We believe in God, but we can't *see* God. But thanks to the ancestors, we're here on earth – that's tangible. So why would we forget them? Why wouldn't we honour them, touch them?'

A wave of family members arrive and greet Rafaely. All evening people have been turning up for the evening meal, which they eat at several long planks of wood set up to be tables and benches behind a pale pink tarpaulin acting as a windbreaker. The meal is boiled pig intestines with rice, but Eric says we're eating with Lala at her friend's house. Lala never eats at Famadihana; Eric says she once saw a bloated corpse as a child and her young brain made a connection between that image and the flabby pink flesh of pig intestines. Edmond doesn't approve of Lala's refusal to join in, so we're discreet as we slip away.

Lala cooks on a coal fire on the floor of a concrete room. Multiple bunches of corn hang in rows from the ceiling.

It's food storage for the rainy season, when the potholed road we arrived on becomes impassable. The room is gently wreathed in smoke, lit only by moonlight through the window and the lights on our phones. Eric and I sit on a couple of upholstered stools on straw mats laid across the floor. Lala turns to him as she plates up the food and asks a question anxiously. He replies no, and waves it away as nonsense.

'She's asking if you need to eat at a table.'

I laugh. I know there's nothing I can do about the perception of tourists – that we're high maintenance, germophobic, and weirdly insistent on things being familiar – especially when it's so often true.

'I didn't come to Madagascar to act like I'm in England,' I say.

'That's exactly what I told her!' he laughs.

Lala's *zebu* (beef) stew is delicious. Eric does a beautiful job of translating the conversation back and forth, as we all sit in a sleepy, comfortable reverie after the long day. He reclines against the concrete wall, the smile lines around his eyes catching the shadows. He sighs into the darkness, as if taking in a humbling, sweeping view, tilts his head towards me, and says, 'It goes so fast, this fucking beautiful life.'

I share a bed with Lala. The mattress and pillows are satin sheets stuffed with straw. The air is chilly, and I can't shut my brain up about the following day, so I don't sleep much. After a breakfast of leftover stew and the incongruous experience of using an electric toothbrush at the edge of a rice field, we walk back over to Edmond's house, through long grass and on muddy ledges of rice fields. The music from a neighbouring house has been distantly blaring all night, the night sky lit with disco lights – and it's still going. They are, like almost everyone in the village, Lala's extended family, and we stroll right through their party. There's a festival atmosphere; as well as the music and lights, there are stalls set up with dough-nuts frying. We buy a few and continue along the paths between the fields.

We stop several times as people pass and greet us, and the same conversation ensues:

'Hello! Who are you exhuming today?'

'We are guests of Lala,' Eric tells them. 'This is a *vazaha* journalist; she is writing about Famadihana for a book.'

At this point, they usually shake my hand with both of theirs, and say, 'Welcome, thank you for coming, please take lots of pictures and tell everyone what you saw.'

When we get to Edmond's house, it's lively. A twelve-man band is playing joyful music on violins, banjos, drums. It's not even 9 a.m. and people are already danc-ing and singing. Henri spots me and waves his arms, indicating I should come down and join in.

'Are you going to dance?' Eric grins.

'Well, I did promise.'

'*Andiamo.*'

It's absurdly fun. A circle forms and people take turns jumping into the middle to dance, egged on by cheering and clapping. The band play right next to us and between dances I drift in and out of the circle to take photos and videos. After a couple of hours, Eric and I sneak off for a walk – we've spent days on end in a car and our backs are starting to let us know. We walk down the valley, across the rice fields, past a couple of bulls having an altercation, and up the winding dirt path to the village.

We climb some steps carved into the mud and come to a *hotely*, which is a tiny shop serving coffee and food, usually rice-based. A woman in her twenties stands on the dirt floor under a distressed wooden structure, frying little doughnuts. Smoke rises from the fryer and dances languidly in slanting shafts of light, beaming like lasers through the roof slats. She pours a shockingly sweet cup of coffee from a thermos, and Eric orders another round of doughnuts. Behind us some village children stand in the road, staring at me as if I'm a blue horse making a real go of mastering the tango.

'Are they staring because they don't get many *vazahas* here, or is there some extra layer of strangeness about me? Is my outfit weird or something?'

'It's that you're a *vazaha*,' says Eric simply, popping the rest of the doughnut into his mouth. 'But also,' he says, swallowing, 'it's that you're standing and drinking coffee at a *hotely*, like a country person. Even rich Malagasy people don't do this.'

On our way back to Edmond's house, we pass someone selling discs of sugar cane, and buy a bag. The
texture is like a tightly packed toothbrush, shot through
with unprocessed sugar. You chew it up and spit the spent
fronds onto the ground. It's a pretty good way to floss.

'In England it's rude to spit,' I tell Eric, spitting a
mouthful onto the ground, 'so this is delightful.'

'Ah,' says Eric, spitting and waving his hand dismiss-
ively, 'it's just nature.'

I'm following Eric up a ladder to the top floor of the
cottage. Lala and her relatives are sitting cross-legged in
a big circle on straw mats laid out on the floor. Rafaely
gives a speech, followed by Edmond, who welcomes me
to the family for the day, and thanks me for the *lamba*.
Then I'm invited to give a speech.

I stand up, and Eric translates. 'Hello, everyone, I'm
Erica, the *vazaha*.' They chuckle. 'Um...I brought some
rum for the party, just a few bottles, just to say thank you
for inviting me.' As I go on to thank them sincerely for
the warm welcome to their family event, the invitation
to take photos of everything, the openness with which
they answered all my stupid questions, I am absolutely
shocked to feel a lump in my throat. I must be sleep-
deprived. I put my hand on my heart, quite without
meaning to, smile, say, '*Misaotra betsaka.*' Another speech
of thanks is made in return.

But the day is getting away from us, and there's no
time to do things *mora mora* because the moment has

213

arrived: it's time to turn the bones. So they decide to skip the ceremonial shot of rum. Instead, we all climb down the ladder and, with the brass band in tow playing their instruments, the entire village heads uphill to the tomb.

'Would you like to stand on the tomb?' A bizarre question to be asked in almost any context, but here the one-storey tomb is already populated with several drunk, dancing men who seem only too happy to make space for me. The crowd of thousands is dotted with rolled-up straw mats, babies on hips, arms waving to the music, and the air is made of shouts. They shout over the music, shout over the shouting. As the minutes wear on and people get more excited to see their dead emerge, the space gets tighter. Below us, the dirt is being shovelled aside in search of the slab to open the tomb. The view from up here is astonishing. There are easily two or three thousand people here. It's strange to think that many of them will end up in this very tomb, will be exhumed for Famadihana in years to come, and when no one remembers who they are, they'll get pushed to the back of the tomb to make more space, and finally, as we say, 'rest in peace'.

'Eric,' I say, gripping the dusty pink Cross on top of the tomb, 'did you say this is all *one family*?'

'Yes,' Eric nods, taking my backpack and slotting it on to his front so I don't drop it on the corpses that are about to emerge, 'Lala has fifteen siblings, and that's normal. So if they all grow up and get married, and *they* each have fifteen children...' He indicates the crowd. It's simple maths.

'Do they all know each other?'

'No!' he waves his hand. 'That's one of the most important reasons to have Famadihana. So they can meet each other.'

The men toss aside their shovels, having uncovered the slab. They slide it back and dive into the tomb. A very drunk young man sways before the gaping dark hole, his eyes closed, his arms raised to the heavens. People step forward and pass their straw mats past him – the same mats we were just sitting on in the cottage. It's a sign of respect, not putting dead people straight on the floor. The men disappear into the tombs, place the ancestors on the mats, yell out their names, and pass them up to their descendants. The names are still visible on the earth-stained shrouds, scrawled on the side in Sharpie. The descendants hoist them upon their shoulders and walk them to the back of the crowd.

'That's Lala's grandfather,' Eric says, as the fifth body emerges from the tomb. 'Let's go!' We climb down the rickety wooden ladder and jog through the crowd with 'Follow that car!' energy. It takes us a few minutes to find the right corpse, which is not a sentence I ever expected to write. A young man rips strips off a new shroud and mutters, his eyes wet with tears.

'He's saying, "I haven't got a dad any more,"' Eric whispers, '"I'm an orphan."'

I remember Edmond's comment that the over-whelming emotion of exhuming the bodies is sadness, an intense renewal of the loss. Rather than treating bereavement like a flesh wound that heals linearly and with time, Famadihana rips it all open again, if only for a moment. Grief is the small print of love.

They wrap him in a silk sheet, tie it up with the fabric strips. The music swells and all around us, people start to hoist the bodies onto their shoulders. The brass band is louder and livelier than ever, and people grin with delight as they bounce their dead up and down to the music.

I feel a knock in the back of my head – it's a freshly wrapped corpse on the shoulders of three men, who laugh and say, *'Azafady!' Of course*, I think, laughing helplessly, *of* course *I got hit in the head by a corpse*. I briefly wonder if I was kicked or headbutted, but I don't ask.

'Vazaha, vazaha, take our picture!' cries one grinning man, steadying an ancestor on his shoulder.

'Do you have *un stilo*?' Eric asks. I pull a pen from my bag, and Lala's relative proceeds to write the deceased's name in large black letters on the white silk shroud – so they'll be able to recognise him in seven years. The next body over needs one too, so they pass it along. When I get it back, I joke, 'This is a special pen now.'

'It is!' Eric grins. 'You will receive a blessing.'

'A blessing?' I laugh. 'Just for lending someone my pen? That was easy.'

The sun is tumbling towards the hills. It's unwise

to tackle potholes in the dark, so we say our goodbyes. The family members clasp my hand with both of theirs, thank me for coming, make me promise again to share those pictures, and tell everyone what I saw. We hurry through the crowd, *'Azafady, azafady...'* ducking under newly shrouded cadavers bouncing joyfully on the shoulders of their rum-lit descendants.

I shut the car door and gaze into the rear-view mirror, barely able to process what I've just seen. Eric starts the engine. The wheels puff clouds of dust into the air behind us, obscuring the family of thousands, dancing with their dead under a setting sun.

'When someone dies,' Hermann says, putting more roasted pork on my plate, and checking that my drink is topped up, 'we sing, we drink, we play cards, we joke, we *laugh*, to get rid of the sadness.' Eric, who surprised me with a last-minute dinner party at his friend's house before taking me to the airport for my midnight flight, sits at the head of the table.

'You mean at the funeral?'

'No!' he says. 'When the person dies! That very night!'

There is a mix of Malagasy, French and English being spoken at the table, as Hermann's friends and a couple of family members live between Antananarivo, Switzerland and Paris. We get chatting about Famadihana, and how the influx of Christianity has cast tension on the practice.

217

'You know,' Hermann says, hesitating only slightly, 'we had our own civilisation before the French and the missionaries got here.' He says this with the delicacy used by the oppressed to talk about systemic oppression, the delicacy of talking about suffering to the people who've benefited from it. The same delicacy women use to talk to men about the #MeToo movement, the same delicacy people of colour use to talk to white people about race. It's always there, the trepidation that they (or, being honest, as a middle-class straight white cis European: we) might take it personally, make it about our own embarrassment, or get defensive at the suggestion that we didn't fully earn every break we ever got, that any of it came at the expense of anyone or anywhere else. I don't take it personally, of course, because it's true. The sense of Western supremacy, that our way of life is what everyone else is 'developing' towards, still pervades. As such, Famadihana is often covered in the Western press with a grim fascination, mentioned only in the context of the risk of spreading the plague – or as 'dark tourism', as if there's anything dark about any of it. Fear of death and disgust of the corpse makes us miss the point of all of it: that it's rooted in love, and that there's actually nothing frightening about a dead body.

The party spreads from the table to the living room. A karaoke machine appears. Eric sets it up and I laugh helplessly as Hermann tells me how much he blubs whenever he watches *The Notebook*. Then Eric calls me over to the sofa, hands me a mic and tells me we only have a short time before we have to leave for the airport, so what duet are we doing? We go with 'Hotel California'. Our eyes widen when we hear the other sing.

'*Che bella voce*!' says Eric between verses.

'*You* have a good voice – we should have been singing in the car this whole time!'

Sometimes I can't believe the memories I get to store away. I got hit in the head by a corpse this week. I stood on a tomb as a family exhumed their loved ones. I asked questions about people's innermost terror and love, and they answered so fully and openly. And now I'm doing an exit song with Eric, the kind, polylingual, six-foot smile.

As the last chords of the song play, I toss the mic down and give Eric a huge hug. I gather my bags and say my thank yous, my goodbyes. I'm exhausted, delighted, and I ache all over. I dig deep into my reserves for what will be an arduous journey to the other side of the world, where I'll hug my family, share my photos, and tell everyone what I saw.

CHAPTER NINE

The Postal System

I'm on a plane, and I'm fine. It's just turbulence. I am not about to die while writing a book about death. That would be ridiculous. I'm not even going to grip the seat. I might hum a merry tune, just to drown out how fine I am – but that's it.

I'm heading for a Chinese festival for the dead. From the moment I read about Qing Ming (tomb-sweeping day), I assumed I'd see it in Beijing; I have rudimentary Mandarin (I can say 'I'm sorry, my Chinese isn't good' with the cut-glass precision of a damn newsreader) and given that June is the thirty-year anniversary of the Tiananmen Square massacre, Qing Ming is particularly significant this year. I was excited to see Beijing: the smoggy sunsets, the sweeping of tombs across the city's 215 cemeteries – which over this holiday get some 675,000 visitors – paper money burning on street corners, and the sky full of kites as people go out to celebrate spring, the changing seasons, being alive.

But I won't be seeing any of that.

The lights flicker on. Passengers stir with schluffy discomfort as movies get interrupted and the captain's voice crackles over the tannoy, 'Ladies and gentlemen, we will shortly be starting our descent into Bangkok...'

In the seat next to me, Dion smiles and squeezes my hand.

Over half my life ago, before he announced he was moving to Thailand in two weeks' time, my father was a travel agent. He was born in China, and some twenty years ago he met his wife there while on a business trip. So when I first started planning the death festivals journey, I asked him if he'd ever seen Qing Ming. He answered, and I'm paraphrasing: 'Yes, of course. Your stepmother celebrates it every year. It's called Cheng Meng here. Come and do it with us, you idiot.'

After a surprisingly comfortable four-hour coach journey from Bangkok, Dion and I spot the Korat Mall rolling into focus, which is our cue to jump off. Sure enough, there's my dad, who handles hellos much better than goodbyes – he's waving his arms and swinging his hips, the delightful goof.

I was fifteen when he moved. This is perhaps the fourth time I've seen him since. In my mind, his hair is still more pepper than salt and he's in the warm burgundy coat he was wearing when he dropped us off for the last time. But of course, that's just a memory. He's in shorts and a loud linen shirt, and has somehow transformed into a seventy-six-year-old, with a lump of extra skin on his nose transferred there by a surgeon to replace the cancery bits he grew over decades of not bothering with sunscreen. He gives us each a tight hug and an enormous grin, and briefly quizzes Dion about whether he's going to 'continue bothering with this one', elbowing me in the ribs.

'He's right, you know,' I say. 'Check out the grim future of this gene pool.' Dad bursts out laughing, always a fan of a zinger, and leads us to the car, announcing we'll be stopping at the Tesco Lotus for beers.

He parks in the bay in a perfect diagonal line. He doesn't mention it, so I don't know if he can't park straight any more, has never known how to, or if he just doesn't bother in the deserted car park. I hope the latter. Don't get me wrong, he's never been a great driver – something about it makes him want to tell stories, let his knees take the wheel while his hands wave around to make his point. He's an incredible storyteller, so much so that it took years to dawn on me that his very best story is, in fact, about the time he was almost murdered. He charmed his way out of being shot in the head by a Japanese soldier in the internment camp where he lived with his family. He was three years old.

Dad's parents, Fred and Evelyn May, were Salvation Army missionaries and had arrived in China in 1938 with their one-year-old, Kathleen. Beryl was born in

1940, and Gordon – my dad – came along in 1942. The Japanese had occupied China five years earlier, and foreigners had to wear black armbands bearing, ostensibly, their nationality – though 'English pig' seems a bit colourful. Dad's arm was too little for the band, so Evelyn May safety-pinned it to his little sleeve to show him off to the neighbours.

Dad was nine months old when, as he put it, the 'gracious' emperor announced the civilians of their allied countries needed 'protection' in a Japanese-controlled internment camp with barrier walls, barbed and electrified wire, guard towers, guard dogs, and sanitation that would make a cockroach cry. There would be starvation, a risky black market for basic food items, and life-threatening night-time hunts for rats and pigeons to eat. Throughout my life, Dad would get defensive if I ever referred to rats as vermin: 'Don't have a go at rats; you wouldn't be alive if it wasn't for them.'

They were told to report to Tiananmen Square on 29 March 1943 and were permitted to bring as many possessions as they could carry by themselves. Fred made an eight-foot ladder out of bamboo and hung everything he could on it – bedding, towels, pots and pans, baby items. The family wore every piece of clothing they owned, carried everything they could. The women and children were separated from the men and transported in trucks to the camp, but the men had to walk the 300 miles. Fred made it to the camp with his bamboo ladder, having probably shed a little sanity on the way. When he saw

Evelyn May, he collapsed sobbing into her arms. Plenty of others died on the way.

The soldier who nearly murdered my father was not called Captain Bushindi. Unfortunately, he had made a habit of constantly yelling 'Bushindi!', probably an attempt to say 'no can do' in Chinese, so it stuck. Dad insists the exact words the camp commandant used were, 'Anybody in future heard calling Captain Bushindi "Captain Bushindi" will be shot.'

'We had to line up every morning at roll call, bow, and say good morning,' Dad said. 'And the next morning, who should turn up with the commandant but Captain Bushindi. As they approached you could hear all the parents pleading with their kids, "Don't call him Bushindi – it's Captain Yamamoto" – though that's not his real name; I don't remember his real name. Because when they said we'd be shot if we said it again, you must understand they really meant we'd be shot – even the toddlers.' Families had to line up in order of age, which meant as the youngest, Dad had to go first with no one to go ahead of him, which could have served as a last-minute reminder not to call him Bushindi.

'We lined up, and he stood in front of me and I stood tall, bowed very low and said, "Good morning, Captain..."' – Dad froze, made his eyes wide and frightened, like an unprepared actor without a prompt – '"...Yamamoto." You could hear everyone sigh with relief, and Bushindi moved along the line. I was so proud of myself I shouted, "See, Mum? I didn't call him Bushindi!"'

The crowd gasped in horror as Bushindi turned and reached for his gun. But the commandant gave a smile, a chuckle, and then a bellow of laughter. The thousand internees joined in, and started clapping, and Bushindi had no choice but to carry on down the line, presumably smouldering inside at the loss of face and the sarcastic greetings, 'Good morning, Captain... Yamamoto,' each to another round of applause.

I make Dad tell it again, ostensibly so Dion can hear it first-hand, but I never get tired of the story. It feels like leaning over a cliff and wondering about the fall. I often think about the myriad of things that could have pissed the commandant off that morning. A bad dream, a crowing rooster outside his door, a hole in the big toe of his sock; anything might have put him in a temper just bad enough to let the boy get shot. A festival for the dead feels like the perfect time to be reminded that the very existence of my dad, my brother, my sister and me happened almost by fluke, on the knife-edge of a powerful man's mood.

We arrive at the gated community Dad calls home and are greeted by my stepmother, Chanapa, who everyone calls X (pronounced 'eck'). They dated long distance for about a year after they met – I remember taking a photo of Dad to send to her, standing by his car where he'd etched their initials and a heart in the snow on the windshield. When she decided she wanted to move home to Korat, Dad moved with her. They got married a year or so later, in a functional lunchtime ceremony at the mall. She greets us with a huge smile and a hug, and introduces us to her mother, Mae, who's visiting from Sisaket, where she runs a shop. She's comfy on the big leather sofa, watching TV. We greet each other in basic Thai, and X returns to buzzing around her outdoor kitchen. X is a chef and an utterly gifted one; her phone rings constantly for delivery orders from the neighbours.

With a Thai game show blaring on the television, Dion and Dad chat over a beer while I'm wholly distracted by the latest stray X has taken in. Sunday is a tiny black-and-white kitten, so named because he turned up on a Sunday. Dad is grudgingly kind to the contents of their menagerie, while also wishing – frequently and not at all quietly – that they'd all die.

'X is going to eat dinner with us!' Dad says, as if announcing she'll be performing open-heart surgery as a party trick. 'She never eats with me,' he clarifies. 'If I were to count all the times she's eaten dinner with me in twenty years, I wouldn't need my second hand.'

Mae isn't hungry, so she carries on watching TV as we eat a stunning fried river fish X apparently conjured from thin air, and I teach Sunday that yes, I will 'accidentally' drop food on the floor if he meows cutely enough.

'Cookie died this morning,' says Dad. Cookie was one of their dogs.

'She did?'

'Yes, thank goodness.' Dion snorts into his beer. Dad doesn't seem to notice. 'We already have all these cats –

they just appear and my Buddhist wife feeds them, so they stay until they die of one thing or another.'

'What did she die of?'

'Some stomach thing. She was just lying and howling in pain all night, right outside your room, so good job for you we finally found someone who'd put her down. They really try to avoid euthanasia here. It was obvious the vet hated having to do it, even though she quite agreed that it was the kindest thing to do. She sent two nurses the following morning to do the deed.'

Sunday meows, and I drop him some fish flakes. He devours them, purring like a jet engine.

We set off for Sisaket a little late because Dad had to fireman-crawl to pluck Sunday out from underneath the car. The three of us get in the back, and X and Mae take the front. At the traffic lights a street seller walks between the cars. He's completely covered to protect himself from the sun, and his hands are strung with *phuang malai* – floral garlands. A column of jasmine buds with marigolds above and below, strung on a yellow ribbon. X rolls down her window and calls to him.

'*Yîsib bāht,*' he replies.

'Do you have twenty baht?' she asks my dad. He fishes in his pocket and hands her some coins. In the front seat, Mae takes down the old *phuang malai* that's hanging from the rear-view mirror, its petals limp and browning at the edges, and X hangs the new one up as the lights turn green.

'We won't have an accident, now,' says Dad, 'Buddha will protect us.' He's an atheist, but the beauty does the car no harm. And somewhere beneath our layers of thoughts and actions – every veer away from a ledge, every squeeze of a loved one's hand as a plane descends – we're all saying that same old prayer: not me, not today.

This one just has petals.

We stop to stretch our legs, but with the temperature searing close to 40°C, we do it in an air-conditioned supermarket. I ask Dad if we need to pick up any paper money to burn.

'No, we already got it all,' he says. 'Not just paper money – we got paper gold bars, paper coins, a paper suit, I think there's a paper iPhone in there somewhere too.'

The tradition of burning paper money came about because people wanted their dead to have everything they needed in heaven and figured that might involve the need to bribe a judge or two, heaven's 'ghost officials'. A famous Chinese studies scholar once commented, 'Only the Chinese would conceive of the afterlife as a giant bureaucracy.'

In recent years, people have branched out when it comes to gifts for the dead – paper iPads, paper cars, paper claw-foot baths, even enormous paper mansions that cost hundreds and are reduced to ashes in minutes.

A few years ago, X and Mae burned a paper mobile

phone for the first time. Some weeks later, Mae told X, quite upset, 'Your father never called me from heaven.' X put her palm to her forehead, 'Oh *no*! It must be because we forgot to burn him a charger!'

It's the night before Cheng Meng and Dad is in his standard 'relaxing' outfit: a pair of trousers and no shirt. Dion and I sit on the sofa with our drinks while Dad relaxes on the bed and has a lot of fun showing us his 'mountain-range stomach', the untreated hernia he's had since Bushindi hit him with the butt of a rifle. I remember asking him as a little girl why his stomach wasn't round like Santa's, and instead had lump on it, above his belly button. He told me there are two sheets of muscle across the abdomen and his are slightly separated, and the lump is where his intestines are poking out. He didn't mention the violent act that led to it until much later, and correctly guessed that I'd be too distracted by this intestine business to ask. As he's aged and expanded, the sheets have come further apart and now when he tightens his abdominals, you can see the lump now stretches all the way down his stomach, like he swallowed a python head first.

'I'll have to have surgery on it sometime, I suppose,' he says. He starts to tell us about his dad's kitchen duty in the camp, stirring large cauldrons of 'soup', which was, in reality, mostly water. For extra calories, Fred used to sneak out at night to hunt pigeons. He would grab one, wring its neck before it could alert the soldiers with a squawk, creep back via the roof, and drop it silently onto Evelyn May's outstretched apron.

'Pigeons are so tasty!' Dad says, enthused, as if it had been served with a plum sauce. 'And do you know what else is delicious? RATS!'

Dion looks at me and, to Dad's bafflement, we make the Chris-claws, hiss 'RATS!' in unison, and tumble into giggles.

I love it when the dead come back.

X's brother, graphic designer and print-shop owner Ar, has climbed his father's tomb like a cat on a scratching post. His bare feet stand on the marble edging above our heads as he hangs pink, purple, orange, blue and green streamers. They flap and mingle in the breeze.

Down on the ground, Ar's wife – a schoolteacher called Ann – is sweeping away ants with a branch and putting down a mat. Ar and Ann's kids, nine-year-old Bi Pu and seven-year-old Bi Bon, sit cross-legged before the tomb. Bi Bon has a Nike swoosh shaved into the side of his head and sits quietly by his mother as she prays. Bi Pu is playing with some decorative tinsel.

I sit next to X's niece, who we first met last night. I'm already thinking of her as 'my badass cousin Fern' – she has short hair and usually goes about with an SLR camera slung on her back, taking stunning photos. She lays out the incredible picnic X made and teaches me the etiquette around lighting incense – she says after you light it, it's rude to blow it out with your mouth, especially around food, as you'll taint it with ash and whatever viruses you're harbouring. There are three candles at the foot of the grave, all standing upright in sand-filled plastic cups from a popular coffee chain called Amazon. Fern lights a clutch of joss sticks from the nearest candle and shakes them in the air off to the side to blow out the flames. She stands them all together like a burning bouquet in an Amazon cup between the two candles. The thick, fragrant plumes begin to curl their way upwards.

The haul of paper gifts for the dead sit in their packaging at the foot of the tomb – with pride of place given to the three-piece suits rendered in paper, complete with paper tie pins, watches and iPhones.

'X,' says Dad, 'did you bring a charger this year?'

The whole group erupts into laughter. I look at Mae, who is also grinning. I think she's still hoping he'll call.

After some prayers and photos, the whole picnic gets packed up in minutes and we move across to the Chinese cemetery, where X's grandfather is buried, and lay it all out again. The Chinese graves are like thrones carved into mounds, with polished marble, gold Chinese characters and pictures of the occupants. Bi Pu and I talk – by which I mean I speak in English and she responds in Thai – and somehow we decide together to take off our shoes, climb up onto the mound and decorate it with glittery confetti. She grabs a fistful, I count to three and she throws it into the air for a photo. I can't capture it, the joy of it, the way the flecks of confetti glint in the sun as they fall around her beaming face.

'Eri,' Dad calls, 'come down for prayers.'

X explains what to do, that we kneel before the grave with lit joss sticks clasped between our hands in prayer, the lit end tilted forward. Then we close our eyes and pray for the dead.

'What do you pray for?' I ask.

'I usually pray for health and happiness for them,' says Fern.

Dad, Dion and I kneel down. I whisper to Dad – I don't know why I assume this is a situation where whispering is preferred, like church – 'Who are you wishing for?'

'I've no idea,' Dad says. 'Let's see. Who's dead?'

'You're seventy-six, Dad, basically everyone's dead.'

'Oh yeah.' He thinks, then says, 'I think I'll have a little word with Mum.'

Dad disappears into his prayer. OK. I've stalled long enough. Time to talk to Chris for the first time since the altar in Mexico. I close my eyes, feeling self-conscious.

Hi, Chris. Me again. We must stop meeting like this. Ha. That's a joke, obviously. We can only meet like this. Sorry, I shouldn't make jokes while praying, should I? I hope you're healthy and happy. I hope you like my book. Sorry I told everyone about the Liquorice Allsorts incident, but I must reiterate that it's funny. Um... be OK. We miss you. Talk to you later.

I open my eyes, stand up, and give Dion a hug. I ask him what he prayed for, and he smiles sadly. 'General good wishes for parents.'

Everyone sits on the floor and rips into the picnic: beautiful baskets of bananas, apples and plump grapes; steamed buns, glass noodles and rice in metal bowls; roasted ducks and succulent meats glistening in the sun. Dion falls into a foodie reverie, his eyes at half-mast, as he eats the pork. I think if I told him that this has been fun but I'm leaving him for a clown he'd reply, 'Wait, tell me in a minute – this is delicious.' X covers her ears as a family a few graves over let off firecrackers, which explode in little white claps directly under a tree.

I'm chatting to Dad when I realise the fire portion of the party has started. The suit, some gold bars and a pair of high-heeled shoes, all rendered in paper, are already being eaten up by the flames. Ann shows me each item as it's thrown on.

'What's this?' I ask.

'Credit card!' she says. 'And a catalogue.'

'So they can buy things with the credit card?'

'Yes. And here's some money.'

She offers me the bag of paper money, and I sprinkle a few notes into the flames, which are now up to our knees. Here you go, dead people. Go bribe a heavenly judge. Or, to be less of a smartass about it: you're dead, but my love didn't go with you. I will always want you to be OK. I can't believe, like Mae, that these gifts are really being delivered. But that's not the point. Festivals for the dead aren't for the dead, really. They're for us, the people left with an inconvenient connection to an entity that no longer exists. This is a conduit. This is an outlet for love.

The gifts are ash. Ann pours tea on the fire, dousing the flames with a hiss. The smoke pulses one last time, rising in a death-gasp to the sky.

It's been four months since the death festival with Dad, Dion, X, Fern and the gang. I'm back in Asia and, in stark contrast to the cosy family picnic, I calculate that I'm currently the furthest distance I've ever been from anyone who loves me.

Kyoto is a glorious cluster of conveniences; a mass of small, consistent efforts to direct thought away from the mundane ugliness of daily life. In the geisha district of Gion, for example, mounted onto one of the traditional facades is a security camera that's been housed in a little wooden hut, like a birdhouse. I love how it throws a spanner in the thought process of *security camera − surveillance − crime*, diverting it instead to *security camera − in a little house, oh that's so* cute*!* The pedestrian crossing alerts you it's time to cross with the sound of a bird chirping. Are you thirsty? Close your eyes, spin, point, and open your eyes: there's a vending machine, or a *konbini* (convenience store) − which sells balanced meals, has free wifi that actually *works*, and a wireless printer that actually *works*, and snacks and make-up and chargers, anything you might have misplaced. As someone who feels inconvenienced if my train is leaving from any other platform than the one directly in my line of vision, I adore the place immediately.

But there's one inconvenience I can't escape: it's

lonely. I only speak functional Japanese, after a hasty intensive week of lessons. Everyone I love is asleep until about 4 p.m. And while it would be lovely to distract myself by being a tourist, there's a typhoon hitting tomorrow. I'm advised to stay indoors for the eighteen hours or so it'll take to pass over.

During the countdown to the typhoon, I take long walks around the city, looking for signs of the visiting dead. The Obon festival, the festival for the dead which drew me to Japan, begins with an invitation for the spirits to come, and the invitation is good for a week. On Friday, the mountains surrounding the city will be set alight as an invitation for them to leave, huge bonfires in the shapes of Chinese characters (Japanese has three separate alphabets, and one of them uses a number of Chinese characters) that can be seen burning for miles.

Reading about Japan's death culture, it all feels much more familiar than the astonishing practices in Madagascar. While the festival emphasises spirits returning, the corpse seems to be just as reviled as it is in the West, and just as in other parts of the world, has tarnished the people who work with them. Shinmon Aoki's book *Coffinman* details his career as a mortician, and how taking the job brought shame on his family, because nothing is lower on the social totem pole, it seems, than those who work with the dead. His wife refused to let him touch her, told him he was 'defiled'.

While we're not as literal about the notion of defilement in the West, death work of any kind has long been stigmatised – even in journalism. In *Obit*, a documentary about the obituaries section in the *New York Times*, one writer observed that this is only now changing: 'We have the pleasure of being able to come out of the closet as obituary writers. Only a generation ago, obits were very stigmatised.'* They explain that up until recently the obits desk was a place people were sent as punishment when the editor didn't quite have enough on them to have them sacked, or when they were creeping towards needing an obit themselves.

Typhoon minus two hours. I'm in a café drinking coffee and working on my laptop, and the floor-to-ceiling windows are giving the weather report: the wind is picking up. I pack up, run to a convenience store for eighteen hours of supplies, and hotfoot it back to my hotel room. It's a box of stillness, while outside the wind rages and the rain starts to smash down like we owe it money. I check my phone – nothing. Of course there's nothing. It's not even 4 a.m. at home. I bat away the loneliness, bat away thoughts of the last festival surrounded by family, and think about how utterly delighted I'd have been not long ago to be told I *had* to stay inside for a day.

A reluctant cosiness sinks in.

I check my phone again. Stupid.

I sit on the bed and listen to the rain.

*

---

* *Obit*, directed by Vanessa Gould, Green Fuse Films, 2016.

I meet Akari in a hotel café after days travelling alone and eighteen hours trapped in a room with nothing but avatars for company. She's a tour guide and has offered to give me an Obon-themed tour, and all the poor woman says is, 'I ordered a macchiato, but it's quite small.'

'Ah,' I say, 'that's because macchiato is short for "espresso macchiato", and "macchiato" is Italian for "stained", so they've basically stained your espresso with a bit of milk rather than served you a bucket of milk with some coffee in it like Starbucks does HAHAHAHA hi sorry I'm Erica nice to meet you that typhoon was long wasn't it, are they always that long I was worried I'd never get out of that—'

I take a breath, to live.

'Ahem. Sorry. Hi.' I sit down and resolve to be normal, and she kindly acts as if I already am. She tells me we're going to Rokudo Chinno-ji Temple, where between 7 and 10 August, people can ring a 'welcoming bell' to invite the spirits of their ancestors back to this world. I agree enthusiastically, not least because I love the idea of Chris suddenly finding himself in Japan and wondering what the hell happened.

In Japan the dead are like toddlers, in that they're hungry, thirsty and constantly getting lost. People hang lanterns outside their houses to guide them home, and inside the spirits will find an altar with food and sake. 'Children get frustrated when they see the food there, because they want to eat it,' says Akari. 'The mother usually tells them they can eat it tomorrow, after the spirits have had their turn.' I guess that's also a useful lesson in restraint. It seems we never stop learning from our ancestors.

The temple sits at the edge of an old burial mound used during the Heian period (794–1185), which was thought to be the literal border between this world and the world of the dead. At the front entrance a rock carving announces this place as the path to the underworld, and behind the temple sits the well through which the spirits are said to come whooshing out when they're summoned. Akari walks me to the back of the temple, where two smiling men sit behind a counter, and for a few yen will write the name of the family member you're summoning on a *mizutoba*, a thin wooden tablet. When Akari says the name 'Chris Watts', he asks her to repeat it a few times so he can write it phonetically in Japanese. He takes a brush and calligraphs black ink onto the vertical strip of wood.

'So,' says Akari, 'this first line says, "This is for", and here he has written "this world name" – here in Japan you get a new name when you die, so he has written here that this is the name he had when he was part of this world. The line under that is "Chris Watts", and this last line says that he is a soul or spirit.' I smile. It's a thing of beauty, but I won't get to keep it for long.

'Let's go and ring the bell,' she says, and we stroll over to the other side of the temple. The Mukaegane bell is housed in a mini-temple, painted bright white and trimmed with brilliant orange. The knot of a rope pokes out of the front. I grab it and walk backwards until I hear a sombre bell. To me it doesn't sound loud enough to reach the underworld, but what do I know about frequencies? Still, I repeat the action several times like a child let loose on an elevator button, until I'm teetering on the edge of obnoxious.

'So... he's here now, right?' I grin at Akari.

'Yes,' she says, and leads me over to a bank of stone statues, rows and rows of them, each wrapped in a red cloak. They're *mizuko jizo* statues, which are part of a Buddhist ritual for miscarried, stillborn or aborted babies. At the front, people have slotted their *mizutoba*s with the names of the spirits they've summoned, and below the box a few Japanese umbrella-pine branches float in a strip of water. Akari tells me to pick up a little branch, the needles bunched together like a verdant brush, and paint some water onto the *mizutoba*, because Chris will be arriving thirsty.

I slot the little Chris tablet at the very front. 'So do I just... leave him here?'

'Yes. Now he's here for the rest of Obon, until Friday,' says Akari. I smile. I feel rude summoning Chris to Japan and then doing a runner, but he'll just have to deal with it.

'So,' Akari continues, smiling brightly, 'shall we go and get some ghost childcare candy?'

'I'm sorry, what?'

*

Given that most businesses fail within the first few years, I'm very impressed with Minatoya, a 400-year-old candy shop. The woman behind the counter is the twentieth generation of her family to work there (again, amazing that not one of them derailed the streak by going off to try to make it as an actor) and the tourist draw is a ghost story linked to their candy. They are little pieces of golden-coloured, raw-diamond-shaped hard candy, the recipe unchanged in centuries.

The story goes that in the summer of 1599, a young woman started coming to Minatoya every night at midnight (great hours for a candy shop – I continue to be impressed) to buy a single piece of candy. On the seventh night the shopkeeper decided this was weird. He didn't think it was weird to follow her, though – different time – but lost sight of her when she reached the cemetery. There he heard the cries of a baby coming from a fresh tomb. He called the priest and they dug into the earth, and found the corpse of the woman who had bought the candy, a woman who had died while pregnant. Next to her was the crying baby, clutching the piece of candy in his little hand. She had given birth in the tomb, while dead, and her love was so strong she rose as a ghost in order to take care of the baby.

Now, let's not dwell on details like whether it's possible for a baby to be born in a tomb, or why a sharp lump of sugar would keep him alive, even if he did manage not to choke on it. The point of the story is that a mother's love transcends death – and that, Akari tells me, is usually the point of Japanese ghost stories. In the West, what is said to transcend death and form ghosts is usually a want of justice and respect: a violent death, because it's so unjust the victim will stick around until it's avenged; improper burial, because our death rituals matter so much we will imprint the air if they're not respected; or unfinished business, because our earthly projects matter so much we will stroll about see-through if we don't get to finish them.

We're constantly coming up with ways our tiny lives, our tiny priorities, our tiny feelings can transcend our mortality – 'I'll love you until the end of time,' we tell each other, even though, for various practical reasons, we obviously will not. 'May the revolution stay red for ten thousand generations,' says the Chinese government, even though that's longer than the current age of the human race. 'He will not be forgotten,' we say, even though of course – *of course* – he eventually will.

We tell ourselves there are ways we can get around this problem of death, that at least some elements of our existence will transcend it, because the fact that nothing can doesn't compute. In the West, we express that through stories about justice. In Japan, they've settled on love.

Akari gifts me a pack of the candy, and of course I immediately lose it. Dion chats away into my ear as I hold the phone to my face and turn the hotel room upside down. I pick up a towel I've flung, bafflingly, onto the table, and see the packet underneath.

'Aha!' I say, holding it above my head in triumph. 'I found the ghost childcare candy!'

There is a short pause. 'What?'

'You heard.'

Dion laughs, 'Ghost-child care candy? I know all those words *individually* ...'

I explain the story.

'Why did she go every night?' he asks. 'Why buy one piece of candy a night, why not just buy a whole packet?'

'That's your only problem with this story? "Why didn't the ghost do a big shop?"'

'Well. Seems inefficient. Am I mansplaining childcare to a ghost?'

'I believe you are, yes.'

'I mean, Supermum and all that, but I stand by it.'

Today, the dead go home.

In other parts of Japan, such as Nagasaki, the dead are invited to leave with hundreds of fire lanterns floated onto a lake. But this is falling out of popularity, as what must be a stunning tango of fire and water at night leaves a lake full of litter the next day. In Kyoto, the practice is a little different, and no one is quite sure how it started: the city is surrounded by mountains to the east, north and west, and the goodbye ceremony for the spirits takes the form of enormous mountainside bonfires in the shape of huge Chinese characters.

Akari suggested I watch the mountain fires from the bridge by Demachiyanagi Station. I get there an hour early to nab a spot. I'm expecting a couple of hours standing on a bridge, watching some distant bonfires form the shape of the Chinese character '*dai*', meaning 'big'. I do not anticipate feeling forever changed, but of course I must attend the goodbye ceremony of Obon, given that I summoned Chris here without warning (though he did leave without warning, so I'd say we're close to even).

As I approach the bridge, a couple of police officers politely divert me to the right, onto the riverbank. Clearly a much better place to watch the fires. I happily take a seat on the sloping bank in front of a shrub. The mountain is distant but dead ahead of me, and unless a giant wants to sit in a shrub there will be nothing to obscure the view. People start arriving, mostly in groups of families or friends, but a lone Japanese woman in a black sleeveless summer dress takes a seat next to me. I feel a raindrop on my arm and look up.

'Oh, *sumimasen*! Sorry!' she says, holding up a bottle of bug repellent she just accidentally sprayed me with. I laugh.

'That's fine – it's actually incredibly useful,' I say. 'I forgot mine and I'm delicious to mosquitoes.'

She grins and hands me the bottle. Gratefully, I take a few sprays, delegitimising myself as a buffet option for the little fuckers.

The scarring of the *dai* symbol is visible on the mountain year-round. Right now, it's piled with kindling on which people have written their wishes – for the dead, for themselves, for the people they love and have loved. The divine postal system. It's amazing how easily we take on symbols from other cultures – if I was to take a wish you'd written and burn it before your eyes in, say, Stoke Newington, you'd probably take it as an act of violence against your wish. 'Ah, health and happiness, you say? UP IN FLAMES. How do you like me now? Less, I imagine.' And yet both here and in Thailand, it seems perfectly sound, with a moral weight on its beauty.

An orange dot sparks to life in the middle of the scar, and spreads into the limbs of the symbol. The crowd gasps and oohs. Phone screens rise into the air all around, like a choreographed act of worship. With no one to ooh to, I put my headphones in, and watch the ancestors hitch a ride on bonfire smoke. Of all the festivals for the dead I've seen, only Obon puts any emphasis on a goodbye ritual at the end, a full stop to make sure the dead won't outstay their welcome. I wonder if everyone else just assumes they'll take the hint, or if here in Japan they've simply worked out that grief doesn't heal like a cut, that it's healthy to carve out a moment to relive the losses past, that a festival for the dead is really about saying goodbye again. And again, and again.

And I feel it. My tear ducts start to prickle. I glance at the woman beside me, who watches the fires with pure love in her eyes, tinged with sadness and joy. It's a 5,000-story expression. She's in her own world – and so, I realise, am I. Once again, I've put thousands of miles between myself and anyone who knows or loves me. I'm alone here. Invisible. So I let it happen. I let down the Brit barrier and tears silently whoosh down my face and drip off my cheeks, just like they did that Tuesday.

Grief comes in waves. The wound opens and closes over years. I get that now. And I can restitch this later.

'Go on, trooperoo,' I whisper as the fires fade, 'off you go.'

And I think of Mae, 2,500 miles southwest of these flames, still waiting by the phone.

CHAPTER TEN

A Corpse in the Bedroom

'Husband slept in same room as wife's body for six days.'

'Man who slept next to his wife's dead body for six days recommends the experience.'

'Grieving husband slept next to wife's corpse for six days after cancer took her life.'

'Husband writes viral post about why he kept his deceased wife's body in his bedroom for six days.'

Russell Davison is everywhere. He's plastered all over my Twitter and Facebook feeds. There are pictures and op-eds and clips of his appearances on morning television. A week ago, he was a grieving husband. Now he's a viral sensation.

I'm one of many journalists who contacted him when the story broke, but I specify that we should speak in a few months when the press has died down. I don't tell him I'm worried about him, because we haven't met and that would be weird, but I don't want to add to the dogpile of journalists banging down his door when he's at the apex of grief.

So it's months later when I arrive at his front door, a beautiful townhouse in Derby, and he walks up behind me accompanied by an old black cockapoo.

'Erica!' he says, smiling like we've known each other for ever. He's stunningly tall with wavy grey hair. He invites me to follow him and leads me into a bright kitchen with a glass conservatory roof. He fetches me a glass of water. The dog, Elvis, snuggles up to me on the sofa at the edge of the kitchen, and I prepare to ask Russell about his wife's corpse.

'I don't believe in facts,' says Russell. I'm surprised to note that I find this mildly endearing, even though I check facts for a living. Maybe it's because he *looks* like someone who doesn't believe in facts, with his long hippy hair and the easy, open manner of someone who thinks everything is up for debate. 'The only certain mind, in my opinion, is a closed one. I think science is a belief system; we believe which science we want to believe, and there's always a money trail. So I wouldn't profess to know anything, but we found out that people who live natural lives – in the Amazon basin for example, people living from the land – don't get cancer.'

He's referring, I think, to the Tsimané people living on a tributary of the Amazon River in Bolivia. They have been found to have the least heart disease in the world and very little evidence of cancer. Which isn't entirely surprising – cancer and heart disease are two of the biggest killers in the West and both are linked to poor diet and lack of exercise. The Tsimané spend 90 per cent of their waking hours doing physical activity: their staples are corn, plantains and home-grown rice, and if they want meat, they have to go and catch it. The average hunt lasts eight hours and covers eleven miles.

With this in mind, three or four years after Russell's wife Wendy was diagnosed with cervical cancer, they decided to make their lives emulate, as closely as possible, a 'natural life'.

'Is this mainly food-based?' I ask. 'Because obviously your life isn't completely natural. For example, you live in a house...'

'No, it's not mainly food-based, but food is at the centre. We both have science backgrounds, Wendy did a degree in genetics, but we'd kind of had enough of the contradiction in science, of not knowing what to believe. So, when we found out that people living natural lives don't get cancer, it was something for us to latch onto, to really try to achieve. We started to undo anything we believed that had been learned academically and not passed through oral tradition. Animals aren't told what to eat or how to bring their young up, but they know, so that innate "knowing" is something we tried to tune in to.' I decide not to point out that animals also live short and brutal lives, on the whole. 'We said, "What would we do if we were living in a hut in the middle of a savannah or a jungle?" And one thing's for sure: we wouldn't be watching TV.'

'What did you do, of an evening?'

'Read. Which I know we wouldn't be doing either, but it felt more natural. It's our oral tradition, really.'

'What about food?'

'We went raw for a while; that was quite challenging. But basically, we ended up with an incredible organic wholefood diet, which I've stayed with. We've not had sugar for seven years, no alcohol, nothing processed, nothing out of a tin; if there's a list of ingredients on it, we don't eat it.' That seems to remind him. 'Would you like a piece of chocolate? It's a hundred per cent cacao. It's the one non-organic thing I allow myself.' Russell hasn't had chocolate for seven years, save for this bitter, sugar-free variety.

'I actually love one hundred per cent cacao choco-late,' I say. I don't tell him that I, too, started eating it as a meagre indulgence when, after losing Chris to heart disease, I found myself terrified of food. Though rather than eschew anything with 'ingredients', instead I stared at them, calculating, always calculating, googling 'how much sugar a day men/women', typing out baffling equations on my phone's calculator, constantly bargain-ing with the food industry not to kill us.

'So you've had it?' says Russell.

'Yes,' I say. 'It's actually my go-to writing snack.'

'Have a whole bar then!' he says, handing me one, and tells me he'll be right back because he has something else for me, and ducks down to the cellar. He comes bounding up the stairs with a jar of fermented beetroot and cabbage, gushing about the process as if it's an elixir. He takes me down to see where it's fermenting: a dark, tiny space that smells of vinegar. He opens a jar of sauerkraut for me to see. It's a dewy mixture of red cabbage, seaweed, garlic, caraway seeds and salt.

'My belief is that we probably put six or seven years on Wendy's life,' he says when we're back in the kitchen. 'I think cancer was going to get her, and we hoped not for a long time, and eventually we accepted it. I would say for most people if they choose the natural-health road, the chances of survival are really high. In fact, I've read information that says your chances of survival are around ninety per cent if you do your own research into natural health online; it doesn't really matter which road you take.' I baulk at this suggestion. Your chances of survival are 90 per cent as long as you meander through the internet, making your own mind up about what you believe?

He's quoting Ty Bollinger, an accountant and body-builder who became angry when several family members died of cancer – or, in his mind, of 'false treatments'. He never explained which cancers they had, what the treatments were or why they were 'false'. He then went on to interview a very narrow selection of people: only those who agreed with his premise and who didn't base their arguments on science. He then published it all in a book called *The Truth About Cancer*.

While Ty Bollinger is one of many anti-intellectuals I'd like to put in a blender, I understand his appeal to people facing treatments as grisly as the diseases they fight. And four years before she died, Wendy was given six months to live – there's no way of telling whether their lifestyle is what extended her life, of course, but it can't be ignored. That said, there's something heart-breaking in hearing Russell wax lyrical about it. He still nibbles on sweetness-free chocolate; his home is pervaded with the smell of the fermenting basement vegetables; he quotes unverified and outright inaccurate figures on cancer survival rates if you just abstain from this and that. Russell believes that 'nature will provide', just as the transhumanists believe technology will provide, and the *santamuerteros* believe La Flaquita will provide, and much of the British public believe the NHS will provide: those of us plagued by mortal terror latch on to an amulet to keep death at bay.

Except we're not keeping death at bay. Not really. Death has no idea what we're doing and couldn't, I think it's safe to say, give a flying, farting fuck. All we're truly keeping at bay is the madness of knowing it's coming.

Wendy refused chemotherapy and radiotherapy; her medical records said, 'patient is refusing Western medicine'. Since their four sons (two were Russell's, two were Wendy's) were in their twenties, Russell and Wendy decided to go travelling in a campervan. Russell, a land-lord, worked remotely, adjusting his working day to start at 4 a.m. and finish at 10 a.m., so he could spend all day with Wendy. For three years they travelled around Europe in their campervan. They called it the Gypsy, and had it spray-painted with flowers by a graffiti artist. It's still sitting in his driveway.

'We did fifteen countries from Bosnia to Sweden,' says Russell. 'We did two full seasons of snowboarding in Austria. It was amazing.'

For most of the trip Wendy was fit and well, but the September before she died the pain kicked in, and they came home.

'The doctors were wonderful,' says Russell, 'but they pussyfooted around; they wouldn't say "die" or "death". We brought up Wendy dying and the GP cringed and said, "Are we OK to talk about that?"'

'Are you joking?'

'No! I was like, of course we're OK to talk about it – Wendy's *dying*. We've been talking about this for *ten years*,' he becomes very animated, waving his arms and raising his voice in frustration and disbelief. 'It's *incredible*. THIS IS YOUR JOB. YOU'RE A PALLIATIVE CARE CONSULTANT! I understand that some people might need treating with kid gloves, but when you're faced with people who don't, can't you change your game? They couldn't.'

We shake our heads. I tell him one of the reasons I decided to write this book was seeing death cafés in the news, that people discussing death openly is worthy of a headline. He nods.

'I think fearing death is just part of a fear culture that's been promoted. And it's nonsense. I feel for you in your story with your father-in-law, because I don't believe there's anything to fear in a dead body that's been distorted by a natural process.'

'It's true,' I say. 'The amount of time I focused on that, and not the fact that he died in his sleep, as we'd all like to.'

'Peacefully.'

'A book on his chest. He looked clever.'

Russell laughs. 'Absolute dream way of going! But of course your husband was doing what he thought was the right thing by protecting you, because he'd been disturbed by it. I wouldn't be blaming him.'

Wendy died on 21 April 2017. Her body was due to be cremated six days later. In the interim, they kept her at home, on the floor of her and Russell's bedroom. They made an altar for her, with incense and candles and a Buddhist mantra playing, and put fresh flowers all over her every day. He shows me a picture. She looks beautiful.

'Why do we hand our dead loved ones over to strangers straight away, as if they're something to be disposed of?' says Russell. 'The connection that we maintained with Wendy was so healing for us. We were really given this opportunity to be able to authentically connect with the process, being with her from the moment she died, right up until we pushed her into the furnace.'

'So you weren't worried about the realities of that, like the smell?'

'As it happens, Wendy didn't smell, but we said if she smells, bring it on – it's nature and we'll deal with it. We discussed the possibility that the dog might take a bite out of her. That's how real we got.' Elvis is cuddled up to me on the sofa. I stroke his woolly head as Russell continues, 'He was part of the vigil process; he sat by her side. I said to the boys, "We're leaving Elvis to look after Wendy, this is a possibility. He could bite a big chunk out of her face. If that happens, it happens: it will be nature. Let's not be horrified or catastrophise it."'

'You know you're unusual, right?'

'Yes,' he grins.

Nine days after Wendy's death, the story broke. Russell used to be a DJ and bar owner, and as a result has a huge network of Facebook friends. He was never particularly enamoured with social media, but Wendy was, and would post beautiful photographs and descriptions of what they were doing on their travels. 'I thought, if we're not careful it's just going to be pictures of me and Elvis, and Wendy's not going to get her story told,' says Russell. 'So I decided to take lots of photos of her and post once a week, and she liked that. So I started a Facebook page just for close friends and family, because it was too intimate to share with thousands of people. We shared quite a bit about her cancer, and when Wendy died, two days into having her laid out in our bedroom, I felt compelled to reach out to the wider community, people who didn't know our story, and tell it.'

Two days after Wendy died, Russell wrote a long, heartfelt piece on Facebook. It started from ten years ago, when Wendy was diagnosed, went through their belief in natural health, right up to what was happening with Wendy's body in their bedroom.

'I got hundreds of Facebook messages, text messages, emails. They were all lovely and so supportive; people were overwhelmed by the story. We'd taken Wendy to the crematorium on the Thursday; on the Friday I got a phone call from the local newspaper saying they'd come across the Facebook post because it had gone viral, and they asked if they could publish a precised version to make it look like a letter. I had to think about it: part of our life was to disengage with mainstream media. But it's a lovely story and it had been moving and empowering and maybe even life-changing for some people already, so I said OK. He said he'd run the letter by me, and bless him, he even asked me about the headline: "Husband sleeps with dead wife for six days". I said, "Yeah that's fine. That's true." I know it's sensationalist, but that's headlines.'

On the Monday the story came out in the local papers and online. News agencies jumped on it. By 8 a.m. the next morning Russell was being bombarded with calls from the national media, with journalists and photographers knocking on his door. At first, he refused to speak to anyone but the *Guardian* and the *Independent*. 'I wouldn't speak to Murdoch's press, or any right-wing press or gutter press. But I changed all that on the third day because I realised the story was bigger than my personal politics, and why shouldn't *Daily Mail* readers have the benefit of this story?' It was the *Sun* newspaper's most-clicked article of the day. Later it became the most-clicked story in the *New York Post*, with 93,000 clicks.

'We knew the story was lovely, but there's no way we felt it would have that sort of magnitude. So we had Wendy's body in the bedroom for six days – so what?'

'Why do you think it went so crazy? Because ninety-three thousand clicks is the least of it, Russell – you were *everywhere*. I couldn't go anywhere on Twitter, Facebook or even switch on the TV without seeing your face.'

'I think a lot of people would have clicked on it for some sort of voyeurism, maybe thinking it would be about necrophilia. I've had a lot of feedback from producers and journalists; people started by reading it going, "That's weird," and it turning into, "Actually that's wonderful." I found it quite sad that people said, "We didn't know we could do that." Something that's perfectly legal and wasn't that hard to arrange didn't, in my opinion, need much out-of-the-box type thinking, yet people are so disempowered they couldn't put that simple process together.'

It's true; there's surprisingly little regulation when it comes to dead bodies, yet everyone assumes there must be lots. In fact, there are more regulations when it comes to dead animals. In a culture of silence around death, false assumptions grow like mould. When I told a friend I was interviewing a man who kept his wife's body at home for six days, his first question was, 'Was he prosecuted?' But there's no legal limit to how long a dead body can be kept at home (though there are practical limits, which I might have mentioned in Chapter One). You can even bury a human corpse in your garden, if you own the property – though it might affect how easy it is to sell.

When Wendy died, Russell grieved heavily. 'I cried every day for months, but when I wasn't crying, I was happy. I cry two or three times a week now.' I'm fascinated and impressed by how willing he is to feel his pain. It seems so... mature. The fact that I ever thought trying not to grieve was the right decision seems ludicrous by comparison. I feel like I've been scooping water from a jug to a cup with my hands, and someone's come along and introduced me to the concept of pouring. And it seems I'm not the only one who's pleasantly surprised at the positive effects.

'When people came to see Wendy there was general sobriety, paying respects, sitting down, maybe a few tears – and *always* it would end up with some laughter,' says Russell. 'My friend Jason came round to see us, and he would not go in the room. He said he was in a choir when he was seven and had seen too many dead bodies during funerals. I thought, "That's just an excuse – you're scared, dude. I understand." I tried to coax him to come into the room; he wasn't having any of it. He left the house, walked to the gate, turned around and came back. He came into the room and within moments he'd melted and was totally relaxed. He could see it for what it was: beautiful, full of love. And then, after being too afraid to come in, he said, "Do you think we could clown her?"'

'What does that mean?' I ask.

'Put a clown nose on her.'

'*What*?'

'I said dude, that would be fucking ace, she'd fucking love that. He said, "Not all the time, just maybe an hour in the day. A clown hour." We didn't do it, but the idea was so fucking funny. This is my point: why *wouldn't* you laugh your fucking socks off? Our sense of humour was brilliant throughout our relationship; it was one of the unifying factors for us – why wouldn't that continue when she's dead?'

I'm sad to hear that Wendy's friends did what many British people are said to do when they discover a friend or loved one is terminally ill. They disappeared. 'Because they're frightened of saying the wrong thing,' says Russell, 'and what people don't understand is they can't say anything that will make it worse, not when it comes from an open heart and love. You might put your foot in it – so what? Say it. Because by withdrawing because of that fear, you take away the very thing that's essential to a lot of people's experience, and that is their support. People also say, "We thought you'd be inundated with other people," or, "We thought we'd give you some time." But bless them all, when they were challenged on it, they became phenomenal.'

'It's almost as if there's no protocol in our culture for this,' I say, 'and people are left flailing, letting fear make their decisions for them.'

'Right,' says Russell. 'We're very good at saying, "If there's anything I can do, let me know." I know I mean it when I say it. But it's hard to say, "Could you come round now and give me all that support you were offering?" That never happens.'

On the one hand, I see Russell as someone who is terribly afraid of death, someone who has structured his entire life around nature providing – even though nature is the very thing that, one way or another, cuts through all our efforts in the end. And yet, I detect very little anguish in him as he talks about it, and I tell him so.

'You're right, because on a spiritual level I still feel so supported by Wendy,' he says. This sense of having a continuing relationship with the dead is the nucleus of the death festivals – and I once saw it as little more than a fundamental denial that death has taken as much from us as it has. I thought it meant denying their disappearance, denying that death is the end of a person. *How am I supposed to have a relationship with the dead if I don't believe they actually* exist *anywhere?* I wondered, missing the point. It's not about literally believing they're in heaven, or reincarnated, staring at us from the soulful eyes of a neighbour's cat. It's just understanding that the love remains. If grief really is love with nowhere to go, then my God, what's the harm in giving it somewhere to go? And why did I resist it so strenuously?

Russell continues, 'We pursued spiritual beliefs that would support our desire to think that we'd been together in former lives, and that we'd be together again in future lives. We pulled bits we liked from different religions and came up with our own belief system that still guides me now. This might sound weird, but with the attention that I've been getting from this story, and how healing it's been for other people, maybe she chose to end early because of that. Who knows?'

'Who knows?' could be Russell's entire philosophy, guided as it is by, essentially, what he'd like to think. But I can't say it's done him any harm.

As I make a move to rush for my train, he makes sure I don't forget my jar of fermented sauerkraut and the 100 per cent cacao chocolate. I tuck them into my satchel, thank him, and hug him goodbye.

I don't know if I'd have the nerve to do what Wendy did, to throw out everything I've been told will save me for a shot at something that might. And despite her confounding doctors by living years longer than they predicted, it would be easy to be cynical, to say their natural philosophy must be bogus because, in the end, it didn't save her. But I don't want to make the same mistake I made with Chris; I don't want to focus on the wrong thing.

And on the train home, I don't. The moment that echoes in my head is a conversation Wendy had with

Russell while they were travelling around Europe. He told me that most days he would ask her, 'Is there anything you'd rather be doing?' and she'd say, 'No, this is it.' A year or two before she died at age forty-nine, he asked her, 'Is there anyone you would trade places with?'

She told him, 'No. No way. I nailed it.'

CHAPTER ELEVEN

The End of Your Story

If nothing saves us from death, at least love should save us from life.

– Widely attributed to Pablo Neruda

I have found where the British unease with death goes to take steroids and do a Hulk smash. It's the comment section of the *Sun*, under an article about the exhuming of corpses for the ceremony of Ma'nene in Tana Toraja, Indonesia. I don't know what possessed me to go below the line on an article so clearly designed to draw out the terrified and the angry – the headline says the tribe 'keep their dead relatives at home, feeding and cuddling their rotting bodies'.

'Disturbing – very disturbing,' says one comment.

'Creepy,' says another.

'This article is either a joke, or these sick people need

to be wiped out.' I shudder. Just the two options, apparently. Joke or genocide.

'I guess it's better than being a terrorist like their countrymen in other parts of Inbrednesia,' says another commenter, to which the person who just called for literal genocide replies, 'Bigot.'

I close the window.

I'm in Bali on my way to see some corpses that have been left to rot in the open air.

Butu doesn't get in the boat with us because he has to go to temple later. My guide Made (pronounced 'mah-day') explains that only spiritual masters can see rotting corpses and then pray without needing time to mentally recover. We just spent a pleasant hour with Butu and his family, sitting on his porch with coffee and snacks in the lakeside village of Trunyan. Butu walks us down to the lakeside where a little boat is waiting to take us across the water to Trunyan (sometimes spelled Terunyan) Cemetery.

In the boat, Made explains how pervasive memories of the dead are in the Balinese day-to-day. 'In the morning we cook, and then make a small offering of rice and meat and vegetables on the shrines of the ancestors.'

'So thinking about the dead is part of your morning routine?'

'Yeah. Have you seen the offerings, a little coconut leaf with food and some flowers?'

'Oh those?' I say, amazed. 'Yes, I've seen those

everywhere! On the floor outside shops, I've stepped on them! Oh God, am I in trouble with the ancestors now?'

He laughs. 'Don't worry – everyone steps on them. Yes, we make those every morning. We think about dead people all the time. We pray for all the ancestors, even the ones we don't remember; we have a huge celebration for them every six months. They're not lost.'

'So are you afraid of dying?'

'Me?' The question clearly surprises him. He laughs.

'Yes.' I smile. 'You. Made. Here, in this boat. We're on our way to a cemetery, it seems a good time to ask.'

He laughs more, and admits, 'Yes. Of course I'm afraid!'

I tell him about the taxi driver in Mexico, who said he fears death because of concerns for his family surviving without him, and that he'd prefer not to die in pain. Made nods in agreement. I continue, 'And I said, what if I could guarantee you'd die without pain and your family would be fine, would you be afraid then? And he said no.'

'Right,' says Made. 'I'm afraid more materially, for my family and children.'

'Where I'm from, we're afraid of *being* dead. Do you feel that way? Are you afraid of not existing?'

'Umm...' Made makes a face that says, 'No, obviously not; that's stupid.'

'He made that *exact face*!' I say.

Made bursts out laughing.

*

A man called Wayan holds out his hand to steady me as I step off the boat onto the jetty. The view behind me is all blue; blue lake reflecting blue skies, and a blue volcano – whose dark rock now stands in temple form across the lake, and whose constant threat of eruption means houses in the surrounding villages are constructed crudely from cement, sand and corrugated iron. There's no point in building them too expensively when they could be enveloped in ash any day.

The entrance to the cemetery has a wood-framed sign: WELCOME TO KUBURAN TERUNYAN. Underneath, two jawless skulls sit atop a smattering of coins. The other side of the entrance has a bowl overflowing with money, with two more jawless skulls resting on top.

This is Trunyan Cemetery, where villagers leave their dead to rot in the open air. There are eleven spots, which mirror the eleven pagodas in the village temple. The bodies lie under woven bamboo cages to protect them from being broken down by scavenging monkeys, rather than the air. A huge banyan tree dominates the space. Its Balinese name is *taru menyan* or 'nice-smelling tree', emitting a fragrance said to mask the smell of the decomposition. Though that, ultimately, is decided by the direction of the wind.

On the jetty, I tell Made and Wayan that I have a strange question.

'I read that tourists have been coming here and picking up skulls and taking selfies with them, and that other tourists are outraged at the disrespect – but that locals find it funny that anyone would find that offensive. Is that true?'

Made relays this, and Wayan says, 'For us, it's fine to take a selfie with a skull, yes. It's not a problem at all. It's not offensive. I just say you can adhere to whatever your own beliefs are about the dead when you come here.'

'In your life, how many dead bodies have you seen?' I ask.

'Hundreds,' they say, as if it's a weird question. I confess that I've seen hundreds too, but only in places like this. Made starts to translate, then says, 'Wait, what?'

'Outside a tourist context, I've never seen a dead body.'

He pauses. '*Never*?'

'Nope.'

He relays this, and they look surprised – but there's something else in their reaction I can't put my finger on. As Made and I turn to enter the cemetery, it hits me. I think it's . . . *pity*.

Made and I step inside and he begins to tell me about the cemetery. It's small, set on a slope, with strange, life-sized dolls at the entrance, sitting on a wall. The trees rustle. A familiar smell appears, as if sidling over at a party, an unwelcome touch on my arm, *Hi there, do you remember me?* My hypothalamus stabs me with a flashback of walking through the hall in Chris's house, enveloped in the smell, in grief and terror, in the absolute certainty that I would never feel right again. I draw a sharp breath.

'That's a dead body, that smell, isn't it?' I say, my muscles tensing. There is a note of panic in my voice.

'Yes,' says Made, kindly, holding my gaze. 'No problem.'

He's right.

'Yes,' I repeat, calmer, relaxing my muscles. 'No problem.'

The slope curves up to the left, to what looks like a pile of junk. On closer inspection, it's a pile of belongings – clothes, baskets, handbags, a little Cath Kidston satchel, old lipsticks, toothpaste tubes – and the odd femur. Since there are only eleven spots, once the person has decomposed, their remains get taken to an open-air ossuary, and their belongings get chucked onto the pile.

Opposite are the eleven woven cages, like small tents packed closely together. I approach, slowly. There's a huge plate covered in coins and old leaves at the foot of one of the cages, a black-and-white umbrella lying open behind another. I peer through the bamboo and see clothes and plastic bags of belongings, and a skull at the other end, the jaw stretched into a wide yawn. A closed umbrella with flowers and red and white polka dots leans on the inside wall just over the person's head, as if they might grab it on their way out. A beam of sunshine through the branches dances across their face. The skull in the next cage is bare and black.

'Cemetery isn't the best word, because people here aren't buried,' says Made, 'but many visitors find this place shocking; even Indonesians feel sad when they see the bodies lying there. Sometimes they ask, "Why did you do this?"'

Next to the cages are three deep stone steps, the top one home to three rows of skulls, tinted green with a thin layer of moss.

'It's not part of the practice to display the skulls like this,' Made says, 'it's just for the tourists.' Then he says something surprising. 'Why don't you pick one up and I'll take a picture, so you know it's really OK?'

I laugh, much like he did when I asked if he's afraid of being dead. But now he's suggested it, I have to do it. Gingerly, I pick up a skull, and apologise as I do it. My hand shakes a little as Made takes the photo.

'Great!' he says, smiling.

I turn to the skull, and brush some dirt off the side. 'Thank you,' I say. 'I'm going to put you back now.' I place it back down, and it tilts forward. I can't leave it staring at the dirt until the next tourist comes along. I adjust it so it's looking up.

'OK?' says Made as I come back down the steps.

'Yes,' I smile. 'No problem.'

A flight to Makassar and a ten-hour overnight bus journey later, I arrive in Tana Toraja at 6 a.m., in the absolute shitting rain. The place where my Airbnb host Meyske told me to get a bus to her house is, because of

the absolute shitting rain, absolutely shittingly bus-free. I
shelter under the roof of a garage, wondering what to do.
I feel like an idiot as sleep deprivation pours out of my
eyes in the form of exhausted tears. A motorbike winds
its way up the road and stops in front of me. A man in a
poncho introduces himself as John and offers me a lift. I
gratefully accept. I have only the vaguest sense of where
we're going, so we stop and I give him Meyske's number;
she gives him directions. He hands me the phone and she
switches to English. I take her condolences for the absolute shitting rain and ask her how much I should give
John the Poncho-ed Angel for the ride.

Meyske's house is a *tongkonan*, the traditional house of
the Toraja tribe. A house on bamboo stilts, the most striking feature of which is the curved roof, which sweeps up
to the north and south like the bow of a ship, to symbol-
ise the tribe's origins: immigrants who arrived in South
Sulawesi from South Indo-China by boat. Meyske's
house is at the end of a kind of cul-de-sac, with ten more
tongkonans flanking the path. Many of them have a totem
pole of buffalo horns and are used to store rice – and
dead bodies waiting for their funerals.

I am greeted by Meyske's mother, who sits me down
on the sofa and brings me strong, hot coffee and banana
pancakes sprinkled with cashew nuts. Her wizened
mother – Meyske's grandmother – sits opposite me and,
though we don't have a single word of language in common, we somehow chat for about ten minutes.

My room has a bed with a mosquito net, and a

window that is a literal hole in the wall, looking out over the *tongkonan* corridor. I pull on a warm jumper, listen to the rain, and plan the strange days ahead.

This nap isn't happening. A German tourist, Mareike, is also staying in the *tongkonan* and she's playing her ukulele on the balcony outside. Over the next week, I'll try numerous times to relax on the balcony, and fail for various reasons – the too-strong smell of cigarettes from the last occupant of the hanging chair, a whirl of rain chasing me inside, and the impossibility of concentrating on a book while the neighbours slaughter a pig.

Mareike is friendly, and when I tell her I'm here to learn about the death culture, she asks if she can tag along. In the morning, Anto arrives. He's a young tour guide in training: polite, informed, smiley and usually smoking.

In the car, we wind along roads too skinny for two-way traffic. We're like a lumbering hippo, with mopeds buzzing around us like flies. Anto tells us we're going to Tambunan, the village where he grew up, to see their unique ceremony for the ancestors.

'You know the story of why we worship the ancestors, right?'

'No,' says Mareike.

'OK,' he starts, holding his cigarette out the window, 'many years ago, there was a young man who wanted to hunt wild pigs in the jungle. On the way he found a bone, and saw it belonged to a human. He wrapped it' – Anto mimes wrapping the bone with a care and gentleness

that most people would save for an injured kitten –
'and looked for a cave. When he found one, he placed
the bone inside it. When he turned around, he saw all
his spears had pigs on them, and when he got home,
all his rice seedlings grew within a week.'

'So he was rewarded?'

'By the ancestors, because he took care of them, yes.
You can believe the story or not; it's a tale that people
here believe, and now that they look after the ancestors,
all the people in this area are successful.'

I'm sure it can't be true that there's no poverty in
Tana Toraja, but it certainly isn't as visible as in other
parts of Indonesia. My iPhone, for example, is the oldest
model I've seen since I got here.

Anto walks us into a clearing in a forest. I recognise
pigs' blood on the ground. Clusters of family members
kneel over two giant banana leaves that have been spread
across the ground to make a mat. They smear smaller
banana-leaf 'plates' with turmeric rice, and roll different-
coloured sticky rice into tasty cones. Two men then lift
the giant platter, walk it a few metres away to where a
priest waits for them, and place it atop a palm leaf on
the ground, at the foot of a huge cliff where many of the
villagers' ancestors – including Anto's grandfather – are
buried. There's a stick driven into the earth bearing a
roasted pig's ear and tail.

'So, you make an offering of food for the ancestors,'
says Anto, 'and then you apologise.'

'What do you apologise for?' I say.

'In our whole life, there might have been a moment we didn't respect the ancestors, so we apologise for the actions we took.'

'It sounds like the ancestors are something you're a little afraid of?'

Anto laughs. 'Oh yes. Ancestors are the keeper of the land, so we're afraid if we insult them, the land will be broken. You see this, here?' He gestures to a large, marshy patch of mud. 'When I used to visit here when I was a kid, this was a natural pool. I visited again when I was seventeen and it had all dried up. I asked my grand-father, "Why is this place I visited as a child dry now?" and he said, "Because so many of the people have now turned to Christianity, there aren't enough of us to take care of the place and perform the rituals for our ances-tors. And our ancestors got mad."'

People start to approach the food offering. They take some rice and drop some money, which will all be gath-ered and saved for next year's ceremony, to buy things like pigs, betel nuts and tobacco. They leave the back row of food alone; that's for the ancestors to eat. Anto says if anyone takes from that row it'll anger them, and they'll make the transgressor sick. People here get brutal when they die.

'So where will *you* be buried?' I ask Anto.

'Sorry?!' he says. I repeat the question, and Marieke lets out a startled laugh. If Anto was surprised by the question, it doesn't last.

'I prefer to be buried here.'

'So you've thought about it?'

'Yes, I've already prepared because I know I want to reunite with my father and grandfather, here.'

'So, you're twenty-five and you've already thought about after your death?'

Anto nods.

'That's extremely surprising to me, because I'm in my thirties and if someone asks me, I say, "I don't know, shut up."'

He laughs and nods. 'That's the adventure of life in Toraja; you decide your answer.'

Anto films all the rituals on his iPhone. He's been learning intensively for five years, knowing the duty will be passed to him when his aunt dies.

'One day she will become sick and predict that she doesn't have long; my auntie will call me and the priest, and the priest will take the bamboo and plant it into the ground facing east.'

'Why?' I ask.

'To baptise me; to let me know that I've taken over.'

He is, to put it bluntly, shitting himself at the prospect of filling those shoes. When he was nineteen, Anto got in trouble with the ancestors and was punished – twice, he says. During his grandmother's funeral, his grandfather spoke into a microphone, asking him to bring the buffalo up to get some water.

'I thought it wasn't really important, so I didn't bring it far enough,' says Anto. 'I was just lazy.'

The next day, the buffalo ran away. The villagers helped him to catch it, but it became angry and wild. That was, says Anto, his first punishment. Afterwards, one of the priests communicated with his dead grandmother – 'What is the right punishment for your grandchild?' – and reported that she'd told the priest he must sacrifice a pig right now, and a rooster in the jungle.

'Why should I do that?' Anto asked them, terrified and crying.

'To separate the bad things you did during this funeral ceremony from what comes after.'

'And after that,' says Anto, now a wise twenty-five-year-old, 'I really started to care about the ancestors.'

The definition of death varies according to culture and time. The stopping of the heart was long considered the best indicator of death – though even this was tricky to measure before improvements were made to stethoscopes – but when medical science advanced to the point of measuring brain activity, a debate ensued. Which organ, by ceasing activity, was the one that turned us into a corpse?

In Tana Toraja, this debate holds much less interest, since your physical death isn't counted as your death at all. In fact, your death isn't official until you've had your funeral. Since funerals are days-long, festival-like affairs, it rarely even happens in the same week or month as the physical death, since both gathering the money and organising the logistics are substantial undertakings. Also, everyone in the family has to get along; you can't have a funeral amidst family dramas. So the time between a physical death and the funeral could be weeks, months or years.

Anto unlocks the front door of the *tongkonan* and mutters, '*Tabe*' – 'sorry'. Mareike and I remove our shoes, climb the wooden steps and follow him in. In the back room there are three coffins with red-and-blue patterned sheets placed neatly over them. Beside them are offerings of money, cigarettes, an old Nokia mobile phone. A Zimmer frame rests by the window.

'This one, the nephew, has been resting for five years,' says Anto, indicating the coffin on the right, 'the middle one is the daughter – she has been here for nine years, and this one is the father. He has been here for twenty-four years.'

'This person has been dead for *twenty-four years*?!' Mareike and I say, amazed.

'It's not really a dead person,' Anto corrects, gently, 'but a sick person. We still feed them three times a day.' The meals that are brought only stay around two to five minutes; the last thing a room with three dead bodies needs is an ant infestation. 'We serve them coffee and tea,' Anto continues. 'If someone in the family gets sick, we talk to them, we ask, "Why are they sick?" We ask them to please make good things happen for us.'

I ask if it's normal for someone to be 'resting' for so long before their funeral.

'It's normal for us. Sometimes it's caused by problems

with the family – I see they have a mat on the floor; we only lay down this kind of mat when there's a family meeting. Last time I was here there was no mat.' This suggests they're working up to an enormous triple funeral.

'If you have the, er, "sick" people here, there's no one living with them, right?' asks Mareike.

'Sometimes people live together with them.' She digests this, and then asks why there's no smell.

'Before, we had a traditional mummification process,' says Anto. 'We'd wash the body, scrub it with the leaves of the betel nuts, then cover it with banana-tree sap to make it sticky. Then we'd take fermented palm wine and put it in the mouth of the deceased. After that, we take banana-tree trunks and make a V shape for the body to lie on, then take a bamboo stick and punch a hole in the back of the body to drain the liquid. So it's not really a mummification; it's more removing the liquid from the deceased. Now, with modernisation, for the past fifty years we've had formaldehyde injections. We usually take them to the hospital for the injection, or we call out a nurse to help us with it.'

'Does formaldehyde work better than the old method?' I ask.

'Not always; sometimes they rot almost completely within a few months. I think that happens when it's poorly administered. The people we'll see on Saturday at Ma'nene were mummified with leaves and pepper, and you'll see it's worked well.'

A private question I have is whether Torajans have,

in any capacity, the same disgust of dead bodies I was brought up with. Can what feels like such a visceral reaction really be entirely cultural? I decide to probe.

'This might be a stupid question,' I say, 'but why do you embalm the bodies?'

It is, of course, because of the practicalities of keeping a dead body at home. Even if you're willing to face death this head-on, you couldn't eat or even think about anything else with the smell of a decomposing body in the room. Also, the practice of exhuming them for an annual party wouldn't be possible with a corpse that nature had fully claimed. I explain that in the West, particularly in the States, people embalm bodies only to burn or bury them the next day.

'Really?!' says Anto, baffled. 'But that's pointless.'

'They've been known to call it "hygiene services" to make people think they need it, that it's a legal requirement. Because people don't want to talk about death, they never have the conversation that reveals that it's unnecessary.'

'The only tribe for whom embalming is appropriate is Torajans, because we keep the body for a very long time in the house,' says Anto, decisively. 'For those who are getting buried quickly, it's not really appropriate.'

A day before the funeral, the body is placed in one of the little *tongkonans*, ones that are used mostly for storing rice.

'So you take the rice out and put a dead person inside?' I ask.

'We don't take the rice out; we just move it and put the dead person on the floor.'

'So the rice we're eating has possibly been next to a dead person?'

'Not *next to*!' he laughs. 'The rice goes upstairs, and we put the corpse on the floor of the rice barn. The rice is *above* the corpse, not below! Otherwise we'd be disgusted to eat it.'

Aha, I think.

'So you still have that disgust of dead bodies, even though you've seen hundreds of them and talked to them and brought them meals; you still find them a bit disgusting?' I probe.

'Well, just when we want to eat,' he says. 'I never want to touch a dead body during Ma'nene, and I don't like to shake people's hands because they've touched dead bodies.'

Thinking I've got even more evidence for my everyone-thinks-corpses-are-gross hypothesis, I ask, 'What are you worried about? Catching a disease or just "ew, death"?'

'I worry about catching illnesses – but just because I don't *know* these dead bodies. If it's my family I'm not worried. Same as with the living, if I don't know them.'

'So it's not really because they're dead bodies, it's because they're strangers? That's funny – in the West we'd be afraid to touch *any* dead body.'

'Really?!' he says, incredulous.

'Yes! We have an aversion to even *talking* about death, because it feels as if we're calling it to our door.'

'If you touch it you will *die*!' he says in a mock-foreboding voice. 'You know, some of our young generation have been affected by this kind of attitude from Europe. They say things like, "Don't say that, it's bad luck," and I say, "No, in our culture it's something that should be faced, not escaped. Our ancestors teach us to not be afraid of facing death."'

I worry about Anto growing old in a country where these traditions are dying. Even the Torajan language is diminishing; he already has to use simple grammar when he speaks Torajan to his younger family members, which will of course make it all the more difficult to pass on the traditions. It would be unfair for him to have put in all this work to learn how to take care of the ancestors, only to be immediately forgotten when he becomes one.

'Excuse me, miss.'

I move aside and a pig passes me, suspended by ropes from a large stalk of bamboo. She's kicking and breathing heavily, as if she knows what's about to happen. Pigs are intelligent, but I don't suppose you have to be to realise the situation is pretty dire. Mareike asks how many animals will be slaughtered for celebratory food at the funeral today. Countless, Anto says, and if she's squeamish, she might want to look away.

Tourists with digital SLR cameras mingle among the family members at what feels like a music festival. Hundreds of people mill around on a hilly patch of land, surrounded by *tongkonans* under the bluest of skies. Anto takes Mareike and I up some wooden steps to a little viewing platform, with a roof and straw mats to sit on. From here we can see the entire ceremony, the gathered crowd, and the family members walking the coffin around the hilly compound as a master of ceremonies, on a central *tongkonan*, talks incessantly into a microphone. The deceased was a ninety-year-old woman who had been sick for a long time before her physical death two years ago. The coffin is a beautiful object, a rounded red box with gold patterning, mounted on a wheeled *tongkonan*. At least a hundred family members are walking the coffin around the patch of land. A long line of people hold a strip of red fabric above their heads, leading her along. The hills make moving the coffin a little precarious; it's clearly incredibly heavy, containing both a body and her belongings, not to mention the awkward structure of the *tongkonan*, which they pull along with huge bamboo sticks like a chariot. Occasionally they stop for a break, and start bouncing it up and down, jumping into the air, splashing in the mud while making high-pitched hollering noises. More than once, the structure tilts dangerously. Last year at one funeral, Anto tells me, the deceased's own son died beneath a toppling coffin.

Nanni, the deceased's thirty-year-old granddaughter, brings coffee and snacks, and we get chatting.

'Is this a happy or sad day for you?' I ask.

'Oh, sad day!' she says, as if it's obvious, and then adds, 'But also a celebration.' She says she's not joining the procession today because it's hot and she's feeling lazy.

Off to the right, a man begins to sacrifice a pig. Mareike turns away and covers her ears and asks me to tell her when it's over. It's so much worse than I expected. He doesn't just stab her as she lies helpless with tied trotters, he slices her right open and begins pulling her insides out while she writhes and screams. When he takes a huge, dramatic blowtorch to her skin, singeing all the hair off, I exhale with relief that she must surely now be dead. She lies blackened, motionless, pooling blood, bordered by burnt grass.

The incessant mic-talk switches to English: 'Tourists, please be careful when they sacrifice the buffalo; the family doesn't have insurance for you.' I don't go over to watch the creature being felled, but plenty of other tourists do. The violent spasms as it bleeds from the throat, the indignity of doing so while tied to a post by a rope threaded through its nose ring, a crowd surrounding the spectacle – even peripherally, it's tough to see.

When it's over, we emerge from our little shack and walk around. Someone has left a pig, still tied to bamboo, lying in the sun until it's time to be killed. Around fifty men stand in a circle holding hands around a tree, with the mountains and blue skies as a backdrop. They sing a haunting song, moving their hands up and down and dancing gently. The microphone chatter goes on throughout.

'Look,' says Anto, 'the families are meeting.' He

points to a group of people walking into a *tongkonan*. Even from here, the atmosphere between them seems stilted. I ask Anto how families get along at funerals if they've had issues in the past.

'Usually they will resolve the problem before they run the funeral. Because if the soul of your father or grandfather or grandmother sees you in problems, they might get mad at you and make bad things happen to you, to remind you that you should apologise.'

'And after the funeral do the problems come back?' I ask.

'Not really, because there are more rituals later, so they have to remain peaceful.'

'So death fixes problems?'

Anto laughs. 'Yeah! That's why we're not afraid, because after facing death, we become a semi-god. We have the power to forgive people, to give blessings.'

I can understand that. Why would you be afraid of death when you know you're going to be so important? We have this maxim that you shouldn't speak ill of the dead, presumably because we think it's the ultimate in kicking someone when they're down. But here, they can defend themselves: speak ill of a dead Torajan and they'll make your buffalo run away. I tell Anto that where I'm from, we think that when you're dead you lose all your power; that essentially, you don't matter any more.

Anto looks at me, thoughtful. 'We remember every single thing the deceased did. But I guess in your country, when you're dead, it's the end of your story.'

*

My quads are burning and shaking with the effort of staying on this motorbike. Meyske let Anto and I borrow it for the two-hour drive to Pangala', but the combination of potholes and almost-vertical downhills means I'm holding myself up by pressing my entire weight on flip-flopped feet into the foot peg for minutes at a time.

We're driving all the way to the north Toraja village because that's where Ma'nene reliably happens annually. Because of modernisation and changes in religion, the ceremony is becoming less common. Meyske's family gather to kill a pig, pray, and remember the dead. At Londa, where people are entombed in an ancient burial cave, there are life-sized puppets of the deceased, which have their clothes changed every three years. At Lo'ko' Mata, where tombs are bored into the side of an enormous roadside boulder, they change the clothes of the entombed bodies and the puppets every four years. But in Pangala', Ma'nene is observed annually.

The word '*nene*' means grandmother, and the prefix '*ma*' means playing or communicating with. So essentially, Ma'nene means 'hanging out with Grandma'. Anto and I stop at a shop to buy some cigarettes for the adults and some chocolate biscuits for the children, as a thank you for letting us come and hang out with their grandma. I'm wearing colourful clothes and was careful not to wear any black because Anto stressed that black is inappropriate: this is supposed to be a happy occasion.

If you'd like some tips on how to prepare to meet a woman who has been dead for four years, leaning against a wall between her living granddaughter and her husband who has been dead for seven years, I've got nothing for you. Except, perhaps, the reassurance that it takes mere minutes for the situation to seem surprisingly normal. The grandma is wearing diamond earrings, a brand new bright blue shirt, a red necklace, sandals and a handbag hanging casually from her right forearm. Her hands are folded on her front, her right fingers resting on her left. The veins on her hands are still raised, the wrinkles on her knuckles visible with dust, her nails still neat and trim. She still has her hair, eyebrows and eyelashes; though her skin is dark, dry, almost sandy. Her husband is more deteriorated, his skin peeling, yellowing and with a few holes, but his features are still recognisable, and he also sports new clothes. The trio lean against the blue-and-pink wall of a tomb, as family members and tourists snap photos. Another girl joins the photo shoot with a framed picture of the man when he was alive, and the granddaughter holds one of her grandmother.

The granddaughter's phone rings. It's a FaceTime call. She takes it and holds the phone up to the grandmother's face. The family member who couldn't make it squeals in delight at seeing her again, waving hello.

'As I told you, they still care about them,' says Anto.

We pass around chocolate biscuits, particularly to the children present, and Anto tells me they talk to their ancestors. I ask what they say.

'They make requests, like, "Oh, Grandpa, please give me good grades, let me get into a good school, let me have good health" – sometimes they say, "I really miss you."'

Two young men lift up the grandmother and grand-father and walk them past their own open coffins to the edge of the hill, so everyone can take pictures of them against the lush mountain backdrop. Anto is keen for me to know that as they moved her, they said, 'Excuse me, Grandma, we will put you over there now, just like we did last year.'

'When we make them stand like this, we always ask their permission. If you don't talk to them, you can't move them. It's basic respect.'

'That makes sense,' I say. 'If I was paralysed and couldn't move, I'd expect you to ask me before you moved me.'

I'm half-joking, but Anto says, 'Yeah, exactly. You treat them just like you did in their lifetime. Death is not the end in Torajan culture.'

At first, the boys crouch behind the body while peo-ple take pictures – even now, when I look at the photos, at first glance they look like a couple posing on holiday – then they stand and put their arms around them and pose for more pictures. Afterwards, they carry them over to where the granddaughter is sitting by an open tomb, her legs dangling from the ledge. They stand her grand-parents next to her.

I hit record on a video and capture a moment that

changes me. The granddaughter turns her head, looks at her grandmother and seems to spot something. Lovingly, almost absentmindedly, she brushes some dust off her grandmother's hair. Two strokes of her hand, and then she goes back to looking at the view in companionable silence.

Five years ago, I sat at my kitchen table, grief-stricken and anxious, and read about a festival for the dead, a remote place in Indonesia where they exhume corpses, dress them up and walk them around. I read pieces that called them zombies, called it morbid, creepy, disturbing. I arrived thinking I was past the idea that a corpse is frightening, that engaging with the reality of death and mortality is morbid, or even brave.

And yet at no point did it occur to me how visible the love would be.

They are placed gently back into their coffins. The granddaughter replaces the sandals, a comb, a make-up bag and the framed picture in the coffin, then kneels beside it, talking softly to her. She strokes her hair lovingly with one hand and pats her hand with the other. She readjusts her necklace, then lays two blankets over her and tucks her in. She does the same for her grandfather and places his baseball cap beside his head. Two young men replace the lids on the red, gold and blue coffins, and two more help to lift them back into the tombs.

Ma'nene highlights, more than any other festival I've seen, one of the harshest and most brutal ways we're getting death wrong. A few months ago, I spoke to Laura

Green, a lecturer in palliative care at the University of Manchester, who said people have a social death and a physical death, and that when people are dying they are 'almost treated as though they're dead bodies, even though biologically things are carrying on'. It reminded me of a letter I was read over the phone by Liz Rothschild, a celebrant and burial-ground owner with a one-woman show about death. The letter, written to her local newspaper, read, 'Since being diagnosed with advanced prostate cancer eighteen months ago, friends I've known for years have disappeared, my sister is no longer in touch. Worse yet, a partner I have known for thirty-one years left me shortly after we attended the oncologist interview. She did not tell me she was leaving. This is at a time I need her more than ever. Prior to being diagnosed I was a reasonably healthy man for my age, almost eighty, tall, slim and active. I am still reasonably active but greatly troubled by being treated as untouchable . . . The partner I had and I used to enjoy going out for lunch and dinner . . .' Liz broke off, and told me, 'He goes on to talk about realising he's in a world that caters for couples and he's obviously not had any periods in his life of being single. He dreads being asked the question, "How many will there be, sir?" and says, "Recently when asked that question, I answered, 'Just one, please.' He led me upstairs to an empty dining area. I said, 'I prefer to be seated in an area where other people dine.' He said, 'We must keep those tables for two or more, sir.' I said, 'I have to eat alone at home.' I walked out."'

Every part of that letter made me want to bawl. I revealed my coddled naivety about attitudes to death in Britain, telling her, 'I had no idea that was happening to people who get diagnosed with terminal illnesses, that suddenly everyone walks out. I suppose people just don't have the...emotional equipment?...to watch someone die.'

Our mortal terror consumes us so entirely that we're dying our social deaths before our bodies give out. Worse than that, we're killing our loved ones socially before they even die, because we 'don't know what to say', or 'want to remember them as they were'.

Here, people are still part of the community years beyond their physical death. Their importance augments and their power grows. The love that sustained them in life is still there, bringing them meals, buying them clothes, brushing the dust out of their hair.

I'm zipping up my bag when I get a WhatsApp from Dion.

'Hey! Can't wait to see you. Are you on your way to the airport yet?'

'Leaving for the overnight bus in about fifteen minutes,' I reply.

'Yaaaay!'

I send a hug emoji, and then, 'I went to Ma'nene today. It was pretty astonishing.' I send him the video of the girl stroking her dead grandmother's hair.

'Wow,' he replies. 'That's actually incredibly beautiful.'

'It was.'

'Were you OK with it?'

'Absolutely.'

'You've finished. All seven of them. I can't believe it. So proud of you. You've seen a lot of death now, hon.'

I read the text, and smile.

'Yes,' I reply. 'No problem.'

CHAPTER TWELVE

Death vs Love

One way of imagining life is that it's a competition between love and death. Death always wins, of course, but love is there to make its victory a hollow one.

— Robert Webb, *How Not to Be a Boy*

The funeral home calls, after several years of storing Chris's ashes for us, and says it's time. We have to take them. Naturally, this re-sparks the conversation about what we're going to do with him. Since he never told us what he wanted, we have to guess, and we don't want to get it wrong. The conversations over the years have gone something like this:

Me: 'Why don't we scatter him in Australia?'

Dion: 'But he left Australia, then chose to set-tle somewhere else, and rarely went back. If he chose not-Australia in life, we should probably go with not-Australia for his death, shouldn't we?'

Me: 'What about Cape Town, so he can be with your mum?'

Dion: 'He definitely never chose to be there; I'd feel weird leaving him there.'

Me: 'What about Greece? He loved ancient Greece!'

Dion: 'I'm not sure about choosing his final resting place based on what he was reading when he died.'

Me: 'OK, let's narrow it down. What should we avoid?'

Dion: 'Roads. Once he got into cycling, he started hating cars – well, mainly the people driving them. Ooh, could we find some way to scatter him that would inconvenience a motorist?'

It is exhausting trying to guess at the wishes of a dead man. This is where the constant epithet that 'we don't talk about death' is truest: we don't talk about our *own* deaths. And the reasons we give are often prudish notions of it being 'morbid'. Meanwhile, to cater to this noble distaste for morbidity, TV and Hollywood cannot commission enough on the topic of murder: there are around twenty shows and movies about zombies on Netflix at any given time, and east London is stomped over daily by tourists who simply must know exactly where a Victorian serial killer disembowelled some prostitutes. As Jules Howard said in his book *Death on Earth*:

> We humans have an inherent interest in life-threatening situations. We like telling stories about it. We like

passing it on... Pick up a newspaper: you'll read about disease, war, plane crashes, earthquakes, drownings, murders, suicides, injuries, car crashes and plenty else to do with death. People who say death is taboo are mostly wrong. We *love* talking about death.

And yet when it comes to our own, we blanch. We demand a subject change. We imply our daughter is ruining Christmas dinner (sorry, Mum). When our loved ones mention their own demise, we shout them down, and when it happens we retreat to the kitchen, call the police, call for help, because not one part of us feels equipped for the task at hand: the problem of the body, the problem of wishes you spent years skirting around, the problem of goodbye.

Why are we like this? And more importantly, can't we just decide to overcome it? Can't we just admit we're obsessed with death and turn a little of it on ourselves? Some people can. I searched Spotify for funeral playlists when I started writing this book, and found hundreds – many twelve- or twenty-hour lists with 200 or 300 songs, which is perfect: it's not enough to try to extend your life, some people are apparently picturing their funerals going on and on. We all just want to exist that little bit longer, but at some point, you have to let people go home.

We decide on Hampstead Heath, where Chris used to walk Troy. It's a place he loved, close to home, away from traffic. Having moved out of London, we're staying in an Airbnb on Highgate West Hill. The host is meeting us at the door to let us in. I can't help wondering about the etiquette of casually bringing a dead body into someone else's home.

I turn to my Twitter followers with a poll:

What should we do if the host asks, 'What's in the box?'
Option 1: Just say, 'My dad.'
Option 2: Lie! Obviously lie!

To my surprise, most people plump for the honest response, with only 17 per cent voting for option two. Luckily our host shows no interest in the box of Chris, so we dodge the bullet of having to admit we've brought a corpse on holiday, and now, on a gloriously sunny Saturday, we step out to say our final goodbyes.

Chris's ashes sit in a paper bag, packed in a box, which was presented to Dion in a strong, emerald-green carrier bag, the kind you'd get at a high-end department store. Chris was heavy in life, and is heavy now in death, and the bag's golden-thread handle is etching a groove into Dion's palm. He's too chivalrous to let the weight of his dad cut my hand in half, so he carries the ashes and I hold the dog lead – we have a dog now, a spaniel. His name's Ludo, and with his melting expression and big old Disney eyes staring pleadingly up at me, I can never again decide not to go out.

We come to the zebra crossing at the top of Highgate

West Hill. Just as the cars stop to let us cross, Ludo, who has no sense of occasion at all, curls his little body and starts to take his morning poop on the pavement. I fumble for a bag and car horns sound off the fury of Londoners who've been delayed almost six entire seconds. As a lapsed Londoner, I understand – they've gone to all the trouble of obeying the pedestrian-crossing law, only for me to obey the picking-up-after-your-dog law on *their time*. The woman at the front of the queue is driving one-handed while angrily eating a doughnut and is clearly yelling and swearing at me from inside her car between mouthfuls. She speeds off, her engine snarling.

'Sorry, lady,' I mutter, tying the poop bag. 'Not picking up after your dog is an eighty-pound fine, but there's no fine for—' I gasp. 'Hon!' I call out to Dion, who's already on the other side. I point at the dog, and with utter glee, say, 'Ludo! He . . . he inconvenienced a motorist!'

Dion puts down his dad, grabs a treat from his pocket and kneels down, opening his arms as the dog runs to him. 'Good boy!'

Under flecks of sunlight through the trees on the heath, Dion pulls out the brown paper bag, just like the ones that used to arrive at Chris's house containing Friday-night takeaway. But it's neater, stapled even, free of fat stains from onion bhajis, and instead of a receipt reading the same old order, there's a label reading 'Cremation remains of the late CHRISTOPHER WATTS'. Dion pulls the bag open, and a cloud of dust bursts out, as if it had been feeling claustrophobic in there. When it disperses, he peers inside.

'Wow. Yeah. That's ash.'

He hands me the bag, and I stare down into it. My eyes lock upon one tiny fragment, that unmistakable honeycomb pattern of the inner bone.

Dion takes out his phone. His dad used to wake him up for school by reciting a poem through his bedroom door, and on the drive down Dion spent an hour googling any snippets of it his memory threw up. Because among the many questions he never asked his dad was the name of that poem, those few lines that roused him for so many years, so gently and with so much love, while the rest of the world whacked the heads of alarm clocks for just five more minutes.

My face is already wet with silent tears as Dion begins reading. I start to pour the ash onto the undergrowth, putting Chris to rest to the sound of the poem he recited to wake his son. The ash lands and sits on top of the leaves. I brush at it to get it to settle. Ludo jumps back and shakes ash off his little head. I turn to Dion. He wraps his arms around me and sobs, just like he did on the Worst Tuesday. I hold as tight as I can, as if I can squeeze the sadness out of him. After a few minutes, he pulls back, composes himself, and kisses my forehead.

He takes the bag. There's so much left. He turns it upside down, shakes it, and nothing happens.

'It's like a brick,' he mutters.

'Use your hands.'

He walks the path through the trees in front of me, reaches a hand into the bag and begins to scatter the ash.

'Wait, wait, wait!' I say, running in front of him. 'There's a breeze and some of that – PEH – some of that went in my mouth!'

He laughs, sweetly. 'Sorry, honey. We did say we didn't want a *Big Lebowski* situation.' *The Big Lebowski* is Dion's favourite film, and the scene in which they try to scatter their friend's ashes and end up getting caked in every last bit of it thanks to a gust of wind is fresh in our minds.

I walk ahead of Dion. He scatters his dad in great handfuls. The sun catches the dust as it blows in the breeze and settles to the earth.

Dion offers the bag and I reach into it, pulling out a handful. I walk and walk, Dion scatters and scatters. I carry on into the woods, still clutching my handful of Chris dust.

Now, trooperoos.

Move in here.

Oops, sorry!

Come on, cho-ree-toe.

RATS!

Does that interest you at all?

Thanks for moving in.

I stop in a lush, sun-dappled clearing. I close my eyes and open them again. I take a deep breath, and smile.

I throw my hand aloft and let go.

Acknowledgements

In the early stages of writing this book, I had a dream that my teeth were falling out – a common death anxiety dream, I'm told. In the dream, I rushed, as you would, to a dentist. The dentist was my agent Laura Longrigg, because my unconscious is brilliant at casting. Thank you, Laura, not only for signing me when I was a whippersnapper of a trainee at the *Guardian*, but for being such a wonderful and encouraging agent and friend.

Thanks to the incredible team of editors at Unbound. Joelle Owusu, my commissioning editor, saw a viral tweet of mine, researched who I was, found the project and asked if Unbound could publish it. This is not an ordinary way of getting a book deal and I don't expect to ever get so lucky again. Thank you, Joelle, for immediately understanding everything I was going for with this book, for your faith and kindness throughout the process.

Enormous thanks to my manuscript editor DeAndra Lupu and my development editor Rachael Kerr for all the time, attention to detail and enthusiasm you put into this book.

Thank you to all the guides and interviewees who were so helpful and informative, and even delved into their own lives and memories to help me understand the death festivals: Jaime Hernández Balderas, Barbara Anderson, Victoria Ryan, Sandip Bhujel, Junu Shrestha, Adriana Patelli, Silvia Marrone, Giusi Cataldo, Sandro Dieli, Lucy Talbot, Sarah Chavez, Andrew Chesnut, Zoltan Istvan, Michelle Acciavatti, Cindi Richardson, Dartanya Croff, Luke Siddall, Bloody Mary, Eric Ralison, Rojo Johnarson, Raharimino 'Lala' Lalasoa, Edmond Rakomalala, Hermann Andria, Akari Murata, Russell Davison, Made Sukana, Capriyanto Tandipau, Meyske Latuihamallo, Liz Rothschild and Laura Green. Thank you to all the interviewees whose incredible insights, for reasons of length, didn't make it to the final cut, but who guided the tone and spirit of the book: Gwen Nelson, Bella Heesom, Amy Pickard, Dr Phil Hammond, Katie Williams, Jesse Karmazin, Eugenia Kuyda, James Norris and Jason Moore.

Thanks also to the many writers I hold in terrifyingly high regard who encouraged me while I was writing this: Rhik Samadder, Stuart Heritage, Karen Smyte, Steve Kettmann, Elmaz Abinader, Deepa Narayan, Barbara Tran, Debi Goodwin, Jean Shields Fleming, Jeannette Brown, Nívea Castro, Rita Juster, Courtney Young, Tanushree Baidya, Anita Gill, Paulette Livers, Rashaun J. Allen, Christy Stillwell, Christine Maul Rice, JC Hallman, Kristina Marie Darling, Jackie Munn, Diana Whitney.

Much of this book was written, workshopped, developed and edited at writing residencies; so huge thanks to the Wellstone Center in the Redwoods, Vermont Studio Center, Hedgebrook, Faber, and Virginia Center for the Creative Arts for gifting me time and space to write. Thank you to the staff at various cafes in Cheltenham (where I lived for three years) – Scandinavian Coffee Pod, Coffee Dispensary, Baker & Graze, The Hive, and Botanica – for never reproaching me when I sat and wrote for much too long, for giving my dog treats and for always asking how the book was going.

Thanks to the *Guardian Weekend* editors Melissa Denes, Abigail Radnor and Ruth Lewy, who took my grief-addled pitch and gently nudged it into the memoir piece that sparked this project. Thanks to Kristian Brodie at storytelling night OneTrackMinds, Todd Hannula and Lisa Renee at DaCunha, Lucy Talbot at Death and the Maiden, Jemima Kiss at Medium, Arifa Akbar at Boundless and Jessica Mitchell at Cruse Bereavement Journal for publishing early excerpts of this book.

Writing is maddening, and those of us who are kept from the brink usually have a team of misfits to thank for it. My best friend Stephanie Spiro, you are one of very few loves of my life. I'm excited to continue the conversation we've been having over Facebook Messenger for almost a decade. Thank you for believing in me to a frankly absurd degree.

Toby Finlay, you're a brutal man. I've seen you dissolve people with your words like rain on candy floss, so your decision to do the opposite to me is both baffling and wonderful, like a scorpion deciding it likes you and wants a cuddle. You make me a better writer, and I love you very much. (Also thanks for story time – I think you'll find it's your turn.)

Alex Morgan, when this book happened, you had me come to your house in my pyjamas for champagne. Let this be a blueprint for all writers' friends. Thanks for always picking up the phone. Drive slower.

Robert Powell, thanks for sending so much support and encouragement, funny tweets and the occasional well-timed suggestion that I get a grip.

Simon and Claire Watts, thank you for cheerleading this project from the start. Thanks for your unending kindness, and for the daily videos of Simon playing the fiddle when I was neck-deep in the edit during the coronavirus lockdown.

And Mum and Chris, thank you for all your support, even though I'm pretty sure being the daughter of medics and writing about death qualifies me as a major disappointment. Sorry! I think I'm making up for not rebelling enough as a teenager.

Can you thank a dead man? Because if so: thank you, Chris. For everything.

And there's one last person to thank, who read my early drafts and encouraged me to say more, be more honest, reveal even more; who talked me down from the ledge many, many times over the years of researching and writing; who made me holler with laughter every day; who took care of everything at home while I was cavorting with cadavers and gallivanting with ghosts. He knows who he is (and so, I suspect, do you). The hero of this story is him.

Quotation on page 109 from *The Captain Is Out to Lunch* by Charles Bukowski © Linda Lee Bukowski, 1998.

Quotation on page 290 from *How Not to Be a Boy* © Robert Webb, 2017.

Extract on pages 291–2 © Jules Howard, 2016, *Death on Earth*, Bloomsbury Sigma, an imprint of Bloomsbury Publishing Plc.

Unbound is the world's first crowdfunding publisher, established in 2011.

We believe that wonderful things can happen when you clear a path for people who share a passion. That's why we've built a platform that brings together readers and authors to crowdfund books they believe in – and give fresh ideas that don't fit the traditional mould the chance they deserve.

This book is in your hands because readers made it possible. Everyone who pledged their support is listed below. Join them by visiting unbound.com and supporting a book today.

Jason Ballinger
Nicola Bannock
Hannah Barham-
Brown
RJ Barker
Chloé Rose Barley
Thomas Barron
Kevin Bart
Rachel Bass
Debbie Bassett
Soumya Basu
Teodora Beleaga
Coste
Richard Bell
Rebecca Benedetti
Chris Benston
Belinda Benton
Stig Berg
Matteo Bergamini
Chris Bethea
Marco Bettoni
Emily Bevan
Julian Birch
Andrew Bishop
Tom Black
Dan Blackett
El Bladukiene
Nicholas Boalch
Katie Boehm
Becky Bolton
Jen Bowden
Becca Bradford
Marianne Bragge
Jill Brandwein
Joanne Brennan
Andy Brereton
Stephanie
Bretherton
David Brimble
Jill Brinkworth
Kate Britton
Kristian Brodie

Lee Brookes
Gary Brooks
Dan Brotzel,
Martin Jenkins
& Alex Woolf
Jeannette Brown
Maureen Brown
Brian Browne
Jason Buck
Eric R. Buist
Mike Buist
Tristan Buist
Ed Burness
Charlotte Burnett
Lazlo Burns
Marc Burrows
Ana Isabella Byrne
Brenda Caley
Elaine Cameron
Tim Campbell
Beth Campbell
Duke
Melissa Carlson
Ela Carpenter
Lis Carter
Amy Casey
Maria Catamero
Kevin F.
Cavanaugh
Ivan Cenzi
(Bizzarro Bazar)
Andy Charman
Katrina Chatterton
Imran Chaudhry
Jesus Chavez,
MSW, ASW
Abby Chicken
Jamie Chipperfield
Ric Christ
Adrian Clark
Sue Clark
Philippa Cochrane

GMark Cole
Stevyn Colgan
Rebecca Collins
Heather Combe
Tamsin Comrie
Philip Connor
Cat Cooper
Mark E Cooper
Hannah Costigan
Asha Coutrier
Saul Cowen
Simon Cox
Becky Craggs
John Crawford
Elena Cresci
Paul Crinion
Alasdair Cross
Laina Cross-
Harris
Eric Crump
Cruse Bereavement
Care Notting-
hamshire Area
Catherine Curtis
Heidi Daehler
Chris Dale
Kristina Darling
Steph Davies
Laura Davis
Russell Davison
Martyn Day
Vicky Deighton
Dan Deville
Andrew Dickens
Glenn Dietz
Kate Dobinson
Kathryn Dowling
Billy Dowling-Reid
Bethan Downing
Nicole Doyle
Frances Drinkall
Alexis Dubreuil

Chelsea Duke
Daniel Y Durrance
William Dyson
Scott Eakin
Alys Earl
David Edick Jr
Hannah Edwards
Diane Eichorst
Stinne Elkjær
Robert Elmer
Inigo Escalante
Erica Etelson
Casey Evans
Cath Evans
Nigel Exell
Louise Farrow
Nicole Farrugia
Terri Faulkner
Tom Faulkner
Charlotte
   Featherstone
Jacqui Fernie
Ankie Ferry-Damen
Patric ffrench
   Devitt
Annie Fielder
Toby Finlay
Catriona Fitchett
Lori Flask
Jean Fleming
Foldingpapercranes
Rebecca Foster
John Fraser
Susan Fraser
Tasha Gallagher
Neelam Gandevia
Nicky Gardiner
Robert Garza
Chris Gibb
Mary Gibbins
Elizabeth Gilbert
Anita Gill

Shenagh Gilliard
Ashley Goff
Maria Goldsmith
Debi Goodwin
Heide Goody
Amita Gore
John Gorman
Emma Grae
Joni Graves
Mike Grenville
Eamonn Griffin
Fee Griffin
Xowie Grist
Liz Hadaway
Paul Hadfield
Glyn Hadley
Cris Hale
J.C. Hallman
Marjorie Hamilton
Todd Hannula
Michael Hargreave
   Mawson
Pete Harris
Rachel Harris
Regina Harrison
Mandy Hart
Brian Hartland
Maximilian
   Hawker
Hayley Haynes
Sam Haynes
Anwen Hayward
Sue Heady
Adam Heath
Michael Hebb
Cathy Henderson
Aby Henry
Stuart Heritage
Tara Herman
Martin
   Hetherington
Emily Hodder

Amy Hoddinott
Misty Holland
Jennifer Hollis
James Horner
Hotel Casa
   Encantada Ryan
Caroline Howell
Neil Hughes
Laura Hutchings
Pamela Hutchinson
Ashley Hymel
Jessica Irvine
Oscar Irvine
Bruce Irving
Cat Irving
Zoltan Istvan
Hannah Jackson-
   McCamley
Oli Jacobs
Jackie James
Jenna James
Jo James
Leah James
Harriet Jane
Laura Jellicoe
Michael Jenkins
Paul Jinks
Mike Johnson
Emmy Maddy
   Johnston
Anatole Jolly
Gareth Jones
Leanne Jones
Bergþór Jónsson
Dawn Joosten,
   Ph.D.
Alice Jordan
Jorge Kageyama
Victoria Kainz
Jamie Keen
Samantha Kelly
James Kennell

Anne-Marie Keppel
David Ketchum
Steve Kettmann
Dan Kieran
Patrick Kincaid
Oliver King
E Kinsey
Lisa Knapp
Edmond Knight
Jo Knights
Andy Knott
Elizabeth Kohen
Daniel Kontos
Marta Kowalska
Inna Krieger
Alexander Kumar
Paul La Planche
Mit Lahiri
Hugh Langley
Stephanie Lawrence
Ewan Lawrie
Nick Lee
Rebecca Lee
Rebecca Lee-Wale
Martin Leslie
Christopher Lewis
David Lewis
Life. Death. Whatever.
Roslyn Lindner
Sandra Ling
Paulette Livers
Nikki Livingstone-Rothwell
Polis Loizou-Denyer
Amy Lord
Michael Lovan
Harriet Lowther
Anita Luby

Johanna J. Lunn
Judy M Cherish Ceremonies
Cait Maddan
Naomi Malan
Santiago Marin
Angus Mark
Christan Marsh Pierce
Michelle Marshall
Marie Martin
Slavko Martinov
Laura Mason
Chris Massey
Victoria Mather
Sebastian Matthews
Christine Maul-Rice
Jessica Maybury
Andrew McAvinchey
Nuri McBride
Bryony McCarry
Charlie McCay
Megan McCormick
Peter McCowie
Lawrence McCrossan
Rich McEachran
Kate McFarlane
Sarah McGrath
Layla McKane
Jeanne McKnight
Aidan McQuade
Bairbre Meade
Rich Mehta
Amanda Mellon
James Mellor
Michelle Mellor
Ben Melton
Rachel Menzies
Nick Meredith

Carlene Metcalf
Alyssa Millbrook
Gemma Milne
Marina Milner-Bolotin
Amy Mimer
Andrea Minurka
Sonny Minx
John Mitchinson
Lucy Moffatt
Virginia Moffatt
Hillary Molloy
James W Monroe
Dee Montague
Adam Montgomery
Richard Moore
Zaki Moosa
Amanda Morales
Alex Morgan
Ashley Morgan
Patric Morgan
Ruth Morgan
Dominic Morley
Eric Morris
Lesley Morris
Samantha Morrish
Kate Moseley
Katie Moseley
Scott Moseley
Tim Mountford
Blair Mowat
Marko Muhar
Muhammad Mulla
Jackie Munn
Alan Murphy
Christina Murphy
Laura Musselman
Danielle Mustarde
Sachin Nakrani
Claire Nally
Deepa Narayan
Katie Narey

Carlo Navato
Gwen Nelson
Tiff Nield
Kristin Nielsen
Julien Nightingale
Helen Noakes
Sophia Noelle
Amy Nolan
Gemma Norburn
Victoria Nowlan
Tim Nthambi
Áron Ó Dubháin
Adam O'Brien
Ciara O'Sullivan
Gregory Olver
Matthieu Oostveen
Flavia Orsi
Kate Orson
Joelle Owusu-
  Sekyere
Lisa Pahl
Tim Parker
Kate Parsons
Travis J. Pashak
Lisi Perner
Adam Perry
Martin Petersen
Amy Pickard
Emma Pickering
Jemima Pickering
Nev Pierce
Emily Pile
Stacey Pitsillides
Ian Plenderleith
Justin Pollard
Chelsea Post
Catherine Potterton
Coral Poulter
Robert Powell
Rhian Heulwen
  Price
Ysaan Proks

Hatty Rafferty
Kaitlyn Rak
Esmeralda Ramirez
Claudia Rapp
Rado Ratsima
Molly Rector
Redbridge Libraries
Rebecca Redman
Isabel Rees
Alicia Renner
Phil Reynolds
Loren Rhoads
Cindi Richardson
Karen Richardson
Leslie Rieth
Eddie Riff
Liam Riley
Obed Rivera
  Muciño
Kirsty Robb
Alun Roderick
Alex Romeo
Bree Rose
Larry Rosenthal
Amelia Ross
Jim Rossignol
Liz Rothschild
Lyla Rothschild
Charlotte Rump
Amardeep Sadhra
Lucinda Sainsbury
Rhik Samadder
Mercè Santos Mir
Oceana Sawyer
Matthew Saxby
Bethan Schaufele-
  Fox
Ericka Schenck
John Schjetne
Janice Schofield
Howard Serlick
Ehud Shapira

Michael Shepherd
Nicky Sherwood
William Shurman
Robin Simonton
Jas Singh
Luke Sirinides
Anja Sisarica
Mhairi Smith
Peter Smith
Edward Smyth
Lili Soh
David M. Som
Jerry Soucy
Phyllis Spiro
Rand Spiro
Stephanie Spiro
Wendy Staden
Laura Steele
David Stelling
Linda Stevens
Heather Stevenson
Christy Stillwell
Tabatha Stirling
Rachel Street
Nick Stylianou
Ronnie Suleiman
Lucy Sullivan
Danielle Summers
Lo Tamburro
Amy Tavano
Colin Taylor
Sr. Bianca Tempt
Rachael Terry
Louie Thomas
Ellie Thompson
Rich Tiffany
Barbara Tran
Julia Trocme-Latter
Natalie Trotter-
  King
Jenny Tudor
Elen Turner

Kate Turner
Alexandra Turney
Wendy Tuxworth
Cara Usher
Rens van Bergeijk
Tony
   Vanderheyden
Robin Vaughan
Roberto Fabio
   Venchiarutti
Joff Verby
Vision Redbridge
   Culture & Leisure
Gina Vliet
T W
Denise Walters
Lisa Warner
Julie Warren
Lizzie Waterhouse
Bj Watson

Jacob Watson
Matthew Watson
   Jones
Simon Watts
Katy Webster
Dan Wedge
Melissa Anne
   Wemple Heritage
Greg Wesson
Teresa White
Mitch Whitehead
   and Anja Sisarica
Philip Whiteley
Diana Whitney
Warren Wickman
Indra Wignall
Michelle
   Wilczewski
Robyn Wilder
   Heritage

Annette Wilkinson
Derek Wilson
Theresa Witziers
Hanna Wolf
Caleb Wood
James Wood
Peter Wood
Russell Woodhead
Wendalynn
   Wordsmith
Fiona Worth
Aled Wynne
Daron Akiko
   Yamauchi
Stuart Yates
Courtney Young
Juliana Zee
Cathy Zheutlin
Pia Zulueta

A Note on the Author

ERICA BUIST is a writer, journalist and lecturer living in London. She writes mostly for the *Guardian* but has also contributed to publications such as the BBC, the *Mirror*, Medium and *Newsweek*, as well as various literary anthologies. She has been a writer-in-residence at the Wellstone Center in the Redwoods, Vermont Studio Center, Faber, Virginia Center for the Creative Arts and Arte Studio Ginestrelle. She has lived in Mexico and Paris, and speaks five languages – mainly to her dog. She tweets @ericabuist

Photos and video footage of the death festivals can be found on Instagram @thispartysdead